Inspirations:
101 Uplifting Stories
For Daily Happiness

Foreword By Kyra Schaefer

Compiled by Kyra Schaefer

Edited by Todd Schaefer and Karen Oschmann

Printed in the United States of America.

Nothing in this book or any affiliations with this book is a substitute for medical or psychological help. If you are needing help please seek it.

National Suicide Prevention Lifeline: 1-800-273-8255

Dedication

To all those who are willing to take the
leap toward feeling more inspired.

Table of Contents

Foreword
By Kyra Schaefer

This book is an absolute joy. There are trials and tribulations, hardships, and successes. You will find loves lost as well as found in the pages of this book. The magic contained within comes from the fact that everyday people just like you and me are willing to share their stories. They have come through the difficulties of life with unshakable courage to deliver a message of inspiration to you.

The best way to use this book:

I recommend reading through the table of contents and flipping to the page that resonates the most with your current situation. You may find insights and wisdom from an author that you haven't read before. You may also find a connection with an author as you learn you are never alone in this world.

I also recommend that you hold the book between your hands and ask a question, such as: "What is the message I need to most hear in my present situation?" Let the book open to any page. You may find the answer comes quickly from the writing in this book.

Your inspiration may come from these stories, or it may be sparked by how these authors share their journeys. You get to decide how you would like to experience this work. We hope that you will get what you need and expand with more positivity and gain new awareness along the way.

What this book isn't:

The articles in this book are not for those looking to get warm, fuzzy, and cuddly feelings. The articles are from real, genuine, and down-to-earth people. They don't sugarcoat the reality of their experiences. At the same time, they are unapologetic in their approach to taking the leaps in their lives that were necessary for their growth and development. I applaud the wit and bravery, the raw vulnerability and the integrity of the authors in this book. This is real life, my friends. It's hard, it's authentic, and there are unimagined gifts that reside here.

When we take the leap toward inspiration or feel a calling to be something more, it's not always easy. In many ways, it may seem impossible. If you have reached for this book, there is something here for you. You are likely taking that leap yourself. The authors in this book can relate to you and are thrilled you have decided to take this journey. It is with great hope that you do find comfort here as well as the necessary boost that will help take you over the top and find all you are looking to receive.

You may like to join our Facebook group and find daily happiness at: www.facebook.com/groups/InspirationsDaily

Kyra Schaefer is the co-owner of As You Wish Publishing where she helps authors avoid rejection. Find her at www.asyouwishpublishing.com

Gratitude
By Rollie Allaire

Gratitude—this is a word that is thrown around a lot. It sometimes feels like it's become one of those *buzzwords*.

Because of the dysfunction in my upbringing, depression and anxiety were a normal part of my daily life. I learned to manage, and quite well, I might add. I've experienced anxiety for as far back as I can remember. Practicing gratitude saved my life. The year 2013 was the lowest point of my life. My father-in-law had passed away three years before that, and we had a number of things happen in those three years.

At one point, I became suicidal. I knew and experienced that low point that many of my clients experienced. I've always been a glass-half-full kind of person, and at that point, I was struggling with keeping it half-full. For about a year or so, I moved through the roller coaster of emotions until November or December 2014—that was my breaking point.

For a good couple of months, I struggled with getting out of bed. As a mental health and addiction clinician, I knew what I needed to do, but it was a chore. I had no will or desire to live. I didn't want to be around, period. I wanted to hide away in my bed, preferably with my head under the blankets. This had been the lowest that I ever had experienced. Getting to my therapy sessions was a chore and a half.

At one point, it was clear to me what I needed to do therapeutically. I understood, at that point, how difficult this was for my clients. "Just do it," I would tell myself. "Mind over matter."

I had an appointment with my psychotherapist, and the knowledge of what she would be expecting me to do ran through my head before the appointment. I already knew *what* I needed to do; I've been going through it with clients for years. *Why* was this so hard? *When* was I going to just do it?

I made a "Recovery Plan." I was going to start physical activity. I was going to start eating well. I was going to start out things. It was time to live my life again. And the only way to the other side was through.

Many knew I wasn't working, few knew why. Some assumed and started spreading rumors. One rumor was so far-fetched—that I had been fired for having an affair with a client! Oh my goodness! That was so absurd, and I couldn't believe that someone would stoop to that kind of rumor.

I couldn't possibly tell anyone that I was struggling with my mental health; that I couldn't even look for a job. I had a number of different excuses when people would ask, and the most that I would share was that I was under a doctor's care. It wasn't a lie, but it was something that I could live with. For nearly two years, I pretended that things were okay. I pretended that nothing had fizzed me, and I was strong. I had overcome many challenges over the years, and this was merely one more.

I had one client who was extremely observant. She knew the whole time that something wasn't okay and called me out on it. We had been working closely together for some time, and she knew. She still reaches out from time to time and checks in. But despite her knowing, I still did nothing about it.

Now here I was, hiding under the covers, wishing the world would simply disappear. But now I had a plan. My plan was big, too big to start. I sent my plan to my clinician by email. She now had the plan. The appointment was coming up. I didn't want to go. She canceled the appointment. "Phew!" I thought. I don't have to start now.

I knew that this plan would not work if I didn't have anything to live for, and at that point, I didn't—or I didn't feel like I did. Years of working the Crisis Line taught me that I needed to find an anchor with the person I was working with. I knew I needed to find my anchor. I had no idea what that was. My relationship, although improved, still had me doubtful. My son was still using pot almost daily, but I came to accept that it was not my responsibility. And I didn't have a job. These were the things that I held dear, and none of them were stable.

One tool that I used with many of my clients who didn't feel they had anything to live for was finding something to be grateful for—no matter how big or small—and also to find those who supported them. I wouldn't talk about it, so my support was limited.

I decided that I would publicly share on Facebook what I was grateful for. I would need to share at least *one thing* that I was grateful for, and it didn't matter what. No one knew why I was doing it, simply that I was doing it. Some days it was tough to come up with one thing, but I did it. I did it every single day for a few months. I don't remember how long into it I was, but a family member reached out and asked, "How long will you be doing this?" My response was—however long it took. She had no idea what was going on in my life. When working with my clients that are struggling with getting themselves out of bed, I can honestly say, "I understand completely." I don't merely empathize with them, I truly understand.

Finding gratitude is the one true thing that helped me recover. I may have recovered otherwise, but it truly gave me the will to live. Try it! It's not as easy as it sounds when you are feeling down.

Love Lives On
By Kim Andrews

July 20. That dreaded call came once again. Was this the tenth time in three years that my father was rushed to the hospital? He was struggling to breathe but refused intubation. I returned to my work, waited for updates. Hours later, Mom called to advise he was admitted to ICU. For some reason, I felt no panic. I searched my heart and mind for the signal that I should get on a plane immediately but came up empty.

July 23. I navigated in a mysterious, yet somehow familiar, haze of quietude. Mom reported friends and family took turns sitting by Dad's bedside, trying to come to grips with the probable loss of him. Finally, the doctors hit pay dirt, and Dad was transferred out of ICU. "Now is your time," I heard deep within, and immediately scheduled my flight.

July 24. I went straight to the hospital. Dad was in bed, an oxygen mask on his face. I waited for his usual protestations that I should not have spent hundreds on airfare and taken time away from my life, but there were none. "I am glad you're here," he said. I kissed him and lingered by his side a moment, feeling a difference in the air around us. I looked for the usual twinkle in his eye whenever I entered a room but did not see it. It seemed I had invaded the room of an understudy.

July 25. It seemed Dad had improved, so everyone went back to their lives. It was just us two. We shared our deepest thoughts. He lapsed into silence periodically and glanced upward for a few seconds as if someone afar had called his name. I perceived an odd shift in time, as if the grand observer had a remote control that clicked us into slow motion. I downshifted in response, vigilant.

At mealtime, I fed him, touched by his willingness to let me serve him. Though he was only six feet tall, he was a giant amongst lesser men to me. Yet now he appeared dwarfed by his helplessness. I searched for the father I knew. I found a new soul who loved me just the same but needed me perhaps for the first time.

July 26. I arrived at the hospital around noon and sought shelter in the cocoon my dad and I had forged. Between naps, he assessed where each member of our immediate family stood in their lives. He judged each like

4

God on the seventh day with, "It is good." Then he looked at me and expressed his joy about my marriage to the son-in-law he loved dearly. He paused and brightened. "Continue to take good care of each other."

July 27. He was asleep when I arrived. I took my usual seat and waited for him to awaken. Our cocoon today seemed darker, oppressive. His every inhalation seemed arduous. The rhythm of it set in like a mantra I didn't care to hear. One part of me wanted it to go on forever, feeling that his last breath would surely be mine too. Another part of me wanted his chest to slow into one last hushed exhale and land him peacefully at rest. One side fought the other, and I began to weep as my desire for his peace started to win.

The flow of emotion threatened to drown me. My chest tightened, and I felt as if I would implode. So, I surrendered to the pull of my heartstrings and floated away on a sea of tears. Hours passed; my sobbing continued. Nothing existed other than me, my dad, and the crushing sadness. Somewhere in mid-afternoon, he awakened. "Don't cry, baby. Everything is going to be all right." He looked at me longingly and drifted back into slumber. He slept the rest of the day, his breathing still ragged. Day faded into night, and I sat and cried until I could summon the strength to leave him in God's hands.

July 28. Dad was awake and alert, and I wondered if yesterday had been a terrible nightmare. He was sitting up in bed, talking. Had the cosmic remote control suddenly clicked us into fast forward? I shifted in response again but felt I couldn't catch up. My flight home was due to leave soon. So, I kissed and hugged him fiercely, drinking him in once again, and forced myself to put one foot in front of the other to leave. "I love you, Dad. I'll talk to you tomorrow." Somehow I made it through the door, my heart heavy.

July 29. I awakened in my bed, glad to be home. Life continues. I was wading through unopened email when the phone rang. "He's gone," Mom said. Her voice sounded like she was at the end of a deep, cavernous tunnel. I heard myself scream, my voice trailing through the air like I'd been shoved off a cliff.

Aug 4. My husband and I sat in the room with my dad's casket. No one else wanted to view its closing. "Are you ready?" the undertaker asked. My dad lay at rest. His chest no longer rose and fell precipitously. That peace I longed for a week ago had settled around us now. I walked to the casket. "I am ready. Can I tuck him in?" He nodded assent. The room fell away. We were back in our cocoon; peace covering us. The fabric was cool and satiny. I felt him letting me tend to him again. I appraised him. One. Last. Time. I felt our love for each other wash over me. I closed the coffin softly.

I return to that cocoon often. Sometimes it's a song I sing, and he's there in every note and rest. Other times it's a movie scene, a father and daughter captured in life's struggles or triumphs together. Some days it's in the eyes of someone else I love appraising me as he often did. Love changes but lives on.

Our Stories Heal
By Linda Ballesteros

Are you moved by hearing other people's stories of mountains they have climbed? I am. Curiosity has driven me as a radio show host since 2008. What I know is that everyone has a story. Most people will share a few select stories to their trusted friends and family, but there is always a story that is too tender to talk about. Our minds, bodies, hearts, and souls thrive on connecting with each other just as the root system of a grove of trees becomes a means of communication.

No one likes to feel as though they are in it alone, but that's what happens when we keep everything to ourselves. We disconnect, and we build walls instead of bridges. It is when we finally start to share our stories that we slowly begin to tear down those walls. By finding other people like us who are going through a similar struggle, we feel less alone and more connected. It is that connection and feeling of belonging that creates an atmosphere of safety.

As we step into our authentic energy, it allows us to feel vulnerable so that others who need to heal will be drawn to us. We become a beacon of light, providing hope for others. However, for that to happen, we must be brave enough to show up as our true selves, and that requires taking off the masks and lowering the walls. Building a community of love, authenticity, and prayers helps us find the strength to move through to the next level of healing.

These are not mere observations or advice I have read from a self-help book written by a well-known author. No, this is my life and what I am doing to navigate through healing after losing my husband. As his caregiver, I saw my world shrink to the point where I felt like a part of me was disappearing each day. When I shared my story with family and friends, I no longer lived in isolation. It was not easy to allow them to see the parts of me that I was taught not to show because it was a sign of weakness. My parents taught me well. They were strong-willed, independent, and the perfect example of the phrase "salt of the earth." I watched my mother care for my younger brother, who had AIDS and my father, who suffered from Alzheimer's. She never asked for or accepted help until she fell and broke her leg, which forced her to allow us in. When

I look back, I realize this brought our family together in a way we had not experienced prior.

Today, I know that my story has allowed me to connect with my "tribe." For many, it has become a page in their survival book. Authentic story-telling is a chance for us to heal even deeper. It is an opportunity to visit those sensitive and uncomfortable topics—the ones that we might keep hidden. I found that it provided clarity and purpose back into my life, and I could see others embrace and share their story after I opened up to them.

When we show up to reveal a piece of ourselves, we create a safe space for others to step into and share their stories. By exposing vulnerable parts of our lives, we take the chance that not everyone is going to love us or our story. We put ourselves out there to possibly experience rejection and judgment. This challenges us to step outside our comfort zone, and because of that, we grow. When we tell our stories about failure, death, or a life's struggle, others can rest assured we are a haven where they can talk openly about their pain without judgement or being seen as weak. We help others while helping ourselves.

In a world where everyone is trying to get noticed and seen as quickly as possible, there are few who are willing to sit down and truly listen, to give someone their full undivided attention. In fact, it's difficult to have a meal without checking our phone while sitting across the dinner table from someone we love. So, when someone takes the time to share their stories with us that last longer than a nine-second Snapchat story, we start to see the real them, and they see the real us.

Unfortunately, we still live in a society where issues like illness (mental and physical), death, and failures are uncomfortable and kept secret. We don't talk about our insecurities with our bodies or our struggles with lack of self-love in our lives. We don't talk about problems with our relationships or the amount of debt we have, because those social media posts will not get many "Likes." The pictures of us sitting by the pool or sharing where we had dinner seem to more popular, giving us the illusion of being more connected.

We don't ask for help, because we think it will make us look weak. In order to eliminate the stigma around our struggle, we must be brave enough to share our story, letting others know that there is hope. I believe there is a story within us—about love, pain, heartache, trust, loss, and everything in-between—and not so in-between. We have our ups and downs, our highest of highs and lowest of lows, our deepest and darkest secrets, and lifelong dreams and desires.

As storytellers, we can break shame cycles and change the direction in which our lives are headed as well as impacting where we are headed as a society. We can set the foundation for future generations to eliminate judgement, stigmas, and labels. The magic of sharing our stories will cause barriers fall and we will finally see that we are all more alike than we are different.

It is time to start showing up as your authentic self. *Be brave, stand up, and tell your story.*

Big Girl Panties
By Pam Baren Kaplan

"**M**rs. Kaplan, your heart is dying," the emergency room physician told me. My daughter, Dani, and I stared in disbelief. "I came to the emergency room tonight because of pneumonia, not my heart!" I exclaimed. They immediately scheduled me for an angiogram the next morning. My family was not emotionally prepared for this. Oddly enough, I was calm.

Results from the angiogram indicated that I was not a stint candidate, but I was at the top of the class for a quadruple bypass. My family didn't take the news well. They tried to keep their fears from me, but they didn't do a good job. I wasn't afraid. I knew in my damaged little heart, no matter how things ended up, it was meant to be.

I had a feeling that my angel, Roxy (my "yella" Lab girl who passed about five years before), was looking out for me. I felt her in my gut. My gut is very intuitive and usually on-point when I listen. I knew I was approaching a crossroad—a wake-up call—and there were going to be a few more "plot changes" in my future. But fortunately, I have an angel for my traveling companion.

After a painful insurance tangle, the surgery was scheduled for the following Monday, March 18th. Just in case something was to end up not the way I wanted, I had to discuss financials with someone who wouldn't fall apart in a million pieces. Who was my best option? My daughter, Dani. After the way she had stepped up to untangle a massive, messed up situation with my insurance, I "volun-told" her.

I was more concerned about her reaction to this subject rather than worried about myself. Starting that conversation was difficult. I couldn't make eye contact without crying. I looked away, but you could hear the tears in my voice.

"In the event that something happens, not that I am expecting anything will, I am giving you my accounts and passwords. Here is a list of people you will need to contact—if." Dani's face melted into tears. I felt so badly giving her this responsibility, but I knew she would manage if I couldn't. We hugged as she whispered to me, "Don't you dare leave me with those two," referring to her dad and brother. We laughed, and I made her that promise.

We had to be at the hospital at five the next morning. I kissed my two girls, Zuzu and Frankie, praying this was not a final goodbye. I felt my throat swell a bit, and liquid love clouded my eyes. I ran back for one more good luck kiss.

While driving to the hospital, I saw my life flash by like a movie trailer. I was reliving the milestones I had experienced over the last few years. So many life-changing events had occurred! They started when Roxy passed, which was followed by the death of a very dear friend. Then, my job got eliminated after 32 years with the same company! A comfortable six-figure salary—gone! I took a job that kept me away from my family, traveling the country teaching professional adult education seminars. I was in an airport at least six, if not eight, times a month. I was beaten up and plagued by pneumonia five times in four years! And now this.

I refused to feel sorry for myself. I chose to face this with courage, remembering a motivational sign in my home office that reads, "Coffee in hand, big-girl panties on, a sparkle in my eyes and a smile on my face. Yep, I'm ready for the day! Bring it on!" I had to keep my promise to Dani; I couldn't leave her with those two knuckleheads—no way.

And then my *Paws to Celebrate* Pack, the community for grieving pet parents that I started the summer of 2015, prayed for me and sent positive thoughts and healing energy. I loved them so much; I couldn't disappoint them.

The next few days after the surgery were a blur. To top off this fun, I got to spend my birthday in ICU, a day to remember, which actually I don't remember at all. As it turned out, I didn't have a quadruple bypass, only a triple—no disappointment there. I was repaired; a little ticker tune-up was exactly what I needed.

After a week in rehab, I returned home to my puppies. I had missed them fiercely, and I was so happy to be home! This little "vacation" allowed me to revisit my next steps. I knew I was grounded from traveling, and I did not want to see the inside of Terminal Two at Chicago's O'Hare airport again for a long time, if ever!

My heart wanted to write a book to honor Roxy (my deceased pet). She was my reason for starting *Paws to Celebrate*. It felt right after helping heal thousands of grieving pet parents. I was inspired to reach more, and to help heal more. I envisioned this book as a roadmap for a rough journey through pet loss grief recovery. I couldn't sleep and I couldn't concentrate on anything else—most likely because my gut kept talking to me continuously for hours. I finally had to tell it to hush up and agree to do it!

Overcoming the shadows of self-doubt that lived within me for decades was nerve-wracking, and those old voices of self-sabotage whispered, "Who do you think you are, writing a book?" This was my time, I had to "woman up" and remind myself of that ticker tune-up conversation. With my angel, Roxy, always a few steps ahead of me, I can confidently trust myself, acknowledge my credibility, and put faith in my best friend—my gut. And I did.

I am so proud to tell you that my first book, *Tails of Unconditional Love*, will be published this summer!

Tie-Dyed Faith:
Revealing Your Authentic Self
By Brooke Bensinger

I love quotes. They keep me grounded. One of my favorites is by the author Kurt Vonnegut. "To practice any art, no matter how well or badly, is a way to make your soul grow. So do it." I did it. By doing so, I acquired the faith to be me.

Three years ago, I decided to make a dream come true and started my business. Starting a tie-dye business in itself was taking a leap of faith (especially since my career was in school counseling), but never did I suspect the changes that occurred. I'm not talking about the typical changes to my schedule or having to be better organized with paperwork. I'm talking about a transformation of my inner being. Tie-dye has been a catalyst for personal growth. My belief and trust in myself are stronger. I'm more confident in my ability to overcome doubts and more comfortable to reveal my true, authentic self to others. Upon reflecting on this, I've learned three lessons through tie-dyeing.

Embrace Color in Your Life

We're surrounded by colors every day, but are frequently too busy to recognize the impact they have on our lives. Color plays a role in how we experience the world. Heck, color psychology dates back to the 19th century. There is even a National Color Therapy Month (March), which was established to promote people finding their light and joy through color. Research shows color boosts one's mood, creativity, and serenity.

I find color to be empowering. I purposely choose hues that reflect the mood I want to project. I might select red to portray strength or blue to convey tranquility. Color can be renewing and revitalizing.

I have a customer who'd always ask me to use neutral colors when creating her clothing. At a Do-It-Yourself (DIY) event, I noticed the item she was dyeing was bright and vibrant. When asked about it, she said she was tired of hiding behind bland tones. She wanted to make a statement and now had the confidence to show her true colors—who she truly was—without concern of others' opinions. She found it liberating to make that change.

Embrace the Purge

Dye needs to be rinsed from an item until the water runs almost clear before washing. This is monotonous and time-consuming. As I was rinsing one day, I heard my father's voice pop into my head: "Find a way to make the menial meaningful." Dad (the wisest man I've ever known) used to say these words to me on Saturday mornings during chores. "Menial meaningful" was a lesson I applied to many aspects of my life.

I discovered how to make the rinsing process meaningful one day as I watched the dye running down the drain. I noted how brown the water looked. It amazed me how beautifully bright my shirts became after the muddy-looking excess was rinsed away. I started to consider the excess in my life I needed to rinse and wash away. Often negative thoughts and feelings clutter our minds. They are unnecessary and prevent us from living the lives we desire. We also have objects that clutter our space. We need to make room in our minds and living space to breathe and to fully experience the positive in our lives. Feeling water run through my hands, hearing the water rush down the drain, and seeing "mud" disappear was a soul-cleansing experience and stimulated clear thinking. The menial had meaning.

I've facilitated DIY events for various groups of youth, and talk about the metaphors of tie-dye. Participants take the shirts home to rinse and wash. Last summer, a teen from a church youth group sent me a photo of her shirt. She told me she thought about her sins washing away when she rinsed her shirt. "It felt so good to watch them go down the drain. I can be forgiven, and I can forgive myself." What a great lesson to learn at a youthful age.

Embrace Vulnerability (As Scary as That Might Be)

To see the beautifully bright design of a tie-dyed shirt, the sinew or rubber bands used for the design need to be untied or cut. There is so much anticipation in this step of the process because it's the first time the colorful design is exposed. Rarely does this step in the process disappoint.

Wouldn't it be nice if we felt the same way about exposing our insecurities and fears? Unfortunately, we often stay tied and bound to old habits, unhealthy relationships, perceived weaknesses, and our brokenness. Staying bound holds us back from experiencing all the joy life has to offer. I've discovered a new strength within myself, one where I look inside myself for reassurance and affirmation rather than outside myself. This prompted me to add a new statement to my practice of daily affirmations, "I allow myself to feel vulnerable so I can experience the life I desire."

While tie-dyeing with a group of youth living in a residential facility, a girl looked at her shirt while she was placing dye on it and said, "It's ugly." I reminded her that it would be beautiful once the process was completed. She stated, "No. My life is ugly." In her moment of vulnerability, she exposed her dark thoughts to me, a complete stranger. She shared part of her story, which included having suicidal thoughts. I motioned a staff person to join us as we listened to her release pent-up emotions. We hugged at the end of our conversation. My heart sank when she whispered, "I haven't been hugged like that in an awfully long time." That moment of vulnerability sparked a breakthrough. She made great progress toward discovering her authentic self.

As Kurt Vonnegut suggested in his book, *A Man without a Country*, practicing an art is good for your soul. It was good for mine. The lessons learned have allowed me to gain the confidence to be authentic as I move forward in life.

Finding Light On Vancouver's Darkest Street
By Kristi Blakeway

W hen you meet Cindy, you know immediately that she is an addict. Her two decades of life on the streets, entangled in a web of cocaine and heroin addiction, have left no doubt in the passerby's eyes. In one glance, her story appears transparent: homeless, addict, street worker. Her skin shows the track marks from recent injections, her clothes are ragged, and her eyes are like tinted windows, masking her light. It's easy to judge Cindy, and most do. City-goers shift their gazes, and commuters lock their doors as they pass through Canada's poorest neighborhood. To most, Cindy is simply invisible. Few know her true story—one of courage, hope, and unwavering love.

As a school principal, I have spent years taking students to the streets to help Vancouver's homeless. In 2009, I began *Project HELLO (Helping Everyone Locate Loved Ones)*, a year-round initiative where students create handmade greeting cards and invite the homeless to reconnect with friends or family with whom they have lost touch. We have helped hundreds of Vancouver's homeless reach out to say hello, often for the first time in decades. I'll never forget the moment a woman in California dropped her phone in shock after I began to speak. Her husband had given up hope, but she had never stopped believing their son may still be alive.

Despite hundreds of mini-miracles, by 2013, I realized I had to go further. I was asking Vancouver's most vulnerable citizens to open wounds from the past. This raw emotion deserved better than a quick conversation on the street. I began *Beyond HELLO*, where I made the personal commitment to take a homeless person to lunch once a month in an effort to connect through compassion and help shift the perception of homelessness. Cindy was the first lady I met.

In a candid conversation, sitting across the table in one of Vancouver's hidden diners, I asked, "What do you wish the world knew about you?" Cindy replied, "I am not the monster you think I am, but I fight the demons that try to make me a monster."

Cindy's addiction helps her hide the pain. She struggles with HIV, Hepatitis, and heroin addiction, yet, her biggest regret is giving her baby up for adoption as a teen in Ontario. With love, she wrote a six-page letter and kissed her baby goodbye. Decades later, despite knowing little more than a first name and birthdate, Cindy lives with unwavering love and hope of finding her daughter.

What had I done? As I drove away to the comforts of my home, the image of Cindy sobbing and hugging a parking meter would not escape me. I had opened a wound so deep I feared I had made things worse.

That night, I stayed up and searched social media for every person named Paige in Ontario. In the middle of the night, I found a match. I clicked on her Facebook profile only to discover that one of her friends was connected to one of my friends. A few phone calls helped me discover that one of my past students had gone to college with Paige's childhood friend. Within 24 hours, a miracle happened, and Paige called me, ecstatic to learn of her mother.

I explained to Paige that it might be hard to hear of her mother's life. Paige understood as she had also struggled with addiction. She credits her own recovery to a book, *In the Realm of Hungry Ghosts*, written by Dr. Gabor Maté, which tells life stories of addicts in Vancouver. The chapter, *Pregnancy Journals*, tells a story of a woman named Celia who wanted to be drug-free to be a good mother. Paige felt such a strong connection that she wrote to Dr. Maté and thanked him for his work.

When I returned to the streets to tell Cindy I had found Paige, I asked if she had ever heard of Dr. Gabor Maté. Through her addicted state, she looked at me with curiosity and mumbled, *"In the Realm of Hungry Ghosts."* Amazed, I asked how she knew the name of this book. "He's my doctor. In the book, my name is Celia." Without knowing it, Cindy had already changed her daughter's life.

After twenty years on the streets, Cindy accepted my offer to fly her daughter across the country on one condition. She wanted to be clean. Cindy checked herself into rehab the very next day. Three months later, Cindy and Paige met, and their reunion was everything the women had hoped it would be.

Cindy and Paige are still connected today. Paige has returned to Ontario and Cindy has decorated her tiny Vancouver home with family photos. Cindy and Paige talk regularly, and Cindy and I frequently meet as friends. Last week, as I hugged Cindy goodbye, I handed her a meal token. She smiled and said, "One day I will help people too." As we parted, a man approached collecting half-used cigarette butts. Cindy reached out, put her hand on his shoulder, and began, "Please have a meal on me—you need this token more than I do." Smiling with confidence, she faded into the troubled streets, connected and content; her spirit light, and her soul free.

Cindy has taught me that miracles happen and that each one of us has a story worth hearing. When we begin to repair relationships and connect as people, only then will we overcome pain and rekindle the human spirit. Next time you meet someone who has lost their connection with society, look in their eyes and see their untold story. Engage with curiosity rather than judgment. The people on the streets may be hungry, but they are hungry for so much more than food. They are hungry for hope, they are hungry for love, and they are hungry for human connection. Please join me and go *Beyond HELLO*. Engage in soulful conversation and let compassion connect us all.

Friends For 40 Years
By Kristi Blakeway

"Become friends with people who aren't your age. Hang out with people whose first language isn't the same as yours. Get to know someone who doesn't come from your social class. This is how you see the world. This is how you grow." —Anonymous

During the fall of 1988, high school friendships, cute boys, spiral perms, and acid-washed jeans consumed my world. In typical teenage girl fashion, I based my friendships on commonalities. My mom would frequently tell me that my friends and I all looked the same, which I would adamantly deny. Looking back at photos, I see that she was right. We knew the trends of high school life and dressed accordingly. I had no idea that one particular afternoon, in our high school cafeteria, would open my world and teach me the beauty of diverse friendships.

Lunch hour started in the same way as most. I headed to the cafeteria to purchase one of the cream-stuffed eclairs before they sold out. I left the cafeteria line with my tray in hand and headed diagonally to "our table." My look-alike friends had already arrived and were seated in the same place as always—three tables in, against the window on the right side of the cafeteria. They looked up in recognition, expecting me to walk towards them. I started to move in their direction until a voice called out, "Hey—what's your name?"

Steven also sat in the same place every day. The first table, directly in front of the cafeteria line, was reserved for students with intellectual disabilities. Steven sat at the end of this table and watched students hustle by.

"Hey—what's your name? Come sit with me!" I paused, not knowing who Steven was shouting at. I looked at his eyes full of hope and curiosity. He was talking to me. I remember standing still for a second, not knowing what to do. Should I accept this invitation, or should I continue on to my table? I made one of the best decisions of my life and accepted his offer, as others looked on with wonder.

"What's your name? What do you have for lunch?" Steven continued with questions as I sat down across from him. I introduced myself and explained I had a cucumber, tomato, and cream cheese sandwich. Steven smiled and asked, "Cucumber and cheezies?" I explained again, but he liked his description best. As we sat together and talked, Steven looked at me with a big smile and optimistic eyes and asked a life-changing question, "Can we be friends for 40 years? I will call you every day!" I smiled and wrote my phone number on a piece of paper. Our beautiful friendship began.

As the years passed, Steven kept his promise. He has never missed his daily phone call, and he has become a special part of my family. He was an usher at my wedding, and as our guests arrived, he shouted, "Welcome to Kristi and Shawn's wedding—*sit down!*" My kids have grown up calling him Uncle Steven. He has traveled with us, volunteered at my workplace, and he has cheered for every sports team my kids have joined. In fact, he has often ended up becoming the water boy or assistant coach. Steven loves to meet new people and brings joy to everyone around him. I am currently a school principal, and Steven has become our most beloved volunteer. He reads to kids, joins in with dodgeball, and permeates our school hallways with enthusiasm.

I don't know anyone quite as authentic as Steven. He is quick to tell you what he loves and what he hates. He was offered a job cleaning up in a food court years ago. After two days, he quit. He will still tell you, "I hate it—the garbage stinks!" He would much rather work for free doing things he loves. In Steven's eyes, connecting with others is far more valuable than receiving a paycheck.

There have been a few times where people around us have not accepted Steven. A restaurant host sat us in a closed section, people stood and moved away from us in a movie theatre, and a border guard was skeptical when I tried to convince him I wasn't working when I took Steven to Disneyland. "You mean to tell me you are taking him as a friend?" Yes. Moments like this remind me that we all have work to do spreading the importance of inclusion. How sad it is to realize some may be missing out on the friendship someone like Steven can offer.

Becoming friends with Steven has enriched my life tremendously. I look up to Steven as he is the happiest person I know. Steven loves everyone he meets regardless of age, gender, or ethnicity. He sees the beauty in others and is happy to include everybody. He knows how to lighten up a room, how to make people laugh, and how to make people feel good about themselves.

It's now 2019, and Steven and I have been friends for 31 years. He has kept his promise, and he has called me every single day. I have asked Steven what we will do when our 40 years runs out. He just smiles and says, "We can be friends for 40 more!"

Deciding to sit with Steven was one of the best decisions I have made in my life. Every day he reminds me what it means to see the bright side and love wholeheartedly. Steven has opened my world and taught me that we are all better when we engage with curiosity rather than judgment. A simple smile can connect perfect strangers. Next time you walk into a room of new people, I encourage you to step outside your comfort zone, take the risk, and say hello to someone new. It may be the beginning of a beautiful 40-year friendship.

Learning To Fly
By Meredith Brookes

In the spring of 2006, I was ready to graduate from the University of Virginia (UVA) after four incredible years. One class opened my soul, not only in the coursework, but also from my classmates and guest speakers.

On the first day of class, I noticed Jack—tall, dark, and as handsome as they come. He had deep soulful eyes that shined and twinkled like the eyes of a child. He was two years younger than me, and me being an arrogant "fourth-year" student, I saw him as a piece of eye candy. We did not talk during the first few weeks of class, but after meeting out on UVA's Corner one night, we began to find ways to hang out through mutual friends.

Spring progressed in Charlottesville, the air was sweet with heavenly magnolia blossoms, dogwood trees were robust, and the apple and cherry blossoms were brilliant in color. Foxfields, the biggest party of the year, an event for everyone to put on their Sunday best, was near.

My friend Barry visited for the event, asking if he could crash on my couch. I agreed, thinking nothing of it. Knowing I had to get up early the next day, I drank little that evening. Barry came back drunk, in a blackout, and forced himself on me. He was a college wrestler, and any attempts to fight him off had no chance of success. At some point, I knew it was over. I had to give in, or the pain would be much worse. In that moment, my spirit splintered. I felt as if I could see what was happening to me from above. I let him have my body, but my psyche was fractured.

The following morning I had to put it behind me quickly. I couldn't think about it; I just kept moving. I showered off and returned to my room, where Barry was hung over, naked and confused. He asked, "We didn't do anything, did we?" I scoffed, "No, don't worry, nothing happened." He was clearly relieved and quickly ran out the door. I told my best friends what had happened, and eventually went to the hospital. When asked there if I wanted to talk to someone, I said no, because I could not deal with what had happened. Instead, that day at Foxfields, I used alcohol to escape the pain. That's when Jack found me. He embodied kindness; leaving his group and getting a taxi to take me home safely.

For the next few weeks, Jack and I were inseparable. I cheered him on watching him play polo; he came grocery shopping with me and cooked me dinner. He preferred me without alcohol; he saw that I was not the same person when I was under the influence. We developed a sexual relationship that could make your toes curl, helping me to recover from some of the immediate impacts of Barry's assault. Jack showed me how to value me again.

We parted ways when I left for a three-month trek through Europe with my sister. When I returned home and started working, the dark hole of the rape grew inside my soul. I lost myself in alcohol again. I eventually flew cross-country to attend a formal recovery program where I broke away from that poison, but my sense of self-worth was gone. I craved love, in any form, wanting to feel safe in a relationship. I made a grave mistake—I picked the wrong guy to marry and have kids with. He abused me in many ways. During and after an ugly divorce, I felt even more alone. I was a shell of a human being when I broke away from my ex-husband. I was in a pit of depression so big, I didn't know how to get out. My parents supported me, both financially and emotionally, but I needed more.

In 2014, Rolling Stone wrote a horrific article about the "culture of rape" on the campus of the University of Virginia. The emotions from my traumatic experience came flooding back.

I remembered how Jack had been my light back then, and I reached out to him via Facebook to get his address, with the intention of sending him a letter. That simple act of reaching out allowed warm, happy, feelings back in—feelings I feared I would never have again. Remember in the old Beauty and the Beast cartoon movie, when the beast is lifted from imminent death, spirals around, and morphs back into humanity with a light shining on him? That is how I felt. When Jack asked if I ever thought about that summer, I had my first real laugh in a long time. Of course, I thought about that summer!

Jack flew to visit me for a beautiful weekend; he once again brought my heart, soul, and body back to life. I told him that I had felt like a caged bird in my marriage, and that my ex-husband constantly scared me. Jack told me life should never be scary. I cried knowing he was only mine for the weekend. When he left, he gently kissed me behind my ear, on my neck, and whispered, "Fly little birdie, fly."

While I continue to fight legal battles for my children, Jack has moved on with his life. He married someone else three years later. In my heart, I will always be Jack's personal cheerleader, but I do not have to watch him live happily ever after. He had brought me back from a dark precipice, not once, but twice; staying friends would hurt me. Jack's last gift to me was the lesson of loving myself, knowing what it should feel like when someone loves you. I honor that gift by living my life as the beautiful bird that he chose to set free. I am no longer that little bird though. Today I am an owl, wiser, wilder and free in spirit.

Maybe I'll Try it Just Once
By Jenny Cabaniss

Two years ago, if you told me that I would learn horseback riding as an adult, I would have roared with laughter. Why? Because I was the poster child for loving the indoors and I avoided nature the way cats avoid water. However, that was all about to change, and in the process, it changed me in the most unexpected ways.

My daughter, age ten, had been riding for six years. She started trying to convince me to take a lesson so I could "see how fun it was." Initially, I was completely against it. *These lessons were for kids. What if I fell? What if I looked ridiculous?*

The last time I had ridden a horse was back in high school. I remembered falling off and not being terribly hurt, but that was a long time ago. As a fellow barn parent told me, "Kids bounce. Adults thump." Through all of this, my daughter kept working on me, "Mom, you could wait until the weather is nice so you won't get too sweaty." "Mom, you can take a lesson in the morning when it isn't too hot." And the guilt laden, "Mom, it would mean a lot to me if you would take a lesson!"

After thinking about it for a few months, I decided, *maybe I'll try it just once*. The rationalization was that I was doing this for my daughter. So, I waited until October, when the weather cools down in Texas. Well, sort of. After talking to my daughter's instructor, I signed up for a beginner lesson where the average age was about eight years old. I hoped I could cut it.

When I got in the saddle for the first time, it was both scary and exhilarating. Scary to be so high up, and exhilarating that this nice old horse was following my commands. By the end of the lesson, I had the basic knowledge of how to avoid bouncing, but I had no idea there were so many abdominal and thigh muscles involved. The kids made it look so effortless! I could barely use my legs to drive home that day, but I was proud of myself. My daughter was so excited, but I wasn't completely sold yet.

I scheduled another lesson to continue testing the waters. And believe it or not, when that Sunday came, I found myself excited. Although still very much the beginner, by the time my lesson finished, I felt so accomplished. I was hooked. My daughter was ecstatic, I was ecstatic, even the horse was ecstatic! Well, maybe not the horse. As the lessons went on, I gained physical strength, which allowed me to not only maneuver the horse better but to eliminate my double bounce. I was getting in a comfortable groove. *If I can keep at these beginner lessons for the next few years, I'll be doing great*, I thought.

Then, my daughter mentioned an upcoming barrel racing competition, and how fun it would be to do the competition together. Again, I balked. An adult doing a kid barrel race? Not only would the kids be watching me, but also all the parents, my friends, the teenage assistants, and some of the instructors would be watching as well. And did I mention my division would include the drill team girls? She kept working on me and threw her final card—"Mom, it would be such a great present for my birthday if you did this with me!" I thought, no way! Well, *maybe I'll try it just once.*

Needless to say, I went to my first barrel racing competition. The horse was pretty tame, which was fortunate since this was my first event, and my first time riding him. Warming up next to the six-year-olds, I felt I was bonding with my new ride. Tahoe and I were becoming one. And then it was my turn. When Tahoe realized this was a competition, he lost his mother-loving mind. Never in my life have I ridden that fast, gone that far, and stayed upright. It was terrifying and so thrilling at the same time! And not that anyone is keeping track, but I got a third place ribbon in my division of six! It had been a long time since I felt so empowered and proud of myself. This also showed my instructor that I was serious about pushing myself to get stronger as a rider and take chances. A short time later, she offered me the opportunity to enter the advanced class. After playing it safe for most of my life, this one event showed me how to get out of my comfort zone. Thank you, Tahoe.

As the months have turned into years, I continue my lessons. Not only has this become my passion, but I have the privilege of sharing this passion with my daughter. Who knew that riding a horse could tap into the inner power and strength I had all along? In the last year, I've received feedback from friends, work colleagues, and family that my voice sounds stronger, and I seem more self-assured.

When I began this journey, I had no expectations about the end result. In fact, I still don't. I only know I look forward to my lesson every week. Society seems to teach us that if we are not great at something, we shouldn't do it. It is intimidating trying something new as an adult; taking the chance that you might be mediocre at it. The end game is not how well you do; it is how you feel about yourself while doing it. So, I hand the reins to you. Is there something you have wanted to try? Find what scares you, what thrills you, what pushes you out of your comfort zone. Learn to paint, water ski, join Toastmasters or take a class. The possibilities are endless. I encourage you to think, *maybe I'll try it just once.*

The Inspiration Trail
By Jeannie Church

Many years ago, I got lost in the dark. It took a while to relocate myself. While I was crawling around in the dark cave of my soul, I noticed these faint trails of light. Little sparks of inspiration that guided me and pulled me deeper into my inner world, where I could truly begin the emotional work of my lifetime.

The inspiration for healing my life came from my third divorce. I was pursuing a master's degree in Boulder, Colorado. At the time, I was also married, and our home was in Los Angeles, California. I was away from our Los Angeles home much longer than I should have been. About that same time, my then-husband began to energetically move away from me. I now see that the marriage was fated to teach me how to break many leftover childish illusions about myself and relationships. I followed this trail of inspiration through poetry and prose, so I could dive deeply into my soul and truly discover who I have been and who I am now.

At first, you may think this poetry is not inspiring at all! However, if you keep reading all the way through, you will realize that each word leads to total inspiration. The inspiration to keep coaxing and healing my soul into the light of this radically divine life.

In 2012, the first words that may be considered poetry revealed themselves to me. Then, the poetry disappeared for a long period of time. This poem from 2012 represents the foreshadowing of what was to come.

04.27.12

Down the spiral

Descending to the depths of nowhere

Light fades, and shadow creeps in

Fear hides in shadow

Impulse to run back to light

Panting, breathing, stumbling for the light

But no don't leave the shadow alone

Shadow needs your embrace

It lives with fear and craves your love.

You will notice a four-year gap here because I was hard at work with graduate studies and trying to pretend like everything was perfectly fine. Then, there was no choice but to face it all. In 2014, my husband and I separated, and I was alone with my karma and my choices. A couple of years later, the poetry came back to help me express some of the devastation.

09.18.16

I need you, my Shadow, to be whole

To deny you is to be fragmented, scattered in all directions

God sees all, and you are part of ALL

Let the light meet you, dance with you

You hold the mysteries of this Universe

You are the place where stars hang their light

You are more than rumors and fear of hellish play

You are the curtain, the backdrop, for life's expression

You are vast darkness waiting to be filled.

My healing process became about finding and integrating the parts of myself that were held in shadow and ready to come home. I was less afraid of what I would discover next, and more inspired than anything else to understand who I was.

10.14.17

Mistakes, regrets, shame

Integrating shadow

It is happening

Allow the flow

Be aware, stay in contact

While the shadow flows freely.

At this point, I was once again not trusting my shadowed parts. I wanted to slowly dismantle and dissect them. This was more about me trying to manipulate and control what I could not see in the dark.

10.14.17

Shadow lives to separate, eviscerate

Deconstruct your shadowed parts if you dare

Let them out, look at them

Listen to them, offer them light

A little piece of light at a time

Feeding them too much light may cause destruction

Emotion, implosion, explosion.

Sometimes there are just hashtags—10.16.17. #Touchingreality #Destiny #Fate

12.26.17

Don't mark me

I've come back to this Self—Proud Spirit

Rebellious to socialize—materialize.

12.26.17

Weaving through relationship

I am a snake side-winding and gliding over this Earth.

12.28.17

Bring her out, let her find her way

Watch her finding her natural way.

12.28.17

I'm not perfect, but sometimes my tarot cards tell me I am.

01.02.18

Keep evolving through all the failures and mistakes, just keep evolving.

01.06.18

I have thoughts of prosperity

Lush green

Sparkling white

Rich brown and red

Deep blue

Strong granite

Clear flowing prosperity.

01.06.18

Trying to catch up, grow up, force up

Here I am

Craving the innocent, fearless curiosity of a young woman

Renounce lack

Given a gift to be that energetic, fearless, creative, confident Maiden

So connected to the Earth and her dreams.

01.17.18

I can see her movements.

01.20.18

Waking unconscious with haunting past

What if it is light and awareness, not heavy sadness

I give my past light and awareness.

01.20.18

You have been holding your PAST as your PATH

No longer my love

Give it your light and awareness

Then, turn in a true direction.

01.20.18

Deconstructing

True wild out

It knows a way

A natural way

Her natural way.

02.25.18

The freedom to stand as ONE

Stand for ONE

The freedom to fully express the SOUL together.

03.20.18

Let me be a visitor

A super-duper shooting star

Let me surrender to the bittersweetness of it all.

The beginnings, the ends

The lovely mess of stardust everywhere.

06.02.18

Resonating reality

Mirroring my imagination

Journeying into Soul's chamber and sweetly embracing your youngest

The ones frightened and lost in the darkness

Bring them home

Bring her home.

So now I am home! Writing heals my journey. I am inspired by the past, not regretting it or trying to forget it. I am inspired by the love I see between couples, knowing that it is waiting for me too. There is no jealousy, coveting, or desperation. There is inspiration as I witness the unique ways we come together, grow apart, and also stay together.

06.02.19

Consciously seeking inspiration

To touch the reality of my destiny.

The Beauty Of Grace
By Tami Close

It was morning, but the curtains were drawn, and the room was dark. It permeated my mind, my heart, and my soul. What I was doing wasn't living. I lived to used drugs, to numb the pain of memories, the pain of broken dreams, and the pain of living. Because I was unemployable, I became an escort. I would take three or four clients a day. They would come to my motel room, the dark one with the curtains drawn. I would get high, put on a smile, and pretend to be funny and confident and alive. But I wasn't. Not really. I was dead inside. It was never-ending. I wasn't living, and I couldn't die. I tried. The last time, being just a couple days before. I took handfuls of pills, yet woke up the next day, just like every day. Dead, but living—completely broken. I hadn't seen my children in months. They were better off without their train-wreck of a mother. That's what I told myself, sometimes repeated over and over as I rocked myself to bed.

One day they came, guns drawn, six or seven officers. I was outside smoking, and they swarmed me. They had come looking for my boyfriend, who never showed up to meet his probation officer several months back. They found him, but they had found me too. Little did I know that the nights I spent praying for it all to end were being answered, just not in the way I envisioned.

In the beginning, drugs were my magic potion. From the age of about five or so, I can remember I felt wrong in my skin. Everyone else looked happier than I felt, more confident than I could understand. Everyone else seemed to have the instructions to life, but I had been born with them missing. I felt scared all the time, like I had to be more than I was for people to like me, and I felt shame over that. I was a mistake, I was sure of it. Otherwise, I wouldn't feel that way, right? Nobody else talked about being scared or insecure or unsure of what they were doing. I knew I was wrong, different in fundamental ways. Those feelings of inadequacy and shame and fear just grew. By the time I was 12 and found alcohol, I would have cut off my own arm if you had told me it would make me feel "normal," and that's what alcohol did. It made me feel what I perceived as normal. It made me feel invincible, brave, funnier, and happier. It made me feel free. For the first time since I could remember. And from that first drink I sought it out, and anything else that my parents told me was bad, because if they were wrong about alcohol being bad, they were wrong about everything else like cigarettes and drugs and sex before marriage. They had to be wrong about it all.

From that day on, I was on a mission to find and do all the things—all of them. I only felt peace and happiness when I was wasted, so that was my only goal. Not good grades, not college, not being a good daughter—just getting wasted. So I did. I was a mess from the beginning, unsurprisingly. I had plenty of consequences, but I couldn't see them for what they were. Alcohol and drugs were my cure and my answer to all that ailed me. I couldn't see them for what they were. Or what they would do to me spiritually and physically. I couldn't see that one day I would have sex with men for money, that I would leave my children, and that I would hate myself so deeply that I would know in my heart I deserved everything I got.

That's the slippery slope of addiction. You don't know what you are signing up for. Because no one thinks to themselves, "This is how I end up a junkie," while taking their first hit or doing their first line. Maybe some people do. But I sure didn't. I was sure I could control myself. I mean, I was a good girl from a good family. I had morals, character—a good solid compass. But none of that matters. Addiction doesn't care where you come from or who you are. It will take every shred of your decency and laugh when it's time to give more. So that's how a good girl, from a good family, becomes an escort and a felon.

I was booked into jail and time went on. I stayed in jail for six months, and I went from jail to treatment at an inpatient facility called House of Hope. All of it was hard. I was there for six months and, once graduated, did four more months in their outpatient program. I had several other probations that I completed over the next couple of years, all the while staying sober and raising my girls. I struggled to find a decent job that could support us; I struggled to find housing because of my limited income and felony record. I struggled to be a mom when some days, I barely felt human. With little help from anyone, I somehow managed, but, God, it was hard. I felt alone, scared, and absolutely exhausted from trying to keep it together so much of the time.

The thing that kept me going was this absolute knowing that I had literally been saved from a life of degradation and demoralization by something or someone greater than myself. I knew it in my bones. There was no other explanation for the way things happened for me. I could have gone to federal prison for up to eight years for some of the things that I'd done, but instead, as I kept putting one foot in front of the other while I moved through the terrifying process of cleaning up the wreckage I had created, and accepting the consequences for my actions, I kept encountering this beautiful grace. Grace that was given to me by almost everyone I encountered. There is no explanation for why I didn't go to prison and lose my children, except by the grace of God. There is no question in my mind it was divine intervention.

That grace has continued to follow me. It's nothing I earned, but that is the beauty of grace. Today I have almost eight years sober. I have a good job, my daughters are happy and healthy, and I own a home and enjoy a life that is something I could have never even imagined eight years ago. What is even more important than the outside success is that I don't hate myself any longer. I know I am here for a reason: I belong in this world among the living. That I have value and purpose. After being lost for so very long, I am finally found, and that is the greatest gift I have ever received.

Beginnings
By Gilda Jill Cook

It was a simple, two-story wooden white house with a white picket fence around the exterior. Three bedrooms were upstairs and one on the main floor. A traditional kitchen, dining room, living room, bathroom, and an enclosed front porch that Mom finished in knotty pine wood and country curtains on the windows. This was one of my mom's favorite spaces. Here she had her desk, sewing machine, deep freezer, washer, and dryer.

On the wall, hung the traditional black rotary dial phone, complete with a "party" line. In our small Midwestern community of less than a hundred people, neighbors often shared phone lines. You might pick up the phone to dial and hear someone talking. This meant that the line was in use by the other party, and you would need to wait until they were done.

Clearly, it was not an easy task to figure out exactly when the other person was done on the phone, so you would end up picking it up over and over and hope, by chance, they would get the hint and finish up their conversation sooner rather than later. And yes, sometimes, we lingered and listened to the neighbor ladies chatting up a silly storm about small-town events.

The memories of my early childhood deeply involve the simple white house I write about. I was born there, born in the house that was once a church, and later disassembled, moved and refurbished. My parents took great pride in our home, and my younger brother and I were frequently enlisted to help paint and repaint the white picket fence each summer.

The yard was lined with a wide variety of bushes. Flower gardens with large flat rock edges lined the sides of the house with Mom's favorite flowers and ferns: daisies, roses, and many wildflowers. The rocks were carefully collected from the streams running in the woods not far from home.

Fifty-eight years later, I still think of the simple house where my life began. Where my journeys started small—collecting blueberries, cherries, and apples from the trees we planted and watched grow. I was the little girl with the perpetual purple face due to climbing the mulberry trees and eating more than I ever managed to bring home in the berry basket. My knees were a constant eyesore. Each was a scabbed-up brown mess from apparently being an inept bike rider. But my efforts to balance my bike and my life, started there—in the little white house in the middle of the United States—and my early efforts would see me go on to finish high school, college, and journey to countries my parents only read about in books and magazines.

All of us begin somewhere, and life takes us along unique turns. We learn. We grow. We fall. We get up—over and over. What I still find fascinating, is how my perception and deeper understanding of life events still unravels, decades after. I find inspiration in the unexpected recesses of my memories from my parents and their struggles and persistence.

Despite neither having a high school diploma, they became diligent small business owners. They were hard-working, true nature lovers, and wise enough to teach me to push forward to be the best I could be in the areas that brought me joy. Money was always sparse, and our clothes came from rummage sales and second-hand stores, but they were always mended and clean.

From their humble and, at times, extremely difficult beginnings, my parents persisted. My maternal grandmother died from a ruptured appendix when my mother was only three years old. My mother went on to experience a terrible accident where she was badly burned over much of one side of her body, and had to live with a variety of different family members and, finally, a foster home.

Sadly, my father experienced early physical child abuse, and was removed from his parent's home to then be raised by his grandparents and devoted aunt, about whom he would tell countless funny stories.

Like most people, I look back and think of many things my parents could have done differently, but what I have found, is that with the passing of time, I continue to have deepening gratitude for all that they did for me. I am proud of them for all they accomplished.

I have dissected my childhood memories, and am now uncovering the joyful childhood memories that were concealed underneath traumatic abuse from extended family members. I now live free of the darkness that clouded so many of my days.

Each year, my flower gardens expand—daisies, wildflowers, and more rose bushes. Perhaps I will be planting a mulberry tree soon, where I can send my grandchildren with their berry baskets.

We Can Still Have Christmas
By Joann Cooper

It was the winter of December 1965, and I was seven years old. We had recently moved from Kansas to Worland, Wyoming, as my mother wanted to be near her family. My father was a truck driver and was going to join us later in Wyoming, because he was still working in Kansas. You might say our family was blue-collar, as my mother was a waitress and we were barely getting by.

My brother and I could always find ways to have fun, whether it be riding bikes, riding his go-cart, or exploring. He was six years older than I, and was my protector, but was sometimes mean to me (though not really). A perfect example would be when we hiked to the outskirts of town to ice skate on the canals that ran through the city. We weren't allowed to do that, so out of town we went! Our three cousins joined us on the journey. We arrived at our favorite spot, and we inched our way down the hill to the canal. We all put on our ice skates, and off we went. We knew we had to be careful to not skate too close to the edge, as the ice may be too thin. But I was following my brother as always, and when he went dangerously to the edge, so did I. Then—crash! I fell through the ice, and everyone stopped and laughed uncontrollably at my predicament I was so upset, I starting crying and realized that I was freezing. Our fun had ended. My bother helped me out of the cold water, and we started our way home. Swoosh - swoosh was the sound of my frozen pants as we walked home. And, of course, continued laughter from everyone. We arrived home, and my mother was mortified! How could my brother let this happen to his sister? He shrugged his shoulders, and my mother sighed. At every adventure, I was the one who got hurt or suffered somehow at the hands of my brother! I know not intentionally, but it sure seemed that way.

It was getting close to Christmas, and we still did not have a Christmas tree. I kept asking my mother, and she kept putting me off saying "We will, sweetheart, we are waiting for your dad to send us some money." This was the normal story with my dad. We were always waiting for him to help us, but with him being an alcoholic, he would always drink up the money. This was another reason we moved, so my mother could get support from her family.

Finally, on a Saturday, our mother came to us to say, "I am so sorry, but we won't be able to get a Christmas tree this year." I was mortified! I started crying, as I couldn't understand why. My mother explained that our father had been laid off from work and wasn't able to send any money for Christmas. I learned later that he had been arrested for a DWI and fired from his trucking job. This behavior from him would continue during my childhood.

My mother could always find a way to make things better and fun! She said, "Let's make our own Christmas tree! We have this old tall lamp pole, and surely we can find something to make it look like a tree." We had a pink chenille bedspread that we put on top of the lamp pole and arranged it to look somewhat like a tree. We didn't care that it was pink! Obviously, the ornaments we had wouldn't work on the bedspread, so we decided to make paper ornaments from what I can recall were camels, Santas, and similar items. We also used aluminum foil and popcorn to loop around the tree. My brother and I were so proud of ourselves—we had a Christmas tree! We both felt that we wouldn't have any gifts from our parents, but maybe Santa would visit us. Santa did not disappoint. We both had one present from our mom and one from Santa. I received the doll that I dearly wanted, and my mom made me a dress as she always did at Christmas and Easter. We received a board game that we played all day on Christmas. That morning, it had snowed, and the entire front yard and street looked like soft cotton balls. Totally covered in snow, unmarked from any cars or anyone walking through it. Truly beautiful. We couldn't wait to get outside. There was such stillness, and the air smelled so clean. We made snow angels in the front yard, made horrible-looking snowmen, and then threw snowballs at one another. My mother made a great Christmas dinner that included her homemade cinnamon rolls and pumpkin pie. Oh, the smell of it all baking was heavenly. She was a fantastic baker, canner, and seamstress. We all felt thankful and blessed! Our house was full of love, our tummies were full of food, and we had each other.

Our mother was the strongest person I have ever known. She taught me that you work hard, show up, don't complain, and put one foot in front of the other, even when times are hard. Despite us being pretty poor, my mom always found a way to put food on the table and clothes on our backs.

We always received a new pair of shoes for the new school year and the summer. She handmade many things and taught me how to sew, can goods, and cook. I know she didn't realize the value of what she showed us growing up and how it would impact our lives, but it did. I have carried these lessons with me well into adulthood and always knew that "You can still have Christmas" no matter what was put in front of you.

From Dysfunctional
Dating To Finding Love
By Liz Dawn

It was another sunny day in Scottsdale, Arizona. But within the walls of my townhouse it was dark and lonely.

I was curled up in a fetal position grasping my knees to my chest on my bed unable to move. I was paralyzed. Panic was taking over my body and there was very little breath going in and out of my lungs. The phone rang. It was Mike, my friend, my therapist. He could hear the despair in my voice and understood exactly where my mind was.

"What's happening?" he asked.

"I can't take it anymore. I cannot seem to find my way out of this pain."

I could hear him taking a moment to assess. Mike had seen me through so many dark nights of the soul and could easily tell what I needed.

"You have to move. Get out and exercise. NOW." He was insistent.

My heart was pounding as I rounded another corner and my legs had a mind of their own. I just had to burn off this feeling, change my body chemistry and get out of this fucking awful place.

It hit me. I have to change. I don't have a choice anymore. I had to figure out a way to move through the abyss of dysfunction and stop doing the same thing over and over again or else I would simply shrivel up and die.

I was in another emotionally tormenting relationship that wreaked havoc on every father issue I ever had. When triggered by a man's abusive behavior, I would spiral into a dysfunctional hell and become unreachable. Although I'd been in therapy for years, I was still not making changes. I knew I had to do something different.

That horrible moment was a pivotal turning point for me. I desperately wanted to be in a healthy monogamous relationship with a man, but had no clue how to go about creating it. I was 46 years old. Never married. Never engaged. No children, just a cat and a thriving business. I loved what I did and felt that my company, Celebrate Your Life events was the child I never physically birthed.

The irony of my situation was I was working with some of the greatest spiritual and personal development teachers in the world, and yet my personal life was a train wreck. I felt completely incongruent. I knew this high-level life coach and went to see him. Dave said to me, *"Liz, you are an amazing woman and there is not one reason that you should not be partnered with an amazing man. I can see exactly where you struggle and if you come see me, I promise I will have partnered within a year."*

He then told me his price which was well over my budget. When I shared it with my wonderful mom, she said, *"Elisabeth, if you want to do this, I will help you find the money."*

I thought about it for a couple of days. Coming up with $75,000 was not going to be easy and who's to say it would even work.

I went back to my mom, *"Okay, here's the deal. I am going to put myself on the 'Liz Dating Game Plan' and if in a year, it does not work, I will take you up on your offer and work with Dave."*

When I get my head set on something, I'm like a dog with a bone, as my friend Victoria used to tell me. I started to write out everything I knew to do to manifest a partner, but the most important piece was putting into action what I was doing wrong. What could I do differently? I went back to some old training and realized that every man I dated looked like one or all of my fathers. They were emotional idiots, alcoholics, unemployed, inappropriate, liars and downright assholes.

Well, that was a beginning. I learned to be discerning and used my head instead of my emotional heart or my libido to make my dating decisions. I learned to intentionally walk away from men that had those "red flags" of danger around them. Meaning, I was wildly attracted to them.

I put myself on every dating site possible. I dated and dated and must have consumed twenty gallons of coffee during those initial coffee dates. I made a list of every quality that I did not want in a partner and tore it up and threw it out followed by a list of what my heart desired.

I took off the rose colored glasses and stopped romanticizing every man I dated and became clear that I was looking to partner with someone for the rest of my life. This thought was sobering. I stopped sleeping with every man when I had the urge. I stopped making excuses to go out with someone again that I knew was not a fit for me. I worked very hard on myself going into areas that were deeply uncomfortable. I got real with me.

And then one day in January, about nine months into my Liz Dating Game Plan, I had yet another coffee date.

I was not wildly attracted to him. He was kind, handsome and gentle. He asked about me instead of me always asking the questions. He was a holistic practitioner, Chiropractor, Acupuncturist and Nutritionist. He came from a much more stable background. He was brilliant, spiritual and in amazing shape.

There he was, everything on my list. He was perfect. And yet, through my dysfunctional lens I could not see him clearly.

My therapist said *"Keep going out with him."*

I kept dating him and he kept showing up. Fully. Completely. With an open heart.

I could feel myself slowly opening to him. Trusting him. Letting him into my world. Falling gently easily in love with him. There was no drama, there was no fanfare, just pure sweetness and love.

At 49 years old, I married him. This beautiful gentle kind handsome brilliant man, Jeff.

Little Red Corolla: Getting a
Handle on Procrastination
By Cecilia Deal

I used to own a 1991 Toyota Corolla. It had a bright red exterior with a gray interior. It was a basic model with a four-cylinder engine that had just enough "get up and go." It had manual windows and door locks, which meant cranking a handle every time I wanted to roll down the window. But it did have seat belts, A/C and an AM/FM stereo.

I loved that car to pieces. It took me everywhere, from California to Colorado and back again, then to Wisconsin. It had a few quirks like a pinhole in the headlight I had patched with clear caulk and a windshield-wiper fluid reservoir that was attached with duct tape to the inside of the engine compartment. It had a slight hitch in the driver's side window when I rolled it down. It was an inexpensive purchase at 3,000 dollars and inexpensive to maintain. A lot like my life at that time—inexpensive.

I couldn't afford much, but made enough to cover my expenses. I had recently moved from Colorado to Wisconsin to be with my then boyfriend. He was gracious enough to pay for rent and groceries, which is how I survived. It was an exciting but financially stressful time.

One day, the inside handle broke on the driver's side. It was a plastic part, but critical nonetheless. The first part of the break still left enough plastic for me to maneuver the door open. But eventually that broke off too, and I could no longer open the door from the inside. I couldn't afford to fix it so I didn't even try.

Every time I needed to get out of my car, I had to roll down the window, stick my hand out, reach around and open the door from the outside. Or I crawled over the center console to exit the passenger door.

I did this for a whole year. Through the Wisconsin winters and with the catch in that driver's side window that required me to pull the glass back up by hand.

Later that year, I got the courage to call a dealership to find out how much it would cost to repair. Without the part it was 250 dollars! I couldn't afford to repair it and resigned to live with it the way it was.

A few months later, I ordered a repair manual for about 15 dollars. I scanned through its pages when it arrived, just for fun. I often enjoy figuring out how to fix things, and what I learned was interesting.

In the first few months I owned that book, I never considered looking up how to fix the inside handle on the door. Then one day I thought to myself, "I wonder if I can figure out how to fix this door handle?" The instructions were easy to find and the repair looked simple—a single screw and a thin metal hook. All I needed was a screwdriver and the new part.

But I still kept thinking, "No way. It can't be this simple." I tentatively called the dealership again, asking what the cost of the part would be: 100 dollars. It was still too expensive, but what if I could get the part somewhere else?

The first auto parts store I called didn't have it in stock but could order it. The second place I called had it available. The cost? Just seven dollars! It took me just ten minutes to get in the car, turn over the ignition and drive to the store. I was so excited!

Part purchased. It was a slightly different color than the original, but it would work. It still took me a whole day to get up the courage to try fixing it.

When I finally decided to tackle the job, I got out my screwdriver. I unscrewed the only screw and shimmied the broken handle away from the door. When the little slim metal hook inside made its appearance, I reached around and unhooked the handle. The old broken part was off!

It took me less time to put the new part on than it took me to take off the broken pieces: one hook and one screw. Twenty minutes and I had a working handle again. I waited a whole year to repair something that took me 20 minutes and seven dollars—a whole year!

Why? Because I assumed it would take a lot more effort and cost too much. I made a lot of assumptions and used those assumptions to procrastinate. I lived with an inconvenience I didn't have to live with if I had the courage to look further. I had let my fear get in my way.

Sometimes the thing you think will be really hard, just isn't. Sometimes the thing you fear the most isn't anything to fear at all. But if you don't look for options, you'll stay stuck in fear, uncertainty, or worse—complacency. And if you do that, life doesn't move forward. I don't know about you, but not moving forward isn't an option in my book.

I learned three things that day.

1. Sometimes the obstacles you make up in your mind are far more daunting than the obstacles in reality.

2. Don't dismiss a dream based on the obstacles you make up, or that others show you. We dismiss dreams before we give ourselves a chance to discover or voice them. Look further, get creative, and decide for yourself.

3. Anything is possible, even with a limited budget and resources. But you have to ask, get creative and think for yourself. Don't let anyone, including the "experts," tell you any different.

So stop procrastinating. Get out there and find your answer, because *what if* the answer is easier, less complicated, and a whole lot more accessible than you could have imagined? What then?

You might have to do something about it, and ultimately you might get what you want.

Step By Step
By Kandice Den

A re you a survivor? Are you strong? Do you know you can make it through whatever life throws at you? Do those questions make you shake your head in denial? Well, you might be surprised. People see stories of tragedy every day and think, "I don't know how that person lived through that." The funny thing is, most of those people wouldn't have thought they could do it either. But they did. And so can you. Here are a few stories from my life.

My aunt was my hero. For many years, she struggled with depression. These days, we'd say it was probably postpartum depression, but at the time, there was no term for it and no support. Her husband was with the Coast Guard and was gone for long periods of time, leaving her to care for two small children by herself. Moving often left her without community, and she was typically isolated. After a particularly bad episode where she seriously considered ending it all, she got help. She took one step forward. And then another. In the years to come, she ended up raising three children by herself as a single parent. She returned to school, and after ten years of night classes, finally got her CPA license. She battled cancer four times. If anyone asked, she would not have said she was a strong woman. She merely focused on getting through the next step, then the next one, and then the one after that. But, she never gave up. She set an amazing example for others, including myself.

My mother didn't become my hero until the end of her life. That's frequently the way it is with those closest to us. We do not see the courage right in front of us in our daily lives. I knew she had had a hard life, but I never realized how much strength it required of her until she was gone.

As a child, my mother endured physical abuse and almost died twice. My grandmother was negligent of her children, and so my mother stepped in to raise and care for her siblings. When she was 14, she lied about her age and went to work to provide for the family. Life wasn't entirely bad, though. As a young woman, she skied with the California Ski Patrol, rescuing stranded skiers. She also loved to fly in thunderstorms in the small planes owned by her employer. She was somewhat of a daredevil. However, during this time she also endured an abusive marriage, finally leaving because she feared for the safety of any children she might have. She eventually married my father and started our family.

After a life of service and caring for her family, she fell multiple times in her 80s and had to be placed in a care facility. She loved being at home, so I couldn't imagine what it was like to fall, go to the hospital, and then never go home again as she was transferred between hospitals, nursing homes, and assisted living facilities. She was in strange places, being cared for by strangers, not knowing when she would see her family next. Eventually, her health challenges got worse. Her mind deteriorated. She lost her husband. Despite everything, every time I saw her, she had the biggest smile and always seemed engaged with her friends at the nursing home. Right before Christmas in 2017, seven months after my father passed, she got sick with pneumonia. She hung on for ten days, but died on New Year's Day. Throughout it all, she never complained that life treated her unfairly. She simply did what needed to be done. She took it one step at a time. Looking back, she was my hero too.

As I look at my life, I've had struggles like everyone else. I worked three jobs to put myself through college, only to hit a recession and not be able to find a job. I went through a divorce in which I lost my business, my home, and my support system which left me working for minimum wage. As an only child and close to my parents, losing both of them closely together devastated me. As I worked on cleaning out their house and settling their affairs, I didn't know how I'd get through it at times. The memories often left me curled up in a ball in tears. Did I think I was strong at the time? No. I merely took life one step at a time. Just like my aunt. Just like my mom.

It's only recently I've realized that no one thinks they are strong. No one knows ahead of time that they can survive life's challenges. All you can do is meet each moment as it comes and do your best. Keep moving forward, even if it's only one tiny step at a time. Sometimes you may need help, and that's okay. No one said you had to do it alone.

When life has settled again, and you have some breathing space, honor your strength in getting through that situation. I believe that's where we lose the opportunity to reinforce for ourselves that we are indeed strong. We move on to the next thing life throws at us. But, we need to take a moment and honor what we have come through, and be grateful for the gifts hidden in the challenges—even if it's only discovering our strength.

The next time something happens, and you wonder how you'll get through it, stop and take three deep breaths, then figure out what the next step is. Focus on only the next step, not every step for the next five years. Complete that one next step. It won't be easy, but you can do it. You are stronger than you know, and someday, you will be someone's hero.

Spiritual Warrior Seeking Serenity
By Katie Elliott

A year ago, I was happy, vibrant, and full of life. I was a kindergarten teacher by day, country dancer by night, and I attended classes several times a week. I loved my life and had no intention of it changing. I didn't know what the future would hold, but I was excited about the possibilities.

One morning at school, I tried to tie my apron behind my back, but my arms just wouldn't reach. I also felt weak, and my left eye was beginning to droop. Alarmed, I reached out to the school nurse for help, and she suggested I contact my doctor. I took the following morning off to see the neurologist, expecting to return to school that afternoon. Unfortunately, that was not to be. Instead, I was diagnosed with Myasthenia Gravis (MG), a chronic neuromuscular autoimmune disease. After several tests, he explained the severity of my condition. I was admitted to the hospital. After a week of treatment, I was discharged and able to return to work.

A few days later, the symptoms returned. I went to the emergency room and was admitted to the hospital again. An advanced form of treatment was administered immediately, but my condition was not improving. After more tests were completed, I was informed that I had Stage II cancer related to the recent diagnosis. This was the beginning of a journey I never imagined taking, and I had no idea how these health challenges would change my life. I have had several surgeries, thirty rounds of radiation, weekly invasive plasma infusions, and never-ending doctor appointments. Eight months later, I reluctantly filed for early disability retirement. After thirty years of service, my career in education was over.

During the last year, I have been optimistic and filled with an attitude of gratitude. I have held tightly to these core beliefs.

Divine Order: *Everything you need will come to you at the perfect time.*
~ Unknown

I know that everything in my life is in divine order. God is revealing His plan for me daily. No matter the circumstance, His will is *always* for my highest and greatest good. He desires my life to be filled with light, love, peace, and harmony. And yet, life presents challenges through which I struggle. I don't believe in accidents or coincidences. There is nothing bad happening *to* me; everything in my life is happening *for* me, based on His divine plan.

Perception is everything. I always tell others: "I don't know what God has up and around the corner for me, but I know it is going to be awesome!" I have been blessed to see how divine order is working in my life.

Faith: *"Man says, show me and I'll trust you. God says, trust me and I'll show you." ~ Psalm 126:6*

When I don't understand why things occur in my life, I remind myself that it is *not yet time* for me to understand. However, the time is *always* right to walk in faith and believe in miracles that are about to come. As I experienced endless nights in the hospital, I knew faith was all that I needed. When I was scared and alone, I could hear God's comforting voice. Even though the doctors and nurses were speaking to me, it was as if we were the only ones in the room. It became overwhelmingly clear that my diagnosis, doctors, and treatments were secondary in the healing process.

Acceptance: *"Happiness can exist only in acceptance."*
~ George Orwell

Acceptance is the answer to all my problems today. When I resist what is happening in my life, I am not in alignment with God's will. Accepting difficult circumstances doesn't mean I have to like them. I can deny the inevitable or open my arms in acceptance of what is. I decided from the beginning that I was not going to fight with MG. Instead, I decided to befriend it. I believed that if I could come to peace with its presence in my body, we could work together in the healing process. I completely turned my will and my life over to the power of God.

When I live life on life's terms, I am in acceptance. I'm unable to change certain aspects of my life. People, places, and things don't always cooperate as I wish they would. I must turn my eyes within to see what it is about *me* that is causing this resistance. Inevitably, it has little to do with the outside world. It has everything to do with me and my attitude. I have had many opportunities in the last year to practice acceptance in my life. I feel serenity and peace today. For that, I am truly grateful.

Blessings: *"Train yourself to find the blessing in everything."*
~ Fiona Childs

I've always been a strong-willed, independent woman. My nickname is "Sassy Sunshine." I prefer to do things by myself, even when I would genuinely benefit from a helping hand. When I became extremely ill last summer, I had *no* choice but to ask for help. I couldn't drive my car for months. I needed rides to and from the hospital daily. I wasn't strong enough to clean, shop, or cook. I needed so much physical and emotional support. I was loved, cared for, and supported by my dear family and friends. *They* were the biggest blessing during this difficult time in my life.

I have secretly wanted to be an author since I was a young girl. I had dreams of spreading hope and inspiration. I wanted to make a difference in the world. I decided to become a teacher and put my dreams of writing on a shelf. Throughout the years, I could hear an inner voice reminding me I wasn't fulfilling my life's purpose. However, being diagnosed with MG has provided an opportunity for me to dust off my dream box and pursue my heart's desire. Becoming an author is a dream come true.

Epiphany
By Juhl B Estar

D o you ever sit in wonderment, in deep awe of how each moment in life is purposeful, even if it does not always feel that way?

Throughout many years of self-exploration (not always consciously), I have experienced the unseen elements of my creation wreak havoc on my life and bring the foundation of it crumbling down around me. Sometimes it felt like life or death. And I could say with heartfelt expression, that there were parts of me that needed to die—to be part of the rubble—so that something new could arise. These periods in my life were rarely, if ever, peaceful, easy, or without an opportunity to surrender to something greater than myself.

My early adult years were my most challenging and some of the most profound. I experienced a pivotal "epiphany" moment at age 25 while separated from my husband. I was living with a friend and working in a department store. I had just received some self-defense training because a young woman in the area had been raped and murdered. I remember thinking, "This is good information and training, but rape will never happen to me!" As I would come to experience, somehow I had managed to create a very powerful moment in which I had to choose—life or death.

Shortly after the training at work, I was home alone. My soon-to-be ex-husband was not around, my roommate was gone, and I was alone in our home, when the cat came running into the room. I noticed and thought it was odd, but I continued to do what I was doing without more consideration.

When I had finished my dinner, I got up and meandered into the kitchen where a dark figure with a booming voice startled me. I thought that it was my roommate pulling a joke on me, but it was, in fact, an intruder. The words, "Do as I say and I will not hurt you," stopped me in my tracks. It was surreal. I faced this unexpected moment that would change my life forever. This man knew what he wanted, and I felt it.

In an instant, it was as if time had stopped. I mentally went through the training I had experienced and all my options. I was hyper-aware that there were knives on the counter; I played out in my mind running out the front door or escaping out the back. I even attempted to bargain with the intruder, offering money or all my gold bracelets that dangled from my wrists. No, he was going to take what he came for—my body!

It was in that moment that a more powerful aspect of me knew "He can use my body, but he will not harm my soul!" At that juncture, my soul left my body and hovered above until the rapist had taken what he came for. Before leaving, he warned me that if I told anyone, he would be back.

This was a pivotal moment. I had a choice about what came next. What I remember was an amazing strength and courage rising up within me that was not mine alone. Alone I felt, yet I was not alone.

I called the police who took me to the hospital. I remember that a policeman questioned me about why this man came into my home. It wasn't until much later that I understood and felt the pain of this accusation.

I returned home that same night alone, except for my cat who had so boldly warned me that something was up. At that time in my life, I did not have the awareness to recognize the signs. In retrospect, I believe what we don't know can be a blessing.

The experience didn't end there. I often wondered if the rape was really the worst part of this experience. When my soul left my body, I did not feel what was occurring. Because of what I call my "out of body experience," I was unattached to the act of what was happening to me.

After this violation, I called my father to seek support. I am not entirely certain what I expected from him, as he was three thousand miles away. He was unsure of how he could help me. I felt unloved and unsupported. Then my roommate suggested I see her pastor for support. What came next, in my remembrance, was far worse than the physical experience of rape. The pastor stated that he did not believe me. As a matter of fact, he went so far as to tell me that I had made up the entire event to gain attention.

Over the following years, I chose to look within, to dig deeper, and to explore the potential that this event was something that I created. One could say, "There was a man, I experienced physical abuse, and it did happen to me!" I certainly had a part in what transpired, and I began to open to the possibility that this was a gift I created for myself; it was an opportunity to rise and remember that I am much more.

Unconsciously, a victim could advance. Consciousness allows awareness and acknowledgment that I *am* here. I have discovered that our life's experiences provide us many gifts. There are many levels like peeling the layers of an onion. I continued to ask for greater insight. More was revealed when I was ready to own, allow, and accept my part in the experience.

You see, in the moment, I rose above the physical violation, and I was given a huge gift. It was more than I could see. It was an inner knowing that I am the creator, I am the observer, and I am the experiencer. My soul distills my human participation into wisdom. It's why I'm here after all.

Facing The Demons
By Ana Evans

I want to say I was surprised when the bottom fell out—when our lives completely imploded. That wouldn't be true. The floor had been unstable and shaky, the cracks in the walls and foundation were becoming impossible to ignore.

We met when I was leaving a violent relationship. I had no interest in a new relationship. He knew this and kept showing up. He showed up for court dates, to hang out with my daughter and me. He showed up when we weren't sure where my perpetrator, who had been spewing violent threats against my daughter and me, was. He slept on our couch to make sure that we were safe. He showed up when I felt utterly alone and beat up by a system that was supposed to be protecting us. He wanted to do what was right by us even though he owed us absolutely nothing. I grew to love him; I had found my home.

Ben and I married, he adopted my daughter, and we had our beautiful boy. Our life was good. He worked hard so I could be home with the kids and pursue a career speaking and writing. He loved his work and was proud to be providing for his family. He was working ridiculously long hours; we were missing him, and he was missing the kids growing up. He began to buckle under the pressure, chronic headaches, back pain, increased anxiety, and more drinking.

When he went to the doctor to find relief, they prescribed muscle relaxers, as well as pain and anti-anxiety medications. We were slowly losing him to exhaustion, frustration, and these powerful medications. I suggested couples' therapy and workshops, anything that would help him find his way back to us. There were short periods when things would be better, he wanted to reconnect. We made an appointment with his doctor to discuss the next steps for his pain management.

When the doctor changed Ben's pain medication from Percocet to OxyContin, I reacted, my entire body jerked. The doctor patted me on the leg and said, "I know it's scary, but it's especially effective for pain management. Everything will be fine." Everything in me knew it wasn't true. He took the first pill, and I knew that we were in trouble. He slid into the relief like an old familiar coat. I was trapped. I knew that the medication was helping his pain levels, and we were losing him. His usage increased; the doctors kept writing prescriptions. He lost his job and went into freefall.

He stopped taking the OxyContin after accusing our son of stealing them. He realized how much he had been taking, and he agreed to go to a psychiatrist to get help. The doctor prescribed Klonopin. He promptly began abusing it and triggered a drinking binge like we had never experienced before. His organs were shutting down. He was dying in front of me.

I reached out to friends who worked in the recovery field. I reached out to another friend whose son had struggled with opioid addiction. I thought if I could only understand what was happening, I could help him. I reached out to his family for an intervention, but the dissonance between who they knew him to be and what our experience had become did not make sense to them. We were on our own.

I was exhausted and terrified. Ben was a husk of the man that we knew. He was utterly broken. He felt betrayed by the doctors, his mind and heart. The guilt and shame that he was carrying were suffocating his will to be. He collapsed into himself, devoid of feelings or motivation. We tried therapy, new meds, I created different getaways to try to reconnect.

He became emotionally abusive. His tone became harsh, his words cutting. He was secretive, unpredictable, and erratic. I didn't trust him to be alone with our son. I didn't know who he was or what was coming next. He stopped looking at me, touching me, talking to me. When he told me that he didn't love me anymore and hadn't for a while. I released us both. He had to learn about his addictions and the way they had impacted him and our family on his terms. I was tired of carrying the entirety of the emotional and spiritual weight of the family. I did not ask him to leave to convince him to get help, or do more, or to realize what he was missing, I had done all of that before. I simply asked him to leave.

He woke up and asked for another chance. I loved him, wanting nothing but good for him. I told him when he was ready to do his work, I would be there for him. I had moved on, I needed him to let me go. My heart ached to see his disappointment. My love for him had not ended, it had shifted from wife and lover to friend and support.

I've had the deep privilege of watching this man come back to himself. He is facing his demons and acknowledging the story that got him here. He is choosing to be the man he knows himself to be. He has a lot of work to do and understands that truth. He is reaching out and telling his family the truth of our story.

Healing and recovery are processes of doing hard work and acknowledging difficult feelings and terrible behaviors. It's facing the shadow side of ourselves and exposing them to the light. If we are lucky, we have a brave soul to walk that path with us to shine their light and help show us the way. I hope to continue to be that for Ben and others who by choice or circumstance end up in a place where they need a little extra light to help them see their path.

Life is not perfect, but it is good. My kids have their dad back. My grandkids have their papa. And me, well, I have a new and extremely good friend. I am grateful.

Love Heals
By Benjamin Evans

I was lost for six years. Can you imagine having little or no feelings for that long? I would break through sometimes, but nothing compared to what I call my "awakening."

I suffer from depression, anxiety, and chronic back pain. I'm an alcoholic, a binge drinker, an addict, and codependent. I am an empath, and I considered myself a Christian. I put all of my self-worth into my work ethic.

It was the perfect storm. Everything came crashing down at once. I was working 80-100 hours a week for two weeks straight, then having a week off. I never had time to rest my body and soul. I lost my job, and I could no longer provide for my family. It destroyed me.

I had quit taking and abusing Oxycontin, which was prescribed to me for pain management. It gave me the false impression that everything was grand. My codependency was telling me that my wife, Ana, was not happy. I believed it was my job to make her happy—another failure. Ana believes that, as an empath, I took on her trauma and internalized it, not understanding that these were *her* feelings, not mine. She was let go from the church where she worked, so I stopped talking with God.

I started to take Klonopin, an anti-anxiety medication. I abused it, and it triggered me to drink. I blacked out for two weeks, going into a dissociative state. I almost died. I became a different person, the complete opposite of who I am. I don't remember much. Ana tells me that I was verbally abusive to her and our son, Benny. I completely shut off all emotions. Over the next six years, Ana and I tried different therapies—she would coordinate weekend getaways for us, and I tried different medications. Nothing broke through this shell that trapped me. I stopped talking to her, stopped touching her, stopped feeling for her. We separated four times, and during the fourth time, something happened to me.

I woke up. All of a sudden, I wanted to be around Ana—I missed and longed for her. It took me off guard. When I saw her, I did not see merely a body; I saw all of the beauty that she is. Everything that I fell in love with and more. For the first time in six years, I could feel love again. I could hear her and feel her. The scales were torn from my eyes, and the cotton was pulled out of my ears. I love Ana! It felt like falling in love for the first time, and yet there was something significantly deeper, profound, and mystical. Then something else happened. I could feel both how hard she had fought for me and us, and all the hurt that I had caused her. I could hear and feel everything that she had been trying to tell me from the beginning of our relationship. Everything was coming at me, all of those memories. I was full of guilt and shame for everything that I had done to hurt her. I cried for hours, knowing how I mistreated her. I apologized over and over. I asked if there would ever be a chance. She said, "Sorry." Our marriage had been dying for a long time. She had moved on. She asked me to let her go.

The more I remembered and felt how she had fought for me and us, the more I loved her, and at the same time, it hurt so badly. Thinking of her with this amount of love is awesome, and knowing that I had repeatedly hurt her is devastating. I had this ball of emotion in me—full of love, hurt, joy, guilt, passion, and shame. How do I let this precious daughter of God, who loved me so much, go? How do I live with myself knowing I didn't take care of this gift?

I went into a deep depression of self-hate. I hated myself for turning into this monster. Everywhere I looked, it was dark. All I could think about was the way I neglected her and my children. For weeks all I did was write about how terrible I was. I welcomed death.

All through this, there was Ana. We talked almost every day, and she listened to what I had to say. She worried about me and did not want me to do this alone. She was there as always. She forgave me after everything and told me I am a good man. She told me that she loves me—she always has. She pointed me toward deeper understanding and hope. She has shown me so much grace. It's through her continuous love that I now understand that God has always loved me even when my worst was my best. She has shown me how to love like Christ loves. It's because of her I can finally say that I love me. I am able to let go of the guilt and shame, forgive myself, and that is only possible because she loves me unconditionally. I cry now, not because of what I have done, but because of what Ana has done for me. I lost my wife, who I was not even friends with, but I gained a closer, deeper profound spiritual partner who saved my life.

Ana,

I promise that my life, which you saved, will be lived to its fullest. I will love the way I have been loved. Thank you for all of it. I love you more than words could ever say.

Ben

1 Corinthians 13 4-8

Love is patient, love is kind. It does not envy, it does not boast, it is not proud. It does not dishonor others, it is not self-seeking, it is not easily angered, it keeps no record of wrongs, does not delight in evil but rejoices with the truth. It always protects, always trusts, always hopes, always perseveres. Love never fails...

Constellations
By Kathryn Ferguson

A ugust 3rd, 2017, was a typical summer day in picturesque Vancouver, British Columbia. The sun shone upon its residents with confidence. Most of my educator colleagues were enjoying the pinnacle of summer vacation. Enough time had passed since school let out to sink fully into the season, and September was far enough away not to hold us accountable for planning and preparation. Local pools and parks hosted joyful children whose delightful squeals of laughter reminded passing adults to take a breath and appreciate the boastful pleasure of the season. Summer was showing off, and it suited her well. For me, summer had all but passed me by. As I sat in an ergonomic neurologist's office, I was not lamenting the loss of lazy summer afternoons. I was waiting for an answer that would change the course of my life and redefine my sense of self. That answer was Multiple Sclerosis (MS).

Getting diagnosed with MS at the age of 40 came as a huge relief. I realize that this sounds counter-intuitive; however, I had been living in a state of physical confusion for months. As a high school English teacher, I was not immune to stress, but this year's fall schedule had left me reeling. In addition to teaching over 200 students, I was also juggling numerous extra-curricular activities and writing my master's degree thesis. Outside the scholastic bubble, I was heavily engaged in local music and theatre, which kept me busy most evenings. Like a lot of educators, I was taking on too much, and something had to give. Well, something did, and it did so in spectacular fashion.

My progression of symptoms can best be described as a slow burn. Initially, I started experiencing numbness and tingling in my hands and feet. This was followed with electric shock-like sensations that would ripple through my body any time I dared move my head. Then, insomnia came for me. On many evenings, I didn't fall asleep until early morning (if I slept at all). I lost my appetite, experienced bouts of vertigo, and struggled with balance, resulting in a kaleidoscopic array of bruises that frequently adorned my body like cruel bric-a-brac. Naturally, I was also suffering from extreme fatigue—a type of "teacher-tired" I had never felt. Recognizing that I couldn't continue living this way, I went to see my family doctor. He wisely concluded that these symptoms went far beyond general stress and demanded answers. Thus, began my medical journey.

Over the next few months, I went for every test imaginable. I was poked, prodded, injected, and squeezed. I was analyzed, studied, interpreted, and deciphered. Finally, several MRI scans definitively portrayed a clear picture of the monster inside of me—a monster that doesn't scare me anymore. Once I could name the unknown, I was in a position to fight and extinguish its power. My diagnosis allowed me to put a name to a litany of symptoms. As I listened to my neurologist explain my new reality, a wave of relief washed over me and crashed against the shore of my psyche. It was in this exact moment that I knew that MS would change my life for the better. This disease, where my body attacks its central nervous system, was sent to make me the best version of myself. In short, this disease has been a gift.

Don't get me wrong. I'm not excited to have MS, and I certainly wouldn't wish this disease on others. I do, however, value the lessons I've learned and continue to process. Often dubbed "an invisible illness," MS can wreak havoc without visually obvious symptoms. For example, people cannot see the burning numbness of the pins and needles sensation in my hands and feet, nor is my internal vertigo apparent to the general public. Even when I'm feeling like an over-sized sloth, I push through the fatigue and carry on. Hence, to most people, I appear *normal*. This experience of battling a disease that hides so insidiously has strengthened my empathy. I have a keener understanding of the pain that many people hide beneath the surface, and I find myself leading a kinder and richer life. Of course, I still take people at face value, but I've learned that occasionally it takes a bit of digging to understand the human condition better. Sometimes, that crabby guy at the check-out counter or the grouchy gal at the bank have valid reasons for having less than sunny dispositions. Is someone unpleasant? Be kind anyway. Kindness multiplies itself.

Most importantly, MS has allowed me to be vulnerable—repeatedly. I continue to share my story (with all its triumphs and setbacks) to raise awareness about this disease and to remind others that many are walking amongst us with invisible pain—both physically and emotionally. Occasionally, life demands us to flip the script. Instead of getting bogged down in negativity, I've chosen to view my MS as an opportunity for personal growth. The first time I viewed the images of my brain, I was introduced to lesions (lovingly referred to as "spots" by my neurologists). This was scary—it was akin to seeing holes in my head. Once I got over the shock of witnessing the intense damage to my brain, I was able to see something else. To me, the lesions on my brain looked like constellations, a recognizable pattern of stars, bright lights of hope that live within my galaxy. These inner constellations have caused distress, but their overwhelming luminescence has lit a pathway towards courage. As I continue to walk along this road of valor, I will occasionally remind myself to look up into the night sky and witness the stars and patterns that make the sky devastatingly beautiful. Furthermore, I will remember that we all hold our constellations within ourselves. Some are vivid, and some are dull, but they create the fabric of our humanity.

Dear Abby: Extraordinary
Advice On An Ordinary Day
By Lori Verbin Flaum

There are times when extraordinary advice comes to us on ordinary days. On this ordinary day, my mother-in-law was arranging fresh bagels, lox, sliced tomatoes, onions, and cream cheese on a platter for our Sunday brunch.

My mother-in-law, Abby, was like Dear Abby, the advice columnist, except she dispensed her pointers whether you wanted them or not. She shook a bedazzled finger at me and said, *"Don't be so meek.* Tell people what you think." My 20-year-old self laughed self-consciously and shrugged her off. I thought I knew what she meant (I did not). At 53, I recognize the epic meek that my mother-in-law saw in me that day.

My grandmother was a Japanese immigrant. She had an arranged marriage and sailed to this country with her abusive husband and generations of cultural subservience. My first-generation mother did her best to defy the expectation of obedience and docility, but was mostly passive/aggressive. Needless to say, my propensity for meekness was embedded deeply in my culture, never questioned. Until that ordinary day.

I envied my mother-in-law's bold nature. I wished my ancestors had taught me to be loud, brazen, and outspoken. Abby's observation was an off-the-cuff remark that turned into a lifetime of overcoming. "Don't be so meek" became my personal goal and mantra when my insides turned inside out with anxiety and fear. Over the years, I discarded old ways and traditions, forged new skills, and acquired a different set of tools. I discovered a deeper wisdom in her words than even she likely intended. So, on this ordinary day, I present to you my tips to blast away your meek and embrace your superpowers.

Don't be afraid of your voice.

You have one, so use it. I would balk at the idea because I feared rejection, condemnation, judgment, and confrontation. Abby's answer was, "Feh, who cares about that? Your voice is there, let it out." Sigh. Her give-zero-fucks attitude was easier said than done. I practiced sharing my opinion with more grace than aggression and it didn't come quickly or easily. Gently remind yourself that you are learning a new skill. Practice, practice, practice.

Don't be afraid of your opinion.

Opinions are squishy things. They bring people together, but they can polarize. Learn to hold on to opinions but not so steadfastly so that you're unable or unwilling to listen, especially in disagreement. Now, when the concept of stating my opinion is daunting, I look at it as "sharing thoughts and ideas."

Don't be afraid to say no.

No is seriously uncomfortable for meek people. As we nurture our self-esteem and build self-confidence, it is vital for us to learn how to say "No" with grace. "No" does not have to be confrontational or aggressive. "No" is not negative, and it is perfectly acceptable to include boundaries and limitations. Establishing safe boundaries builds self-confidence. It is scary and intimidating, but I am more successful when I deliver them calmly, firmly and with love. (Pro tip: please and thank you goes a long way to ease tensions.)

Take care of others but don't sacrifice your needs.

Taking care of someone else's need does not have to be at the expense of yours. Understand what it is to be a martyr and deeply reflect if you exhibit such qualities. Being a martyr is neither noble nor generous.

Being sensitive is not the same as being meek.

I was constantly told I was too sensitive as though it were a character flaw. I spent many years equating sensitivity with meekness. Meek is being overly compliant and submissive, and l felt used and walked-on like a doormat. Being sensitive is a different animal. Sensitivity is an emotion and feeling. It is understanding and compassion. It enables people to open up and share, and it encourages deep conversation. It is my #1 superpower.

Know when to back down and when to rise up.

Embrace your newly found confidence. Feel it in your bones. Know it in your heart. Understand that truly confident people are calm, quiet, and humble. You don't need to be aggressive or loud or beat others about the head to be heard. Trust your truth and allow space and time for others to come around.

Be comfortable being uncomfortable.

Being uncomfortable is being human. It is uncomfortable to make mistakes. It is uncomfortable to be ignorant. It is uncomfortable to be awkward. Uncomfortable is your friend. Take your uncomfortable and marry it with determination. Learn and grow to become strong and resilient.

Be less fearful of confrontation and have more conversation.

Meek people hate confrontation. Use your superpower (sensitivity) and engage in conversation to solve problems. One of the best ways to diffuse confrontation is to *care* what the other person is saying even (and especially) if you do not share the same opinion. Everyone wants to be heard. Listen deeply and connect. This is superpower #2.

Be strong, vulnerable, and loving.

All at the same time. Superpower #3.

Be brave and creative.

Do that thing even though it is scary! There is nothing that you cannot overcome because your three superpowers will protect you. Because YOLO! Dream big! Be amazing!

Abby was a force to be reckoned with. Today so am I. No longer can she field any more of my "Dear Abby" questions or parcel out her wisdom and snark. She has passed the baton, and I willingly received it. My job is to honor the gifts she has given me and continue to pay it forward. Now I meld Abby's words with mine and created a new voice. Someday I hope our extraordinary advice will help someone on their ordinary day.

Don't be so meek. Rise up. Be proud of the person you are today and the person you have yet to become. Own your truths. Embrace your superpowers. And most of all, give and receive abundant love.

Keeping Your Promises
By Karen Gabler

A Gaelic proverb reads, "There is no greater fraud than a promise not kept." We are taught that integrity and commitment are key qualities. Breaking a promise is the utmost act of betrayal. But what happens when keeping a promise will likely destroy us?

I was nearing my 30s, and my peers were coupling like animals on Noah's Ark. Weekends were filled with bridesmaids' dresses and wedding gifts. We danced to one DJ after another on parquet floors in hotel banquet rooms, watching friends make promises to each other.

I was dating someone in my closest circle of friends. I envisioned a future filled with beach parties, vacations, hikes, and all the activities we regularly enjoyed. We liked the same people and the same things. With two servings of pressure and a dash of ultimatum, I pushed for our day of wedded bliss.

In preparing the wedding of my dreams, I selected all the obvious choices. The guest list included over 400 of our closest friends and family. I found the perfect dress; we selected the perfect menu. Days before the wedding, I sat with my favorite women, wrapping hundreds of chocolate-dipped cookies into lavender netting for party favors. I shared that my fiancé and I had an ugly battle about the reception seating chart; my tribe assured me this was normal pre-wedding stress.

On my wedding day, I walked the church aisle, feeling every bit the princess the day was intended to serve. At the reception, I smiled exuberantly from our head table. My new husband said, "You should change your facial expression. You look kind of crazy right now." That night, friends carted him to our bridal suite and deposited him on our bed to "sleep it off."

Three years later, I was lost in a pit of despair. My actor husband asserted that success required waiting at home for the phone to ring. This meant playing video games while filling the sink with dirty dishes that welcomed me home from long days of legal practice. When the phone didn't ring, he became despondent and insisted that buying a boat would improve his mood. Desperate to manufacture the glorious lifestyle I had envisioned, we bought the boat. It sat in the yard, gathering dust and cobwebs like our relationship.

It was clear this marriage promised nothing but misery. I had made a critical error. And yet, I was a "good girl." Marital commitments were not to be taken lightly. The product of divorced parents, I knew that my seeds of discontent could reap a harvest of destruction if left unchecked. I had promised that I would give myself to this commitment for the rest of my days. I accepted that my poor choice was my only choice. I had made my bed, and I would lie in it.

Fate intervened when my husband expressed uncertainty about the future and asked for a separation while he considered his options. He packed his belongings while I sobbed. As I braced for the feelings of failure and loneliness I knew would come, I felt my emotions rising like a tidal wave: relief, peace, *hope*. In his selfishness, he had freed me from the chains I had so willingly padlocked around my soul.

I dove into my future like a dolphin released from captivity. Friends commended me on my strength in surviving a divorce. I tried to explain that it took no real courage to end it; it would have taken far more courage to stay in it. My initial resolution to stay did not reflect my willingness to keep a promise. Rather, it represented a shattering of the promises I needed to make to myself.

Several years later, after much self-reflection, the universe handed me the man of my dreams. Infused with a heart of gold, the ability to see good in everything, and an unwavering desire for my happiness, he listened intently as I described what I wanted, needed, desired for my life. Our wedding was at the beach with eleven of our closest friends and family. We spent the morning chatting, with the ocean as our background music. We were almost late to the ceremony, as we lost track of time, infused with love. We wore casual, creamy clothing and felt the grass under our feet. We laughed as we joyfully committed our lives to each other; the thunderous waves and the resonance of the conch shell sealed our future. I felt relief, peace, *hope*.

As our daughter grew up, I considered how to teach her the importance of keeping a promise. I reminded her that when you make a commitment, you must follow through. Your word is your bond, and reneging on a promise is the utmost in betrayal. And then, I thought about promises I've made, and commitments I've broken. I thought about the jail sentence that could have been, and the abundant freedom I found in its place. I took her hand and explained the true importance of a promise.

You see, sweetheart, integrity and commitment are important, to be sure. Maintaining these values depends first upon finding integrity in the promises you're making. Promise only what will serve you, followed by serving others. Commit only to those things that will make your heart sing. Covenant only to explore an opportunity, but not to carry it out until you feel the seeds of joy stirring within you.

Most of all, remember that the promises to be kept above all others are those we make to ourselves. You came to this earth with promises to your soul: to serve your best purpose, explore your highest good, experience your utmost evolution. If you promise anything to another that compromises these commitments, you have already broken your promise to yourself, and your soul begins to wither. Plant your seeds, decorate your garden, and cultivate your soul. This, my darling girl, is your true gift to the world.

Finding Your Tribe
By Sarah Gabler

When I was entering sixth grade, I was sure I would find my tribe at a local middle school. I grew up with a strong interest in the arts, expressing myself through creativity and performance. I thought that my school, with its focus on performing arts, would be filled with students like me. I was sure that I would find best friends for life; people who would understand my goals and share my interests. I also thought that everyone would be nice to me because people respect people who are like them. I knew that middle school would be some of the best years of my life.

I walked in with great confidence. I high-fived my teachers as I entered through the balloon-filled archway. I smiled widely at my fellow students. I was excited about the new adventures I believed lay ahead of me. On my first day, I saw a student looking lost in the courtyard. She asked me quietly if I could help her find her class. Noticing that we were headed to the same class, I walked with her, smiling and encouraging her. I thought, "Maybe this is one of my new friends!" To my surprise, when we reached our classroom, she walked away from me and sat with other students—no thank you, no goodbye.

As the year went on, I was stunned to find that many students were downright rude to me, and to each other. Despite the school's strong "no bullying" stance, students used profanity, called each other names, and made fun of each other. I talked to my mother about my sadness and distress. My reality wasn't matching my expectations—I was so sure that if I spent my time with people who had the same interests as I did, we would bond. My mother reminded me that just because I was in the same building or the same classes as other students, did not necessarily mean that they shared my values.

In the spring, my mother took me to the True Magic conference in Phoenix, sponsored by Celebrate Your Life. Although I was the only kid at the conference, I was surprised that the attendees were actually interested in what I had to say. They came up to us at breakfast and asked if they could sit with us. They asked me questions and listened to my answers! They asked what I thought of the speakers, and they waited to hear my thoughts. A speaker invited me on stage to participate in an exercise about expressing yourself. As I spoke into the microphone in front of 600 women, I felt the support of the audience in wanting each other to succeed.

After the conference, I returned to middle school, uplifted and inspired. I knew that everything would be different now! Unfortunately, I was wrong. My fellow students were still gossiping, making fun of each other (and me!) and swearing at each other. Nothing had changed—and yet, I felt completely different. There was little support or encouragement; students seemed more interested in dragging each other down than lifting each other up.

Months later, my mother and I went to another Celebrate Your Life conference in Skamania, Washington. The event was filled with spiritual speakers sharing information on quantum physics, personal development, spiritual values, and sharing love with others. I saw attendees from the prior conference, who remembered me and expressed their excitement that I was there. Again, people asked me questions, and again, they cared about my answers. Everywhere I looked, men and women smiled at each other, hugged each other, and listened—sincerely listened—to what each other had to say.

I returned to school in the fall, entering seventh grade. Once again, I was sure that things would be different. After all, we had all matured, right? Spoiler alert: it was no different! I was sure that people would be nicer to me, more open to me, more willing to share. Instead, it almost seemed as if another year together had emboldened people to be even meaner and even more aggressive. I began to wonder if perhaps it was only conference attendees from other states who were nice or cared about who I am. After all, no one at middle school seemed to care about anyone else— at least, not for longer than a day or so, or only when they needed something.

In an effort to begin spreading the love I felt with my Celebrate Your Life tribe throughout my middle school, I launched the Sticky Note Project. Each day, I created sticky notes with various affirmations: "Be Happy!" "The World Needs Kindness!" "Spread Kindness Today!" "You Are Loved!" "You Are Enough!" After school, or when I left each classroom, I left anonymous sticky notes on lockers, doorways, desks, and seats. Since I wasn't there to see the reactions to my notes, I had to trust that putting goodness out into the world—somehow, in some small way—was good enough.

I have learned that no matter how hard you try, you won't change other people. You have to stay true to yourself, and believe in yourself. I also learned that your tribe isn't only a group that likes the same things, attends the same events, or who are physically close to you as you move through your life. Your tribe is not necessarily those who share your space.

Instead, your tribe is made up of those who share your values. A tribe is a group of people you can count on, who will always have your back, whether they know you well or not. Your tribe is a group that envisions the world as you do, even if they live in another state or come from another generation. When you connect with others by sharing your soul, it is only then that you can allow yourself to be seen, and to be truly loved for who you are.

The Unfolding
By JG Delos Reyes Garcia

I had everything planned. I'd migrate to America to be with my parents at 10, earn a doctorate at 29, marry an honest man at 30, have children by 35, and live happily ever after in our plantation home. Life was black and white. I romanticized my future with starry-eyed certainty. Although I stayed inside the lines and played by the rules with religious obedience, life led me into different directions. At 39 and short on academic ammunition, I was an estranged daughter and a childless divorcee burdened by personal catastrophes. It wasn't the life I had imagined. Behind a public fairytale façade, I sank into despondency as I was catapulted into a precipice of shattered dreams and paralyzing agony.

Tragedies visited me every season like a one-two gut punch. Divorce was the knockout blow. Pulling the plug on my marriage and the harrowing days thereafter drove me to recalibrate my priorities, unpack my past, and pivot into a simpler lifestyle anchored in unyielding values. I gained insight into unresolved heartbreaks from hiding in blissful denial, shackles of childhood shame and anger, and the quality of my friendships at my all-time low. With my marital failure under conjecture, I felt the odds stacked against me. Above all, it motivated a journey into self-discovery.

Life is not a rehearsal. It'll take us for a downward spiral and leave us raw without a safe harbor in sight. Even with military precision, we can't circumvent its blast radius unscathed. Not every intelligent risk will pay off. We'll walk into the unknown because a linear path is not an option and sitting on the sideline is not an "out." At some point, with collapsed confidence, we'll fall off the wagon with blind spots and regretful choices then land on colossal consequences. Setbacks will fire in succession like a combat zone. Plagued by unbearable anguish, we armor against psychological traumas with quick and easy fixes to escape from torture. Our desolate, battered hearts reach for surface solutions without long-term benefits to mask the hurt. Moral potholes magnified by extreme loneliness lower our standards to the second-best thing, which alludes to moving forward, to fill the void.

People will bail out when we're in dire need of a lifeline. On our darkest days, more than ever, true friends will be revealed. When times get tough, fair-weather ones will renege on their promises, attack with adversity and criticism, exploit our strongest weakness, and flee with convenient excuses. Intentions without actions is lip-service loyalty. There'll be betrayals that cut through the bones and half-baked stories that divide and destroy.

When life threw me in the deep end, I swam to my own rescue. I picked up the pieces and crawled out of hell. To move on with clarity and peace, I turned within. With small but significant moves, I dove deep into my life's dark domains and felt the greatest pain I've ever known. In stillness and solitude, I reflected on every inch of every root cause of my struggles. The past I've lugged around and accountability I've avoided were deconstructed with brutal self-honesty. Singleness is an empowering choice that surpasses relationship stagnation. Time alone with my thoughts was spent quieting my demons, fueling ambitions, defining boundaries, and knowing who I am. Settling for anyone to have someone is beneath my dignity and below my potential. *"For now"* is an ill-fated substitute for forever. I know my worth, and I'm divinely clothed in strength.

Born of my arduous transformation is the unfolding—a period of looking at an uncomfortable mirror, finding my identity, and aligning my energy with my internal compass. It is rising from the ashes stripped of stigmas and awakening with new heightened self-awareness. Humbled by the privilege to have loved and be loved, I'm thankful for what is and what can be. At rock bottom, I learned pain's purpose. Through my trials, I found my truth.

If you're at the end of your rope fighting havoc and pushed beyond the point of breaking, don't lose your grip. You're a wounded warrior, battle-hardened, and unapologetically unstoppable. Grief is the gateway to a new beginning. Start at any moment at your own pace. Move the needle, shift gear, turn the corner, and change from inside out. Happiness, joy and victory are on the other side of suffering, so stay the course. Life is your test and teacher. Look at it square in the eye. Harness the power to show up, do the heavy lifting, and forgive offenses. Forgive yourself while you're at it. In moments of sorrow, self-love and self-acceptance leverage your empathy and compassion for the highest good of all. Your growth is a gift when used in service to something bigger than yourself.

Be brave enough to fall into beautiful ruins and let your colors bleed. With resilience and heroic efforts, you'll unfold into wholeness with resolve, grace, and gratitude. Cherish those who linger, love, and keep you steady without judgment or lapses in integrity. On similar trajectories and with shared principles, continue to fill each other's cups. Troops who leave men behind create spaces for stronger circle of influence and an upgraded social environment. If it no longer has constructive use, acknowledge its temporary contribution then release.

Everyone gets lost on the wrong track, but there's hope on the horizon. The universe is working for you. Surrender with radical trust and an attitude of abundance. All you have is now. You're exactly where you need to be. Let go of expectations, comparisons, and competitions. Nobody's a paragon of perfection. Life's ultimate command is progress —to be better than you used to be. Feel and embrace your meaningful mess and useful mistakes. It's part of being human.

Under layers of loss are lessons masquerading as hardships. Internalize these lessons. As time passes, emotional landmines become tolerable challenges. Victor Hugo said, *"Even the darkest night will end, and the sun will rise."* And so, shall you. Your future best-self will then whisper, *"When the dust settles, I'll be waiting."*

Learning To Trust Again
By Kim Giles

Sometimes life is especially hard. The older I get, the more I know this to be true. Don't get me wrong, I still believe everything happens for a reason. And I still believe that life is good and beautiful even when it isn't. But it's still hard. Between bills, stress, health, family, friends, loss, heartbreak, and so much more, sometimes it can feel like we are being tested time and again.

A few years ago, I ended a long-term relationship with a man who I thought I would be with forever. I would like to say that it ended smoothly and that we are both moving on without complication. But that would be a lie. I know he is not good for me. I know now (finally) that we are not the right one for each other. And yet, he keeps contacting me. And worse, I keep responding, often against my better judgment. But love is funny like that, isn't it? We can know the right answer in our brains, and even in our hearts, but still, we may react in another way. That relationship broke my ability to trust myself as well as others. How do I learn to trust again?

Within the past two years, I have had to put down both of my Labrador retrievers because of cancer. First, Hunter was an old soul from the get-go, who always seemed to know exactly what anyone needed. And then Bailey, who lost a spark when we no longer had Hunter, but kept going until the end. He was the puppy who never settled down—until the cancer took over. While I am beyond thankful for the years that I had with each of them, and grateful that I had the strength to be with them until their last moments on Earth, it is an experience that I would never wish upon anyone. Their loss reminded me that when we open up our hearts and our homes to others, then we may likely end up with a broken heart. I finally understand why people, who had dogs their entire lives, would say, "I just can't do it anymore." I always thought they meant that they wanted their freedom, less dog hair and mess, but then I realized—no, they can't go through *that* ending again. And I got it.

A home without a dog was scarily quiet. The silence made the loss magnify instead of being reflective. I kept reminding myself to sit with the grief. I would picture the little blue Sadness girl from the movie *Inside Out* sitting next to me as I felt the immense grief that would move through me without warning.

After I put down my second lab, Bailey, people would ask when I was going to get another dog. These comments infuriated me. Didn't they understand that they were not only dogs to me? That they could not simply be replaced? It wasn't about missing *a* dog. I missed *those* dogs in particular. I didn't know if I would ever get another dog or certainly another lab. I remember the first time I saw a yellow lab at the airport after Bailey's passing, and I cried into their fur as the dog quietly stood still and let me work through my grief. I walked away saying, "And that's why I love labs so much."

With time, I slowly opened myself up to the idea of getting another dog. But not just any dog. I did not want to go looking for one. I wanted it to happen organically. One would fall into my lap when they were ready. When I was ready soon after Christmas, I received a social media post that someone had returned a six-month-old yellow lab, and it was in need of a home. Reluctantly, I went to see him, along with my mom and my dad. The dog was bigger than I pictured. He was pacing. He looked exactly like Bailey. When my dad bent down next to him, he even held paws with him, like Bailey used to do. That was probably when I knew that I would be taking him home. This dog needed love. He nervous peed like a sprinkler. He would come towards us and then back away, unsure if we would hurt him like the others. I could relate to his uncertainty. We took him home and gave him the name Lucky. He was not trained at all as we had been led to believe. So I hired a trainer to help us work through his issues.

Training him has been a lesson and an adventure. Teaching him to trust and relax has been a test for both of us. While he still looks a lot like Bailey, his personality is more like Hunter. I love that he is a combination of both of them. Sometimes I think how fun it would have been to have them all playing together, young and healthy.

Getting Lucky was a test of faith for me. Together we are learning to trust again. It isn't easy, but we both know it will be worth it. And someday, I am sure that I will find a man who will love us both and be a reminder of what happens when things are meant to be and when we follow our gut, listen to our heart, and trust that everything will be okay.

Rescue dogs, much like each of us, have a backstory that we likely will never completely know or understand. But with time and patience and love, people, like rescue dogs, will learn to love and trust again. And hopefully, we'll find a huge smile on their face the next time we meet.

Tiny Victories
By Rach Gill

R eality isn't always beautiful. It knocks you to the ground and helps you realize some of the old stories you left on repeat.

I stood in front of my mirror, staring hard into the blue eyes of the smaller version of me. I reached out my hand, welcoming her back, acknowledging all parts of me. The girl from my childhood, and the woman I am, make me the warrior I've become. In choosing to take my power back, I overcame trauma in my childhood.

I was sitting by the window
Watching the stars when the phone rang
I stopped counting the stars
Almost like my heart stopped beating
I put my hand to my chest
listening
I've been told sometimes loss
Rushes at you
Full throttle
Doesn't prepare you
No time before it hits you hard
You wonder
If maybe
If you hold your breath long enough
It will all stop
Pain paused
When I heard the phone
I held my breath
Didn't stop what was to come
So it's the little moments
Tiny victories
You grasp for those times
Hoping they won't break apart
If you touch them
Sometimes life is fragile
A breath
A whisper
You feel like it might break you
Trauma plays its part

Tries to hook your mind
Drag you to the back
Sometimes though
That strength
You think you've lost
Courage
The one thing you try to muster
Plaster your face with fake positivity
You don't dare let your guard down
You think it protects you
It does
For moments
When you surrender
Let it go
Walls crash down
You feel like you may never stop failing
When you look down
It's dark
Seems like a hole of emptiness
Then suddenly all that rage
That stubbornness to hold it all in
Breaks you like a dam
Rips you apart
Only for you to feel like you've been stretched out wide
Like playdough
All directions
Then you realize
It's all resilience
It still exists within you
Reach for it
Take back your power
Stand back up
Be a flame
So when the world grows dark
You share your light
Your voice
So everyone knows they aren't alone. That's where I find my peace.

I've been a raging war with pieces of me floating around, embracing grace and love for me. The light I offer is the light you offer. We are mirrors to each other and reflect the negative and positive things we need to heal in. Even in the mess, we all offer more than we acknowledge in ourselves. Pause and know that no matter where you are in your healing, you offer great light in this world. In the last few years of speaking my truths, I have struggled to speak without stuttering. As I have kept stepping out, my voice has grown stronger. It's become a resilient wall of hope and truth. I have accepted that in my vulnerability, my story is a beautiful one. I have struggled my whole life feeling like a burden, and these thoughts sneak up in my mind, and I retreat to the back again for fear of taking up too much space. I still became someone no one thought I would become. I didn't even believe it myself. I was given an opportunity to grasp the importance of my existence here. In spite of people's attempts to make me feel less than, my courage has risen and my heart has overflowed with the gift of experiences the universe has given me. As a young child, I was able to find purpose in my life under every cloud I lifted. Once you lift those cloud covers, there is always sunlight to be found. My story has tattered edges; the words on the pages have been infused with tears of joy, and pain. I have woven a kaleidoscope of my experiences and funneled them into my passion for life.

I was eight years old when I experienced riding a beautiful, white horse through the majestic mountains. Running my hands along his soft mane, I felt the trust for him. We galloped the trail; I felt surrender and the need to control dissipate. Being on Pete was a life-changing experience for me. I learned it was possible to trust even after being hurt in life. He whispered life back into my soul.

For a moment, I saw my pain in the light
I began to cower
Feeling like I was going to sink into the corner
I felt my pain
It burned in every place the light touched it
I felt like my body was set to simmer
I raised my head
Knowing full well to resist my pain
I would begin to boil from the inside
I felt like I was on a timer
As someone passed me by,
They sent a dagger of words to my heart

I didn't care
let it pierce me
I raised my shield
Watched the words bounce away from my place on the ground
Words have no hold
The freedom to be is my key
This is the first time
I haven't stood up
It's a decision to not challenge things head on
To let them be
I've decided honesty is a good place to sit
Although it shines a light on my vulnerability
Makes me look a bit weak to the outside world
I haven't lost my strength
Or my courage
I've just decided that I have nothing to prove
There are no masks for my emotions
I've put down my guard
Just a little
So, for now, I'm going to sit for a little while
Ignore the stares from people who think I've given up
Really I've just given myself a gift
Gift to be
Gift to feel
Gift to stop fighting
Stopped battling in a fight that isn't even mine
I'm sitting here for awhile just so they know
I haven't given up
I've just chosen to sit
Strength to be what I need for me

Empowering Transformations
By Dina F. Gilmore

L ife will be riddled with challenges, hurdles, and obstacles that will morph you into who you are. The beauty of learning to overcome what shows up on your path will provide access for growth in many areas you may not realize until later in life. I grew up with an angry, biker father who, throughout my childhood, was only present during abuse. He treated me as if I was a boy because he never wanted a girl. Ironically, he ended up with two daughters and later a son he never met. I was terrified of his anger and abusive outbursts that left me battered and what felt like broken for my entire childhood. Actually, I would say it took me the first 45 years of my life to overcome my past, utilizing therapy, transformational course work, and the healing arts. My momma had a nervous breakdown when they divorced, so she told my dad to take me. I spent 40 years of resentment blaming him for the abuse, for telling me my momma had died, and for thinking he had kidnapped me. The biggest event in my childhood—being locked overnight in a storage shed with only the clothes on my body—shaped my entire life until I was 46 years old.

My sister called early October 2016 and said our dad was in the hospital and that I should come to see him. My abuser was dying from cancer, and I had a whirlwind of emotions stirring up, yet I dropped everything to join my sister to be by Dad's side. I had one moment alone with my dad while he was in the hospital, and we were able to say everything that needed to be said. I chose to forgive him and spend what little time we had left, and I understood that he had turned his life around. He had changed over the last twenty years, but I had let my fear stand in the way of ever having a relationship with him or getting to know the man he had become. I wanted my dad to see me happy before he died. I was at my most vulnerable and made the worst decision of my life by marrying a raging, alcoholic woman, which temporarily changed my trajectory. She turned my life upside down in every way you could think of, and left me battered while she fled the state from all accountability. I could have let her abuse undo all the work I had done and leave me feeling broken again. However, I made an empowering decision to reach out to healers, friends, and use Rose Andom House in Denver for domestic violence recovery. Being vulnerable meant I was willing to ask for help, not that I was weak by needing it.

Abuse of any sort is not acceptable, and using the power of your voice gives you strength for change. I share this devastating time of my life with you to make a point—that no one has to become their circumstances. You can choose to become a victor and leave your victim past behind. A person may never forget, but it stops haunting us the moment we say no more. Be patient with yourself during healing because it takes time to overcome heinous actions. You are not alone! There are many of us out there who have lived through it and can share our stories. I know there are people not as fortunate as we are who died by the hand of their abuser, but I want you to work with me in changing that. I want you to stand with me in making a difference. I want you to feel the village standing beside you, with you, lifting you up, and empowering you to live. Even if you never suffered abuse, you can stand to make a difference for those that have.

You do not have to be as others want you to be. Stand proud of the unique and beautiful soul you are because no two people are the same. DNA and science prove that fact. One of my favorite sayings that inspired me to be my quirky and unique self is "be yourself, everyone else is already taken" by Oscar Wilde. Over seven billion people on the planet and think of the difference that would make if all abuse stopped and we stood together. That may sound like a dream, but it is one of the many I have for the world. People are not perfect. That is a false, unrealistic expectation. Mistakes have to be made so we can learn and have the experience shift us. We can teach one another how to grow, transform into becoming better versions of ourselves, connect more, love more, and empower each other. Change is inevitable and starts with one new action toward your desired goal or outcome. A coach once shared with me that we are generally one decision away from a totally different life.

What do you want your life to look like? Are you happy? What is not working that you would like to change or improve? Start with small, realistic goals. It can be as simple as getting out of bed today when you didn't yesterday. One action a day toward your desired outcome can change your mood, energy, and set the tone for change in the direction you wish to go. I coach people all the time that if they can remove expectations of what their life is supposed to look like or who they are told to be, it can give them the freedom to be the person they always wanted to be. Your life is about you. What impact would you like to make on the world? What new action can you take today to move closer to that? An aspiring writer simply needs to start writing, and even ten minutes a day is an action. Keep it simple at first if that helps, take a deep breath, and take action. You got this!

The EFT Hometown Hero
By Michelyn Gjurasic

It's spring. I usually sail through it with a rare tickle in the back of my sinuses.

But three weeks ago, I sniffled and sneezed my way into a full-blown immune response. What the heck was I suddenly allergic to? I decided to try some Emotional Freedom Techniques (EFT), or "tapping," to get to the bottom of it. EFT is a cool way to clear negative energy from the body. I'd been around some different kinds of grasses when the coughing started—could I remember any old traumatic experiences with sniffle-inducing grass?

Suddenly, I see myself at six years old, getting stung on the foot by a bee. A-ha! Now I've got an old story to tap on. I drive to Lou Ellyn's house for our Friday morning EFT swap. As trained practitioners, we take turns rocking each other's worlds. I sit back under her expert guidance, close my eyes, and begin tapping.

"Tell me where that six-year old girl is right now," she prompts.

"She's in her front yard, barefoot, and it's summertime."

"What's she doing?"

"She's wearing shorts. Her mom calls her for lunch, and she's so excited she runs full speed to the porch.

"Suddenly her left foot is on fire! Her foot is burning, and she doesn't know what's happening," I explain. "She's crying so hard."

Lou Ellyn has me "freeze" the scene so that I can walk up to my younger self and begin tapping on her. I was called Mike when I was little.

I offer soothing phrases like "Even though you're shocked and confused, you haven't done anything wrong and it's going to be okay," and "Even though your foot feels like it's on fire, it's a bee sting that will go away soon."

Mike is no longer crying; now she's mad. She's mad at the bee, and she's mad at herself for picking that one tiny spot in the whole front yard to put her foot on. We tap on her anger. Now she's mad at the grass, because it did this on purpose. It hid the bee until she stepped on it. Grass hides things that are painful and can hurt you. We tap more, and she relaxes.

Mom brings an ice cube, wraps it in a towel around Mike's foot, and looks into her eyes: "Bee stings don't last long. If you can be strong for five minutes, the fire will be mostly gone, and you'll be okay."

Mom holds a timer with one hand, and her daughter with the other. Mike feels the ice and stares at the numbers ticking away. She's feeling safe and brave and strong, being held and knowing five minutes is not too long. The timer dings. They turn to each other with big eyes and growing smiles. "I did it!" Michelyn proclaims. "I am brave and strong." Mom hugs her in wonder and joy.

Still tapping, I offer my younger self whatever she wants right now to feel better: a high five. I give her one. Then she adds, "I want the neighbors to know!"

Because all things are possible when tapping, we go further: dozens of neighbors come out of their houses to celebrate the little girl who heroically lasted five minutes with a bee sting. The tapping allows even more: it's a parade! A band plays, confetti flies! The entire hometown cheers!

Here comes the Grand Marshal! Little Mike smiles wide from the top of a multi-tiered white cake of a float. Her throne extends from the top, holding her left leg out straight. Her foot proudly bears a huge white fluffy cotton bandage and a fat red ribbon bow. With braids hanging back, Mike throws her young arms wide in acknowledgment of her amazing accomplishment, accepting the honor and respect of the people of her hometown. Her left hand holds high a shining engraved trophy with a golden bee on top. The city-wide holiday is an over-the-top acknowledgement of her courage and strength, and she is overjoyed.

As the final step in the tapping process, Lou Ellyn invites the adult me to share these celebratory feelings with all the cells of my body. Pride, endurance, strength, courage, and heroism float through my physical body, from head to toe. I'm tingling with the power of it all. I bounce the feelings around my body, pausing at the sites of old injuries. I am in awe of this process as my old scars are transformed into points of pride.

My right knee is no longer a victim of that fifth-grade playground accident. It is now the delight of my body! It has held me up for decades, powerfully moving me forward with walking and running, supporting me to stand tall and proud. Those skin cancer cut-outs on my sun-exposed shin and forearm are no longer burned-out weak spots. Rather, they are shields of silver, raised defiantly to deflect evil rays of invasion!

I visit each body part, seeking out shameful wounds and showering them with this magical, shifting perspective. It takes all of two minutes. My entire body has been repurposed by this glowing, heroic, glittering strength. I will never again feel ashamed of it, for it is my testament to a life well and fully lived.

What I now recognize is that in any circumstance, any event where I am hurt, I can revel in the pain because I am still alive. I have survived it, and I have overcome. I am strong, I am a hero, and I can bring that new knowledge forward with me into the rest of my life.

It's been a week since that life-changing session, and the sniffles are still completely gone. My husband, however, has been laid low, and I bring him hot tea and compassion as he tries to figure out how he caught his latest cold. I can't help but wonder how old he was when he got his first bee sting.

Be Yourself!
By Scott Goodell

In 2014, stopbullying.com released a statistic that one out of three U.S. students say they have been bullied at school, most of them in middle school. The "developmental years," as most will recall, is when we morphed from kids to teenagers both physically and mentally, and we all had our insecurities. Since bullying doesn't have age restrictions, it sometimes starts for some children in elementary school.

In the early '80s, not being accepted wasn't labeled as "bullying." I remember a time when I was not accepted. We were a family that danced. My parents enjoyed dancing so much we would go to the local VFW at least one Saturday night a month. By the age of seven, I could dance the Texas two-step, waltz, polka, schottische, Cotton-eye Joe, ballet, tap, and jazz. Music is what connected us together as a family. I remember listening to lots of different genres of music. My dad was a classical guy, and we would whistle "Hooked on Swing." My mom loved Tanya Tucker and Helen Reddy. When we would go on vacations, we would bring cases of eight-track tapes. We would all sing right along with every song.

Like my sister, I loved getting in the car and listening to music and being able to create dance moves to the rhythm. My parents encouraged us to live life through music and dance—so much so that my sister eventually owned a dance studio.

Do you remember the first time you heard Michael Jackson's song, Billie Jean? I do! I was so excited about it that I tried to choreograph a dance to it. The next day I went to school with that beat stuck in my head. I couldn't wait to go to recess. As soon as the school bell rang, I sprang from my chair and lined up in the front of the line. I thought, "Today I am going to make the playground my dance floor," and I would only have about 15 minutes to make the best of it. The door flew open and I couldn't contain myself any longer. I started humming Billie Jean out loud, and started to mimic the dance moves I had seen my sister rehearsing many times. You know the saying, dance like nobody's watching? Well, I lived it, or at least I was living it until I heard a voice from one of my male classmates.

"What are you doing?" he asked, and started pointing at me and laughing. "Dancing is for sissies! Are you a sissy? Do you wear a tutu?" As he turned to the open field he yelled, "Scott is a dancing fairy!" Then he turned to me and repeated it so loud that the words echoed off the side of the school, as the other kids started circling. I tried to defend myself, but I couldn't find the words. I remember my vision becoming blurry as my eyes started to water, and the laughter got louder. A couple of other boys started chanting it too. I was absolutely devastated. My amazing day had become the worst day of my life. I dropped to the ground and held my face with my hands. Each teacher had a whistle they blew to let us know recess was over. The sound of the whistle couldn't have come any sooner. The rest of the day, I felt disconnected from the world. I was full of emotions. It felt like everyone was looking and judging me. I felt so vulnerable. I was so glad when the last bell of the day rang.

Later that evening, my mom asked me how my day was. I told her it was okay. I asked her if quitting dancing was an option. She replied, "Why would you want to stop?" I told her it wasn't fun anymore, and I would rather do something else. Then I told her I was called a sissy for being involved in dance classes.

Her reply was, "Oh Scott, they are just jealous." "Jealous of what?" I asked. "They wished they were more like you. Don't let them get to you. When you are in high school, it will all be different. Trust me!" It turns out my mom was right. Later, I found out that girls love to dance. From the dance floor, it was cool to be surrounded by the bullies' dates on prom night. "Criticize me now boys, your dates are having more fun with me!" My dad always told me that amazing athletes take dance because it helps them with endurance, balance, and agility. I recall names like Lynn Swann and Tony Dorsett. These amazing athletes would later become NFL Hall of Famers.

Everyone is born to leave this world a better place. I am extremely grateful that my parents encouraged me to never give up on music and dance. It was a hard lesson learned and a real identity struggle, but I am glad I stuck with it. Other people's insecurities should not affect your true calling. Today, I am able to share my passion for music and dance by helping others with their fitness goals. In the last few years, I have helped raise awareness and funds for several non-profit organizations. If you have ever been criticized for enjoying your talents in any art form—whether it be painting, dancing, acting, singing or even playing a musical instrument—the time is now to stand up for what you love. Let the criticism fuel you to be the person you should be. Let's put a stop to the bullying that this country is facing and accept everyone for their God-given talents.

Justin Timberlake didn't give up on his dream. On March 30, 2015, he said, "They called me different, they called me weird, they called me a couple other words I can't say on TV."

We are human beings, accept everyone for who they are, and stop letting someone else's insecurities define who you are! Always be yourself!

Happiness Is An Inside Job
By Nikki Griffin

I used to think that happiness came from amazing events like getting married, having a baby, receiving a promotion at work, winning the lottery, or buying shoes. But when a traumatic event in 2007 knocked me off my feet and forced me to start over, I realized the happiness that comes from those milestone events doesn't last that long. Life takes over, and we lose that sparkly happiness until the next big thing comes along.

It took a big shift in my thinking and my actions, but I now appreciate that happiness is not the result of bouncing from one external joy to the next, but rather is found in the little experiences that happen every day. It's the little things that create the state of well-being or happiness that we all desire. Learning to acknowledge these little moments is when the magic truly happens!

Going A Little Squirrely

As part of a personal re-branding journey over the last few years, I've created a life where I can work remotely from anywhere in the world. That alone brings epic happiness into my life! But even when I work from my home office in Canada, my happiness is not put on hold until it's time to pack again.

At home, I don't work alone. There are three pesky black squirrels that put in a full day right alongside me. My desk is beside a big beautiful window that overlooks a white flowering tree and part of the fence between my and my neighbor's houses.

Every day these squirrels run along the fence with their fat cheeks and bushy tails—and they always stop at my window! They look at me, I look at them, I ask how the nuts are today, they shake their tails and run away. This happens several times throughout the day, and every day, it makes me happy.

Last week, one of these crazy squirrels took a running jump at a branch with so much speed that he launched himself around the branch like a gymnast and broke the branch! He hit the ground (running!), and I'm still laughing at the squirrely theatrics outside my office window.

Happiness is a state, not a trait.

Happiness is more than a positive mood or attitude—happiness is a state of being that involves living a good life! It isn't a long-lasting, permanent feature or trait, but rather a fickle, changeable state that you have to keep working at if you want to hold on to it.

Back in 2007, when I was redefining myself and my life, I discovered the power of gratitude. As part of my healing, I began a daily gratitude practice and quickly started to feel happy again. Being grateful for the things I had in my life, and the beauty all around me, created a feeling of well-being and happiness for me. I loved this state and wanted more! I wanted to be happy all the time.

Happiness is not found, it is created.

Happiness has a huge impact on how we live our lives. We are always seeking happiness. We make decisions based on the perceived level of happiness an outcome will provide. You'd think we'd be happier with all this practice, right? So why aren't we?

Maybe a better question to ask is—how can we learn to be happier right now?

The answer, it turns out, is quite easy—you simply decide to be happy. You create your happiness! It's a matter of changing your perspective and adopting new habits.

Happiness Habits:

1. Gratitude—daily practice
2. Positive mindset—always see the silver lining in everything, especially the problems
3. Don't sweat the small stuff—let it go!
4. Find joy in the moment—don't worry about the future or dwell on the past
5. Live with integrity—be your authentic self and listen to your inner voice
6. Self-love and self-care—know your worth and protect it. Make time to do things you love

7. Celebrate your wins—big and small—don't focus only on what went wrong or the accumulation of possessions or accolades

8. Forgiveness—for yourself and others

9. Surround yourself with other happy people—happiness is contagious!

10. Give back to others—spread the love—giving makes you feel happier

11. Commit to your health in all ways—eat well, sleep regularly, exercise often

Coffee Makes Me Happy

One of my most favorite times of the day is the early morning when the world is still sound asleep, dark, and quiet. I used to absolutely love the 3:00 a.m. feeding when my kids were babies! Nowadays though, I still wake up before everybody and pour myself a cup of coffee in my favorite "Be Awesome Today" mug. I sit alone in front of the fireplace in silence. No phone, no computer, no lights, no sounds. That first sip of coffee always makes me smile. The cozy warmth and the taste are like a big 'ol full-body sigh. It's acknowledgment and anticipation that life is good today! As I sit in this quiet space, my mind starts to wander to all that I am grateful for. Sometimes I write a list, but other times, I grin and move on to the next thought.

After my reflections have slowed down, I get focused and set an intention for the day. I ask myself what is important for me today, and how do I want to do it? This isn't the same thing as making a to-do list. It's higher-level than that. It's more about getting clear on what I will focus on during the day, and my way of being so that I get what I want and need while being the person I want to be. Before my cup of coffee is finished, I have a positive mindset, and my vibes are high! I'm ready to take on the day with happiness as my default setting!

Happiness is a choice that requires effort sometimes.

Your happiness will not come *to* you, it can only come *from* you.

Happiness is a choice; choose it every day!

Believing In Your Faith
By Elizabeth Harbin

It wasn't until the last year of my mother's life that my faith accountability took center stage. There was no going around it, behind it, or over it. It loomed largely, and it demanded my full attention. As of June of 2018, I had been my mother's sole caregiver for over 15 years, and her health and life force were quickly deteriorating. Major life-altering changes were happening to her faster than I could keep up with them. The decision to call in-home hospice had to be made. My days quickly developed into blocks of time. This block of time would be to get her meds ready, or this block of time was to check her vitals. Yes, there was even a block of time for me to sleep for two hours. I laugh when I think about that now because there was no sleeping, only endless hours of watching, listening, and waiting. Sleeping? No. Then, with no great fanfare, that day came. The day she let go of her earthbound body, and let her soul take off to begin her new and wondrous adventure on the other side.

Never in my life had I experienced such silence. I have experienced quiet, but this was deafening! Later on, it became clear that the loudness of the silence was due to no longer having to think in multitasking thoughts. She took all of that with her, and I continue to be grateful.

So how did my faith accountability show up on center stage? Remember those blocks of time? Well, there would be moments where I would be sitting next to my mother's bed, holding her beautiful hand thinking, "Dear God, have I made the right decision on hospice? Will she forgive me? Did I get everything signed that I needed for her? What am I going to do about her cremation? How will I be able to afford it? Will I still be able to stay in this house after she passes?" And it went on and on every day for 14 days. Yet somehow, even when lost in those painful, emotional thoughts, my conscious mind would return to my Reiki training, and I would begin saying my prayers. They are called The Five Reiki Principles, and they go like this:

Just for today, I will not worry.

Just for today, I will not be angry.

Just for today, I will be grateful.

Just for today, I will do my work honestly.

Just for today, I will be kind to every living thing.

I eventually changed the wording to fit my needs at the time, but the message and the faith essence were still there. And it worked. One by one, all of those questions and worries I had were answered or eliminated. The home hospice people assured me over and over that my decisions were sound and in good faith. My worries over cremation information and cost were resolved. All of the other immediate problems and worries that had also weighed on my shoulders literally disappeared. Was it because I had said my Reiki prayers and then let them go?To all of those answered prayers, I say from the bottom of my soul, "Thank you." However, what faced me after my mom's death were two separate situations that, frankly, I had no idea how they would ever be resolved. One was my mother's life insurance policy. Unfortunately, she missed the maturity requirements of two years by two months. Instead of the six thousand I had been counting on for all of her related death expenses, I received half of that amount. Once again, I began saying, "I have to believe in my faith that this will be resolved by any and all sources." I did that each time that thought of lack would come into my consciousness. Then one night, I received a text message from someone I didn't know. She explained that I had a friend who knew my mom had passed, and wanted to stay anonymous. So, she agreed to send me this text to let me know I had a gift bag in the bed of my truck and that I needed to go and retrieve it! "Okay," I thought. "I'm not getting any bad vibes, so what the heck." I found the bag and inside was a beautiful sympathy card. When I opened the card, I found a bank envelope. Inside the envelope I found three thousand dollars cash! Had the difference in the life insurance policy been resolved because I started saying "by any and all sources"?

The second and most trying issue was the selling of my grandparents' home. It had been left to my mother in 2005 by my grandfather. So much energy had been used in trying to sell that place. The difficulty was that the house was located in Alabama, and we lived in Texas. My mom struggled with it, and now it was my issue. How was I going to accomplish this? I decided to call upon my mother. I know from being a psychic medium that they love being called upon to assist their loved ones. So, daily, I would pray, "Mother, I have to believe that you have resources to make that house sell. So I'm leaving it up to you to make this happen." The house was sold in three months! Not only did the house sell, we had a bidding war on it, and we got three times the money the Ugly House Buyers quoted! Was this resolved because I asked for my mother's help? You will never convince me otherwise.

I tell my students, you have to believe so strongly in your faith that if a saint appeared to you and said they thought you were incorrect over an issue, you would tell the saint, "Excuse me, but I believe you are the one that's incorrect." Now that's faith! Believe in yours!

Acceptance
By Suzanne Harmony

I have lived a life of extraordinary events. Yes, I am "the middle child." Lord of wonders, that's a good thing! I am blessed to have been raised by two loving and supportive parents and to have shared them with an older sister and a younger brother. I fast-tracked through primary and secondary school as I loved learning new things, and I had a photographic memory. I excelled in sports and held several positions on the student council; I even led the cheer-leading squad. I participated in the Lion's Club Public Speaking contest and came in second at the Provincial Level. The year our family lived with the impact of my father's diagnosis of cancer, I became our town's carnival queen. My curiosity for life was fulfilled by my enthusiastic participation in all that I welcomed. Life was good!

By my nineteenth birthday, I had been to university and dropped-out; I moved away from my home and family to a city two hundred and fifty miles away. I had a full-time job as a bank teller, and I was paying rent and utilities for my one-bedroom apartment. I was alone and overwhelmingly responsible for myself. Accomplished? Yes! Mature for my age? Yes! Aware? Not enough!

My good intentions to remain "just friends" with my ex-boyfriend nearly cost me my life. He brutally raped me, knocked me unconscious, and left me for dead on my nineteenth birthday! Miraculously, I survived this horrific event. God had saved me so I could save the baby—she saved me! I surrendered to my abuser out of fear for my life. I made numerous detrimental mistakes. I believed his threats and agreed to his terms, including not telling anyone anything! My book, *Because I Didn't Tell*, in my pen-name, I. Katchastarr reveals the details of how my life unraveled from there. I wrote it thirty-five years after that life-changing event with the intention to serve as a mighty ounce of prevention for many and a guide to recovery for those who have experienced abuse.

I leave two gems at the end of each chapter; they are: "I now forgive myself for…" then I leave bullet points for the things I have forgiven myself for. Then I leave "a pearl of wisdom." I am confident these gems and my story have fulfilled my intention to help and to heal.

The curse of migraines led me to a gift. I prayed for a non-medicinal source to manage the increasingly frequent and severely debilitating migraines. Faith in my prayers blessed me with a timely offer from my co-worker who offered to treat me with Reiki. This was a miracle; it aborted the migraine, and I was able to finish that day and that week without pain. I blossomed with each new level of Reiki that Sally taught me. On June 1, 2001, I became a Reiki Master, and on October 1, 2004, I took my leap of faith to leave that busy dental practice and build my Reiki practice. On December 17, 2004, I purchased and established Harmony House.

Today, I am grateful for the wisdom that I am experiencing. I am grateful for the divine guidance that I received on New Year's Eve 2019 that prompted me to choose a word for myself rather than to make a resolution. I stopped making resolutions a few years earlier when I realized how discouraged I became with myself when, each year around March, I would give up on the challenge that I recklessly set myself up for. Without a resolution, however, I discovered that my life seemed to be unfolding without passion or direction. This guidance for choosing a word instead of a resolution was an invitation that I enthusiastically accepted; it also felt much less daunting. "How can I fail?" I thought. "It's simply a word." I meditated upon that idea. I resisted the strong urge to *think* about it. Instead, I breathed into my soul space and waited. Relaxed and confident, it wasn't long before I simultaneously saw and heard it: "*Acceptance.*"

In a few short months, this chosen word has become a promise, an attitude, a prayer, a gift, a commitment, an increased awareness. It has birthed many "A-ha" moments. I realize that acceptance brings simplicity to my life, whereas before this, I was always trying to figure life out: Who am I? What is my purpose in life? What's happening to me and all around me? Acceptance allows me to evolve past the struggle to find answers. This word, acceptance, invites me to be my true self, not solely the person that I became as a result of the choices I made from my life's experiences. It motivates me to live my essence, and my essence is truth. No one and nothing can take that away from me. I am here to live it and to share it in ways that may also help others.

I am grateful for my journey that has guided me to this realization: this blessing, this gift, this miracle that I am, and the purpose for my existence. Acceptance allows me to rise above fear, self-doubt, and self-criticism. I know that I am here until I die, so I may as well live my life fully in my essence of truth. Being true to myself requires courage. I believe that courage is faith in motion; love is the fuel. I love myself; therefore, I accept my role in the circumstances of my life. Acceptance, much like forgiveness, is a process, a choice, an attitude, a way of living. These are not just words; they are life-altering experiences. Even though forgiveness implies that someone did something wrong, including myself, I realize that inner peace requires self-forgiveness—or even better, *mercy*—for my evolving self. Mercy is gentler on the soul and allows a person to heal—guilt-free. This, I know is true; I have lived it.

Fire Starter
By Julia Hawkins

My fifth-grade teacher took my flame and lit a bonfire. I was a new kid, in a small town, when I walked into Mrs. Nash's classroom. The room was full of students in Izod polos, Gloria Vanderbilt jeans, and Nikes reminiscent of the Karate Kid. I took a seat, in my no-name clothes, and kept my focus on my teacher. I was shy, insecure, and worried about fitting in. If only I'd known that before the year was over, I would learn that although I wasn't "Mrs. Popularity," I was still special and valuable in other ways. I would learn that I was ready for bigger, more meaningful things. After all, my age was now in the double digits. Mrs. Nash took my love for childhood books and ignited a passion for reading the grand stories, a love of reading out loud, and the belief that I, too, could become a writer.

Reading had always sparked my emotions. I had bookshelves full of children's books. One shelf even seemed to glitter when you looked at all the spines of the Golden Books. Another shelf was for the only doctor I liked to visit, Dr. Seuss. I loved to get lost in a story. In that moment, I was someone else, somewhere else. Mrs. Nash took my little flame of love for books and blew it wide open. She believed in me. She believed I was ready for more. She asked me to read books with pages in the three digits. Books with stories so big, my imagination soared. The spark of emotions I used to feel was nothing compared to this bonfire. I never knew I could experience all these feelings for fictional people in fictional places. They were described in such depth that they felt real to me. My teacher took that one step further and gave them voices.

Mrs. Nash read to us, a little every day. Our reading area had seven cushions. Each one had a different geometric shape and bold color that was so popular in the 80s. Every day she would pick the lucky seven. They were the most well-behaved, hardworking students of the day. When I was in the lucky seven, I was in the lap of luxury, lying on my cushion, listening to the story. On days when I was with the other two-thirds of the class, however, I still cherished story time. We unlucky remainders would find a place on the floor, lie on our backs, and stare up at the ceiling. Cushion or not, our stares soon turned into something similar to stargazing.

Mrs. Nash would begin to read, and suddenly we no longer saw the ceiling. We were gazing at the same beautiful sky that James saw from his Giant Peach. She narrated with such intonation that the story seemed to come to life. She would then ask us to write about the stories of our lives and the worlds we created in our imaginations.

She taught me how to write in a way that seemed to open up my heart and mind. I began to think about my life experiences, what I was passionate about, and what I wanted to share with the world. I learned that I loved to read and write poetry. No longer was I simply writing book reports or short paragraphs on subjects we were studying. I was learning how to put a piece of myself on paper. She gave me helpful critiques, showered with plenty of encouragement to continue refining my work. I entered writing contests at school and won first place. Then, my poetry was printed twice in the town's newspaper. It made me feel special and talented. It was exactly the kind of thing a shy, nerdy girl needed. It was all thanks to my fifth-grade teacher.

Mrs. Nash had lit my literary path so that I saw the larger spines, began to dream of narrating, and discovered a love of writing. I began choosing the bigger books and read more than I had ever read before. While listening to Mrs. Nash, my classmates and I went on grand adventures. Then, thanks to her belief in me and her encouragement to work harder, I learned to write and to focus on what truly matters. I hope to one day pass the torch to my students and become a fire starter.

Welcome Home!
By Patricia Haynes

"Wow!" The heady, pungent odor of camel dung assaulted my nostrils, as vibrant Egyptian music tickled my ears. It's January 1, 2000, and I'm gazing at the Sphinx and Great Pyramid!

A year and a half before, I was bored and feeling sorry for myself. I started surfing the Internet. I landed on Marianne Williamson's site, and clicked on a link to Power Places Tours, thrilled to learn that there actually are metaphysical and spiritual tour groups.

Curious, I clicked on upcoming tours. There, staring at me from cyberspace, were the Sphinx and Great Pyramid! Although always interested in Ancient Egypt, I had never delved into it seriously. Now, gazing at the Sphinx, something in me stirred. A Millennium Tour to Egypt for December 1999! It included speakers like authors Graham Hancock, Robert Bauval, and Egyptologist and then-Minister of Antiquities, Zahi Hawass. I knew then where I wanted—no, *needed*—to be on December 31, 1999. I called my long-time friend, Nancy, in Los Angeles, and said, "How about Egypt for the new Millennium?" A few days later, after a lot of cajoling, she agreed.

From that day until I left, I immersed myself in all things Egyptian. First, the historical, then the mystical, magical, and spiritual Egypt slowly entered my consciousness. My overloaded bookshelves made way for the Egyptian wing. I absorbed everything I found.

In 1999, many people had "New Millennium Fear." My family and friends questioned why a Middle Eastern country. What about Y2K? Terrorism? The Egyptian airline crash in October? I reminded them about my incurable sense of adventure, and that I have always refused to live my life in fear. Awful things happen, even in the USA. Besides, Egypt was in Africa, not the Middle East.

Nancy and I met at JFK airport on December 27, 1999. Our Egyptair flight was scheduled to leave at 11:30 p.m., so we had time to have a drink and meet people traveling with us.

We arrived in Cairo in the late afternoon, still light enough to see our arrival on the onboard cameras. I gazed out at the desert like a kid at Christmas, nose pressed to the window, seeing an amazing wonderland, including the Pyramids! When I walked off the plane and placed my feet on Egyptian soil, I began to feel and remember Egypt from other lifetimes.

Inside the terminal, as we were being processed, I noticed a man with a kind smile and a funny dollop of white in his otherwise perfectly-groomed black hair. He stood out among the people processing us. I noticed they deferred to him, as ancient Egyptians had deferred to their Pharaohs. He was Mohamed Nazmy, President of Quest Travel, who soon became my Egyptian brother and my friend. His crew was exceedingly patient with our large, unruly, tired group, and got us through customs effortlessly.

As I pointed out my luggage, I looked up and saw a smiling though serious man, not as perfectly groomed as Mohamed, rather rumpled looking, sort of like Columbo, but with a certain aura I found reassuring and approachable. He was Emil Shaker, Quest Travel's Egyptologist, also my brother, my friend.

Anxious to get to the hotel, I was happy to board the bus! An attractive, dark-haired woman named Samar got on the bus. Then she said quietly, "Welcome home." I burst into tears, something I never, ever do. Egypt had called me back home; I was starting to respond.

The inescapable bellow of a camel near my ear jolted me back to the sands at Giza. I had ridden one of the beasts earlier in the day, so I wasn't frightened. They speak their minds, much as I do!

Earlier, we had boarded our buses for the Giza Plateau. If you've ever been to Cairo, you know how bad the traffic is. I live in Texas, so I thought I would be prepared for Cairo drivers. Oh, how wrong I was! Our group was supposed to be in the Great Pyramid at midnight. Before leaving for the Plateau, Mohamed told us the U.S. Government was concerned because of terror threats, and had requested that our event be canceled. We were, however, the first group to enter the Great Pyramid on the first day of the new millennium. What a consolation prize!

We finally made it, anxious about being late. We decided the shuttles to the gates would take too long, so we started walking, the thick sand enveloping our shoes. Someone yelled, "Run!" We spilled out everywhere, laughing, trying not to get bogged down in the sand. At the entry gates, we handed the guards our tickets and kept moving, though we should have stopped to be searched. Great, I thought, I'm going to be shot and die at the Pyramids.

As I ran up the last dune, the skies suddenly lit up with fireworks, the music swelled, and the Sphinx and Great Pyramid slowly emerged from the sand. The camel police atop the dunes became elegant silhouettes, crossing against the Sphinx and Pyramids like ancient spirits.

We collapsed in the sand and talked about feeling like Bedouins in some ancient desert, meeting each other again after a long journey. We lifted our large bottles of water, saluting our family and friends, worrying about Y2K and everything else, while we were at the Pyramids!

It became uncharacteristically cool, clouds began to gather, winds began to blow, and a fine mist filled the air. Although the Pyramids and Sphinx were lit up, the clouds rushed to hug them, slightly obscuring them with an ephemeral, gauzy effect.

I quietly took it all in, lost in my thoughts. I had been in Egypt four days, but felt time flowing through me, streaming in my mind lifetimes I've spent here, maybe as someone important, maybe not. Egypt was divulging her secrets to me, opening thoughts of ancient Egyptian mysticism, magic, spirituality, life. The alchemical healing process of moving Egypt from my head into my heart had begun. Welcome home!

Believe In Your Dreams
By Dr. Debbie Helsel

When I think about inspiration, I think about the influence of my seventh-grade science teacher, who planted the seed and opened up my passion for animals. I did not know at the time how much her love for teaching and her influence on me would change my life forever. She is still in my life to this day, and we continue to inspire each other.

Some of us have always known that our lives were meant to be in service; whatever that would come to mean would be an evolving process for our entire lives. I always knew as a kid that I wanted to work with wildlife, but I didn't know how to make that happen. Financially, college wasn't an option for me, and I went into the workforce. For years, numerous synchronicities led me to my dream of working with wildlife at Back to Nature Wildlife Refuge (BTN) in 1990.

My desire to help the animals led me to practice energy healing and provoked an awakening that I can never turn back on. I have been trained in energy healing modalities and found my path in other things such as rocks and crystals. All of the relationships I have made throughout these trainings, as well as my years in the wildlife field, have helped mold me into who I am today.

So many people have inspired me along my journey, a debt I can never repay. I can only pay it forward by helping others. Spirit leads me in ways that I can't describe except to say, I listen to my heart.

We have four staff members and tons of volunteers at Back to Nature—including several who take an active role in the growth of BTN. I share my gifts with them freely and teach and guide them however I can. My greatest achievements come from watching so many of them thrive and succeed in the field of their passions. Knowing that BTN played even a small role of being a stepping-stone to help them find their dreams is a phenomenal feeling. My classic phrase to our volunteers is, "You are the only one who holds yourself back from learning." I try to encourage them to find their dream, find what makes them tick, find what makes their heart sing, and don't ever give up! If you believe—anything is possible! It won't be easy, but keep sharing your dream and encourage others to believe in it through your passion and your desire to see it happen.

It took a long time—a lot of prayers, blood, sweat, tears, and letting go and believing—for BTN to get where it is today. After starting out humbly behind an automotive garage, it took 25 years for our dream of a new home to come. Now we are thriving for the first time ever on 20 acres of conservation land, and the universe is providing support for our growth.

We recently had a visitor from the United Kingdom (UK). She visited our refuge with her husband, and she was in a motorized scooter, which told me that she had some limitations. I walked with them to the main gate, and told them to make themselves at home and to make sure they looked all around, because the property is part of the wildlife corridor and you never know what kinds of animals you might see.

I went back to feeding baby birds and noticed them as they came out of the gate. I always love feedback from people who didn't know about us before their visit. I walked over and asked if they saw anything good and she said she was so amazed at the work we did. There was a similar place near her home in the UK, so she understood our mission as a wildlife rehabilitation and public education facility.

I mentioned we were about to reach our greatest achievement ever at the end of the year when we will finally be getting new solid structure buildings for our facility. I said if they were around next year, maybe they could come back and see the progress.

She went on about how wonderful the work we do is, how much she appreciated my years with the organization, and how it was obvious that we had dedicated people who truly loved this work. Then she said she wished she could, but she would never be back again. She told me she was dying, and the doctors only gave her a few months, so she wouldn't be able to come back. I started to cry, and she told me not to feel sorry for her or be sad because she had a good life. She said not to worry though, because she would be watching over our refuge from above and looking after us, wishing she could be down here with us. We hugged each other, and then I wished her a safe journey and went back inside.

I realized I didn't ask her name because I was so emotional after the news of her illness had caught me off guard. I immediately ran out to the parking lot to ask her name. It's Elaine. She praised me yet again for the decades of my work, and then I had to watch her leave as I sobbed overwhelmingly for the loss of someone I barely knew. I am positive the angels sent her to give me that message. It was a message of faith and hope as well as self-validation. I started my morning inspiring her through my eyes about our work, and in the end, it was she who restored my faith and inspired me even more.

I have spent my adult life consciously inspiring others through my passions, and I have watched so many of my "students" now doing the same. I couldn't be prouder of the accomplishments of our BTN family! We can achieve anything if we do it together and just believe.

Inspirational Alchemy
By Dr. Vicki L. High

God created me to be an alchemist. When I combine things that happen to me and deal with them, I create a new masterpiece from the fragments. These fragments come from challenges, failed relationships, emotional wounds and devastating situations. When these fragments are healed, they become an integral foundation for my strength and resiliency as a woman and human being. After the fragments are purified in the crucible, something new is birthed into existence.

I am a survivor. I was beaten and threatened. I could have died. Although I was still a teenager and had my whole life ahead of me, I just didn't know if I had a few seconds or a few years to live. Imminent death brings life into laser focus. As I looked at death directly in the face, I realized how precious life really was, and I was inspired to live fully. I begged, and somehow, with divine intervention, I was released.

What happened next? It wasn't easy to break my marriage vows. Staying would have been fatal. Against my pastor's advice, I chose life. My mantra became "fear not." I had been given this second chance to live and experience this new beginning.

Decades passed and the movie, *The Bucket List,* appeared on the big screen evoking the question, "What's on your bucket list?" I realized that because of my desire to live fully, I had already completed many of the things that I would have included on my list. So, I created a "teckub" list (bucket list spelled backward) and tracked my accomplishments. These few fearless accomplishments made the list:

- Wrote and published *Heart 2 Heart Connections: Miracles All Around Us*
- Visited all 50 states
- Swam with dolphins
- Waterskied in Cypress Gardens style with four skiers
- Read the Constitution, Bill of Rights, Declaration of Independence from the original documents hanging in the National Archives Museum
- Taught and initiated students as a Reiki Master Teacher

- Appeared as a guest on the Oprah Winfrey Show
- Served as Mayor, City Council Member, Kaufman County Leadership Chairperson, and Crandall Economic Development President
- Met then future President George W. Bush and First Lady, Laura Bush
- Founded Heart 2 Heart Healing, Empowered Dreams, CE2O, Inc., Kalming Kids, Recovering Humanity, Stop Trauma Drama, Empowered Leaders and more
- Completed my bachelor's degree in Metaphysical Science, master's degree in Spiritual Healing, and my doctorate in Divinity/Metaphysical Counseling, quoting my own book as a resource for both my thesis and dissertation
- Became a professional softball umpire
- Met and visited with some of my spiritual superheroes: Gary Zukav, Marianne Williamson, Deepak Chopra, Neale Donald Walsch, James Redfield, Dr. David Hawkins, Gregg Braden, Dr. Masaru Emoto, Lee Carroll (Kryon), Louise Hay, Lynn McTaggart, James Twyman, and Oprah, who collectively showed me they were regular people on their spiritual journeys, too
- Spoke at Attitude & Attire, Reconnective Healing Practitioners' Conference, Alliance of Divine Love, Lake Michigan Data Trainers, Computer Training and Support Conferences (5 years) and Oklahoma Governor's Tourism Conference, winning an unprecedented three Red Bud awards for innovations and collaboration
- Recognized as Lifetime Member of Strathmore's Who's Who and Who's Who in Professional Management
- Converted software applications and created hundreds of training programs in technology, aviation, financial services, telecommunications, entertainment, healthcare, publishing, diesel mechanics, manufacturing, retail, e-commerce, oil & gas, utilities, transportation, and educational services

Challenges paved the way for me to make tough, but fair calls. As an umpire, I could almost hear the players in men's leagues as they groaned, "The ump's a girl." Then they'd be shocked I could make the right calls even ejecting a player from the game, if necessary. My love of the game made me a better umpire. My love of life made me a better human being. Every aspect of my life was changed from that single encounter with death.

My experiences composed the living encyclopedia of Vicki. I found the courage to fearlessly confront bullies and undertake difficult jobs that others were afraid to tackle. During one financial software conversion, mortgage payments were stacked up because no one could process them. I said, "Give them to me. I will find a way," and I did. It felt good to serve others—to make a difference. In another challenge, I was the team leader for a banking conversion. This project was a brutal baptism by fire for many reasons. I worked 21-hour days learning the system and then applying that knowledge at the client's site, one decision at a time. When my new supervisor remarked, "I didn't think you were going to survive," my words to her were immediate and deliberate: "You don't know me very well. I am a survivor!" I knew I had done everything I could to succeed. That was my truth then, and it remains my truth today.

Looking back, I know the exact moment when my courage became stronger than my fear. The moment I regained my freedom birthed this new life for me. I was determined that if I survived, I would live courageously, saying yes far more often. I would discover and challenge my boundaries. Fear held me prisoner, but once released, I claimed freedom as mine. I owned it! I became a powerful catalyst for change from that moment.

If my younger self asked for advice, I'd tell her:

- Embrace your freedom and live courageously!
- Dream big and make a difference in the world!
- Create your own "tekcub" list and celebrate your accomplishments.
- Turn obstacles into stepping stones for success on your terms.
- Travel and experience the beauty of the planet we call home.
- Dance, sing, and laugh out loud often!
- Lighten up and don't worry what other people think.
- Eliminate guilt, shame, blame, remorse and judgment from your life.

- When you experience heartaches, remember "your people" love you and you are never alone!
- For crusty people with rough edges, love them through it.
- Dump the junk in your trunk! It's easier than you think.
- Let your heart experience the healing miracle of love again and again.
- You've got this!

My Dance With Words
By Dr. Vicki L. High

May I have this dance?
I love to dance with words. Words inspire me. Words are the greatest communication tools. Words make my world a more beautiful place.

I was born a spontaneous reader. It was as if I came into this world knowing how to read and absolutely loved the written and spoken word! My mom told me that she first thought I was mimicking other people, repeating their words. Then, as I stood leaning over her shoulder as she was seated on the floor with a project, I read the assembly instructions to her. In kindergarten, my caregiver would ask me to read the Readers' Digest long before I learned to read in first grade. Since then, words have brought me joy, inspiration, tears, ideas and a remarkable career. As an instructional designer, I have developed hundreds of corporate training programs and authored or contributed to several books. As a book collector and storyteller, I am thrilled to share and broaden the horizons of those willing to listen. Words have changed my life.

Words can paint a picture as they tell a story. Words help me share my experiences with you, so you can sway with the music and follow the steps to the dance of words in your unique way. Words can heal, but they can also wound. Words help us form ideas, actions, and achievements. Words inspire me to create, learn and communicate.

Here are a few words that make my toes tingle and tap to a rhythm from my heart to yours. The first words are **love, light and laughter!** In my mind, the combination of these three words generates pink bubbles to engulf, surround and transform the life I live. I read that the energy frequency of laughter is higher than prayer or meditation and I believe that's true! A good belly laugh transforms the energy around us! This high frequency ignites unconditional love as a catalyst for change that restores me and transports me to the sacred heart of God.

While I'm in silence, I worship the creator who spoke our beautiful planet into existence as the Living Word so we can soak in the majesty and wonder of this marvelous world. I listen to the still, small voice that ever so gently whispers my name and nudges me in the direction of my dreams.

Freedom and justice are words that have engaged my spirit to boldly go into unchartered territory and advocate for those who are imprisoned, bullied, or locked behind rigid rules. Let's fly beyond the restrictions with justice and forgiveness, soaring to new heights that make us giggle with delight as we feel the wind beneath our wings!

Hugs and kisses remind me that family, friends and even followers on Facebook engage and exchange ideas, beliefs, joys, successes, losses, and even defeats. While expressing these human emotions, I am reminded that we triumph against defeats and survive to overcome difficulties. Often a kind, loving word from my tribe reminds me of what remains: support, comfort, and recovery no matter what the challenges may be. There may be haters as well as lovers, but the power of "delete" is still there to wield when needed.

Balance, listening and talking are three powerful words. We think we live in a world of absolutes, but we live in spectrums. We maintain a balance between light and dark, hot and cold, good and bad. Maintaining balance is a different kind of dance. I have a friend that absolutely loves to talk and is great at telling a story. She takes the stage, and we become the audience for minutes to hours, depending on the story. It reminds me of *The Celestine Prophecy's* fourth insight, "The Struggle for Power," which describes the dance of energy between people. My goal is to apply the insight to feel the ebb and flow of energy in group communications and reach a better balance between listening and talking with people in my sphere of communication. I love to talk, but I know others do, too. How do we know what's happening in the lives of our friends if they never get a chance to share their stories with us? When I demonstrate the courage to speak up, I set expectations lovingly, enabling me to talk or listen in more balanced ways.

Empowerment and enlightenment are two important words for me. In this journey of life, I am convinced that empowerment is our sovereign right. When we seek enlightenment, we are expanding our understanding, our ideas and our presence through words and actions. Those words and actions must match to dance and demonstrate empowerment and enlightenment. When we live in truth, we operate in truth, and truth becomes the guiding force for our actions and our words.

I am inspired daily through two sources: *Today God Wants You to Know (Neale Donald Walsh)* and *The Universe (www.tut.com)*. These words of wisdom begin my day with a personalized thought or insight that moves me. The words inspire me to think differently and are available for you to have a personal word from God, too.

Words are puzzle pieces that form the knowledge and wisdom collected and shared throughout our world. As I read one book, a puzzle piece (some obscure wisdom) clicks and fits perfectly into place for me from another thought or idea. How amazing to feel the oneness of the Universe as the steps to a new dance are revealed to me!

Words will continue to provide entertainment and exercise for my brain. I am truly devoted to them, and I recommend them for the joy they bring to my life.

There is a variation of a story that I love about the ragged and deeply gouged footprints in the sand. As I asked the Living Word what caused them, Jesus replied, "That is when we danced."

Would you care to dance?

From Diagnosis To Divine
By Lisa Holm

As corny as it sounds, I used to watch *Touched by an Angel*, and inevitably and somewhat embarrassingly, I would cry every time. I wanted to do what the Angels did—uplift those who had lost hope and help people find their divine nature and connection to God. I liked that the term God was never associated with a specific religion, allowing me to experience the depth of my perception of spirit, the Universe, or source as I understood it. Years later, when I began offering intuitive and healing sessions to clients, I felt as close as I would get to doing that work in this lifetime.

I became a spiritual seeker as a teenager. My journey wove through many paths from Christian youth crusades to a George Harrison concert I attended while unapologetically wearing an Indian sari given to me by the Hare Krishna temple I'd recently visited. Sparked by a "chance" encounter with a handsome, young, guitar-playing member of the Baha'i faith in the stairwell of my college music department, I was invited to explore yet another interpretation of how we are part of the divine.

At age 21, while working at a slightly seedy but popular tavern and music venue, I met a man who told me that he would "just think of something and it would come" to him. I'd never heard of this, though now we all know it as the law of attraction. He introduced me to his teacher, an endearingly chubby, and in the best possible way, slightly eccentric psychic named La Faye, who changed my perspective and set my course in a new direction. She was the first teacher who taught me that "thoughts are things."

After many years of studying religions and metaphysics by myself, and with teachers, I finally found my way. I felt excited to start my intuitive and spiritual healing practice. My journey was about to enter new territory, but the terrain would be different than I had expected.

In 2002, after two intensive trainings with a spiritual teacher who enabled me to open to the power that dwells within and to which we are all connected, I felt a new feeling of magical possibility before me. As well as healing and intuitive guidance for people, I found myself connecting with animals in a new way. This evolved into working with people and their pets as an animal communicator. Clients started coming, and everything was rosy.

Feeling a new energy flowing through me, I decided to rip out the old carpet in my living room. After sanding the wood floors, it seemed I had developed a severe sinus infection or reaction to whatever had been set free from the carpet or the dust from the sander. I started to have a terrible earache and headache that didn't go away. I believed in spiritual healing, but I needed some relief, so I consulted an ear, nose, and throat doctor. I have never been fond of going to doctors, but feel there is a place for all methods of healing. This doctor checked things out and decided I needed to see a specialist. By this time, I had pain in my shoulders. It was so bad one night I called my friend to bring me icepacks. Next, my eye started getting all red, and my vision became blurry.

Getting out of my car at the specialist's office, I noticed my ankles felt weird. I breathed and thought, "Okay, whatever." The doctor told me matter-of-factly that I had a rare autoimmune disorder that would kill me in five years without chemotherapy. Time stopped. I felt like this was all wrong. There was a bit of discussion, little of which I recall now. I do remember saying clearly from somewhere in the depths of my soul "Thank you, but I believe in spiritual healing." I then got up and left. I was in some different state of being. This was simply unacceptable. I was not coming from a balanced state of divine knowing yet, but a resounding *no* was echoing through me. I found a payphone—yes, it was the olden days—and called my dear friend who knew that this was not something I had to accept.

This odd turn of events changed my life. The expense of medical treatment was not an option, nor was it what I resonated with. It was the biggest leap of faith in my life to throw my lot in with source and surrender to divine love.

I did not tell my family about it. I only confided in two friends who were dedicated to knowing the truth that "dis-ease" is a thought held that has manifested on the body. I had to make a choice. Was I in or out? Did I truly believe that the default setting of the body is balance and harmony and knowing that truth can allow the body to return to it? I had to commit, so I did. I meditated with guided healing tapes. I practiced what I learned about energy healing. I sought out healing practitioners, read books on healing through thought, and researched others' healing stories. I also used food as medicine. I ate raw food for a year.

My healing did not happen overnight. When fear welled up, I had to surrender it and be committed to allowing myself to be well.

We can choose any healing modality we are led to. Why can two people have the same diagnosis, receive the same treatment, and one recovers but the other does not? Can it be possible that what we believe is the dominant factor? All forms of treatment are valid and can work. We must choose that with which we are most in harmony.

Seventeen years ago, someone told a story about my health that I chose to reject. With continued focus, belief, and surrender, I am exceedingly well indeed. We all are divine.

The Power Of Fear
By Jillian Holper, CCHt, LC

*F*ear. The word itself is intimidating. When coupled with *worst*, it has the power to send chills down one's spine. Just pause for a moment and imagine facing your *worst fear*. Thankfully, many of us will never have to do any more than imagine this. But if you do, is it possible to use the experience of being faced with your *worst fear* to locate and harness your *deepest strength*? This was exactly what I was about to find out.

I was 20 years old, in an abusive relationship, and 11 weeks pregnant when I got into a serious car accident. I nearly died. Instead, I was "lucky" to come away with nine broken bones—a femur, foot, arm, rib, ankle, and pelvis in three different places. I was confined to a wheelchair for my entire pregnancy, and it took over a year to learn to walk again. However, despite all odds—including the injuries, surgeries, x-rays, and medications—my miracle baby would be born healthy and happy.

Due to the accident and numerous complications, I underwent various surgeries requiring general anesthesia. This included the birth of my son, being that an epidural was contraindicated with my unique circumstances. It deeply saddened me to be out for my little miracle's birth. However, at this point, I had begun to develop a crippling fear. The fear with which this story begins—undergoing surgery while completely lucid. It soon escalated into my *worst fear*.

The way this fear manifested was completely irrational. I constantly imagined the horrific situations in which this could play out. I had nightmares that echoed horror films where I'd be operated on while feeling everything, unable to speak or move. I felt hostage to my mind, paralyzed by this fear.

Despite the hospital being where I had every one of my surgeries, staying there didn't bother me one bit. On the contrary, it felt more like an escape. Everything was taken care of for me, and I didn't have to deal with the mess my life had become. A place where I was medicated enough to ease the guilt I felt for bringing an innocent life into this disastrous situation. Looking back, I see that many of the complications I had were a subconscious answer to escape the stress in my life and find solace in those stays. Still, despite the temporary ease, there was a looming *fear*. This fear heightened with every visit, and I would soon have to face it.

It was a year post-accident, and I had been suffering through a trend of poor healing. The most recent example: a plate removed from my ankle that continued to bother me. I was taking a bath with my baby when he did one of those stand-up-then-plop-down-movements infants do when you're holding their hands. Something was wrong—I knew it as soon as he hit my ankle. The surgeon's office instructed me to get to the hospital, where I was promptly admitted.

Apparently, there were complications, including a serious staph infection. They explained they needed to operate right away. The procedure required the bone to be scraped by a metal brush of sorts. The doctor informed me that because I had ingested water recently, they weren't comfortable with general anesthesia. Despite my pleas, I was assured that with the twilight anesthesia I, "won't remember a thing—let alone feel anything." My *fear* was screaming otherwise.

The anesthesia wasn't working. I had *plenty* of experience in this area and knew that something was extremely wrong. I pleaded with the O.R. staff while crying and shaking, I could still feel everything! They kept repeating that I wouldn't remember anything tomorrow. All I know is that despite the localized numbing shot, to this day, I remember the agony of that surgery. In recovery, they discovered my vein had blown, and in fact, I had not received any sedation. Not only had I experienced my *worst fear*, but it was getting worse.

Painful kidney issues had begun to develop due to the powerful antibiotics needed to remedy the infection. I was told my stay would be at least three to five days. Furthermore, I would be sent home with a PICC line to deliver antibiotics intravenously for the next month. What was once a comfortably medicated and relieving experience was quickly turning into another nightmare.

The pivotal moment arrived that evening while recounting the traumas of that day to my sister. She gently suggested that, according to The Law of Attraction, I could be creating this all on some level—and perhaps I could change it! This conversation forever changed my life. I still remember the anguish of having to admit that I had a hand in creating this all and the intense sobbing that ensued. Most of all, though, I was sick of being sick and—with every cell of my being—I wanted out!

I awoke the next morning to a visit from the doctor with absolute shock. After triple-checking everything, they concluded I had experienced an overnight, miraculous healing. I was released that day with only an oral prescription of "just in case" antibiotics.

It took time processing the implications surrounding this experience. Living through my *worst fear*, thereby realizing the power that my thoughts and feelings have on my experience of life, was like waking up for the first time. I turned that fear into my *greatest strength* by not only facing it, but by obtaining an awareness of my capacity. I began to realize the power that resides in focused thought and the creative energy our decisions hold. I continued to practice utilizing thoughts to create the life I had dreamt of. I soon left the abusive relationship, pursued my degree as a single mom, eventually married the man of my dreams, and now have the career/practice of my dreams. A practice helping others to face *their fears* and realize that *their deepest strengths* reside in the power of their mind!

Ollie Strong
By Rosemary Hurwitz

I stood in shock as I listened to my son's heartache on the other end of the line. "Oh Mom, Ollie's got Leukemia. We thought he had a virus, and I feel so bad I didn't take him in earlier. We are in the hospital." I then heard an intense crying out from this strong, young man who rarely cried in front of me, and then, more sobs, which I let him have and did not interrupt.

Thich Nat Han's *deep listening* lessons kicked in, and I went silent and let him cry. "Just be with them," I heard deep within me.

Gathering some composure, he continued, "He has A.L.L., Acute Lymphoblastic Leukemia, which, if you are a toddler and have Leukemia, is the better one to have, the easier to treat." "Okay, well, that is good, that is something," I hoped. "Breathe, just breathe," I told myself.

In disbelief, I thought, "I was recently there!" His sweet baby boy, only two and a half, was not eating anything but oatmeal during our week. When they asked me about it, I replied, "That is the *twos* for you. One week they only like oatmeal, the next week, they won't touch it. It is okay."

They called me after I flew home, wondering if they should take him to the doctor because Ollie seemed "off." I said, "He seemed okay to me, although a little pale, but listen to your intuition." Yes, take him to the doctor—it never hurts.

They thought maybe he might have a case of anemia because he looked pale, but Leukemia? We were all in shock and grief, with thoughts of "These things happen to other people, right?" and "Yes, but we *are* the other people now." Illness is the great equalizer.

Humbled, we waited for additional tests and their call for us to join them at the hospital. We entered the Children's Hospital, and with anxiety and faith, we put on our masks and found the room that Ollie and his parents had been staying in.

His Mom and Dad were amazing at keeping things light-hearted, even in their grief. With his mask on too, Ollie managed a big smile and an easy hug for his Mae Mae and G-Pops.

We would learn of the three phases Ollie would need to pass through in his treatment. They were: Induction, Consolidation (or Intensification), and Maintenance. There were many difficult times in the first stage of Induction, where spinal taps, steroids, and chemotherapy treatments were taking place.

Supporting a young family going through a critical illness with their child holds a grief and a grace all its own. Ollie's parents were inspirations in themselves, and we couldn't know the pain that they were experiencing.

The first phase of Induction and the entire first year were the most difficult. Treatments were tough, including preparing for them. A typically funny, affectionate, and smiley child, Ollie's personality would change from the steroid treatments. He would be cranky and eat everything in sight, which brought on puffiness and weight. This overeating was good because it would help when he had his low moments, including nausea after the chemotherapy treatments, which would wipe him out. It is so difficult to see a small child suffer. Ollie hated his shots or "pokes" as he called them. He cried, of course, but often he was brave beyond belief. It is so difficult to witness the first-time parents of a small child suffer.

Beyond the physical and emotional suffering, there was the frustration of "bubble boy living." No playmates, park, store, zoo, butterfly house, or church were allowed, and certainly no flying to see his grandparents.

Faith, prayers, and a Go Fund Me Facebook community helped them greatly! I remembered artwork on my parents' wall that said, "Prayer Changes Things," and held onto that belief when I felt like screaming. Relatives, neighbors, and friends gave great support, including providing Ollie with fun new toys or crafts to play with. The love and faith in their amazing medical team helped them in a complete body-mind-spirit way.

"Ollie Strong" was a phrase that inspired my good friend, Beth, to write a song for him. It was the most touching gift. We sang it together at a house party/fundraiser for Leukemia research.

"Snips and snails and puppy dog tails,
They say that's what little boys are made of.
We know that's not true, because we know you.

You're made of light—you're made of might.
You're ready for this fight.
You are made of tough. You're more than enough.
You may be small but don't get me wrong,
All day long, you're Ollie Strong.

It isn't fair that you should be living this reality
But with love and faith and hope and grace
you'll turn out and win this race
You're made of light. You're made of might.
You're ready for this fight.
You're made of tough. You're more than enough.
You may be small but don't get me wrong
All day long, you're Ollie Strong. You're Ollie Strong. You're Ollie Strong."

Before one of Ollie's treatments, he asked me to sing "Ollie Strong," or, *my song,* as he calls it. So as the needle dripped lifesaving medicine into him, I sang, and he squeezed my hand through the "poke."

A full circle moment came a year later. We were in the hammock in our backyard swinging together. "Mae Mae, do you want to hear *me* sing Ollie Strong?" "Oh, yes! I said, "Do you know *all* the words?" Ollie sang his entire song ever so softly in his sweet three and a half-year-old voice. Grinning, he sang loudly, "You may be small but don't get me wrong, all day long, I'm OLLIE STRONG."

Ollie's presence and amazing grace moving through this illness is a gift to behold. No doubt there will be challenging days of monthly treatment ahead until this medical protocol is complete. He is doing so well, enjoying pre-school and all the magical and fun things four year olds do. All who know Ollie will never forget his example of moving through illness, not with judgment but with grace and love.

The Trauma of Becoming a
Butterfly Warrior
By Foxye Jackson, RN, CA-SANE, CRM

Butterflies inspire me to pause and smile in the moment. The flicker of colorful wings, the energy of movement, and the brilliance of their delicateness light up my day with hope and joy. See, butterflies are a lot like me—or maybe I am a lot like them. For I, too, have a colorful energy displayed in the brilliance of my delicateness that resulted from life's major transformations. My transformations were from victim, to survivor, to warrior. It was the trauma of becoming a butterfly.

I sit writing in the comfort of my back porch, with hanging chimes playing lullabies and the wind whispering gently across my face. Damp, cut grass is dappled with random yellow dandelions, and a white bird soars overhead to signal a message is coming. This is the perfect space for reflecting on my life's milkweeds.

Caterpillar Victim

As a young caterpillar, the Monarch's focus is eating milkweed and staying alive. Milkweed is toxic to other insects and some animals because of the cardenolide content in its sap. Cardenolides affect the rhythms of the heart, causing them to slow down, speed up, or stop. However, the Monarch caterpillar is born genetically dependent upon and equipped to handle these toxic substances. Likewise, I was born spiritually dependent upon and equipped to handle the toxins of my life.

A victim is one who has experienced life events that caused harm or trauma. For me, it was parental abandonment, sexual assault, and domestic violence. I was born into a family of women who were accustomed to keeping family business secret. Many had been sexually assaulted and beaten physically and emotionally by those they loved. Because no one spoke about it, no one healed, but everyone learned emotional detachment as a mechanism of survival.

My mother was part of that family of women. She and my father separated when I was a young child. He was later murdered, right before my stepfather began to assault me sexually. Although my stepfather was one of many who would abuse me, his abuse is significant because of the abandonment I felt by my mother and absent father. Despite Mother remaining silent as she was taught, the trauma affected me no less and set the stage for me to allow future abuse.

Toxic relationships bloomed throughout my teen years, which included devastating sexual encounters. Although the caterpillar sheds its skin several times, I feel that I held on to mine. Carrying the traumas of my younger years, I married twice. Together, they fed me physical, verbal, and emotional desecration that convinced me suicide was the best and only solution. Spiraling into the abyss of my soul's darkness, a change occurred, and my soul began the weaving of a silken pad in preparation for my chrysalis.

Chrysalis Survivor

"If I catch you with someone else, I'll kill you." Those were the words spoken to me by one husband. Now, there is no set time for a caterpillar to wander off and become a chrysalis. They just eat, grow, and shed their skin until something sparks an unction within them to be still and shed once more. Those words were my spark.

Hearing those words and feeling the intended fear and worry of my listening children, I replied, "Do it now. If you're gonna kill me, do it now. 'Cause what I'm not gonna do is live in fear." Choosing not to live in fear gave my soul permission to attach to its silken pad and begin the shedding of skins that had held me in the caterpillar stage far too long. I became a chrysalis survivor.

The phenomenal transformation that occurs in the chrysalis stage produces nearly unrecognizable art. The chrysalis covers and protects the Monarch as it transforms. Archangels Michael and Raphael, my spirit guides, and the loving ascended masters all gathered around me and protected me as I changed my thought processes, beliefs, knowledge, and overall mindset. I allowed myself to cry in the chrysalis because it was safe.

The massive protection I felt allowed me to explore my purpose for existing in the physical. I learned how to be thankful for the milkweeds of my life and use them as fuel for my change. I embraced being a victim of abandonment, fear, sexual traumas, harmful words, and heartache and sought a way to use them to affect healing in others and myself. The words of my mentor pushed me out of the chrysalis and into my purpose of being a butterfly warrior.

Butterfly Warrior

While in my chrysalis, I received direction from a psychic, who later became my mentor. She told me I was purposed to heal all the women of my lineage, and this would be accomplished by healing myself. I knew exactly what she meant and understood the challenges I would face within.

Believing I was equipped to accomplish my purpose was the greatest challenge. My inner self reminded me I was born for this purpose and had been given a life of milkweed to strengthen my ability to survive in a world that thought I was expendable. That world included me. The next challenge was to have warrior compassion.

Warriors become great when their compassion for others surpasses their desire to remain silent in word or deed. As a warrior, I learned to have compassion and forgiveness for myself and those souls who agreed to feed me what I thought was toxic because, now, I was able to fly. I am a butterfly warrior.

A butterfly warrior lands in its purpose and spreads that beauty across the universe, constantly replacing outdated beliefs and thoughts with new ones. It embraces each moment as a teacher and seeks to infect the lives of everyone. A butterfly warrior understands that everything and everyone is connected energy. This connection enables the healing of others as I heal.

As you read this, know that it is time for you to embrace the trauma of becoming a butterfly warrior.

Freedom Through Forgiveness
By JamieLynn

A s teens and young adults, we find passions, or at least we start to learn what we like and what we are good at. When I was 13, I discovered I'm good at public speaking, and at the age of 15, I discovered I was good at being bold. What I discovered in my 20s and early 30s was the importance of forgiveness.

After eight years of sexual abuse by five family members, and being raised by a mentally and narcissistic mother, I realized that, with the love and support of my father's family, life could be better. I told my school counselor of the sexual abuse when I was 15, and went to court. Three of the five served time in jail or prison. I watched my dad's older brother defend my healing and freedom when others would have had me stay a victim. Deep within I felt a pull—passion and knowing that my purpose is to do something with all I had experienced. Also, the heart and empathy that sat deep within were screaming to me that these acts of abuse were caused by a deep, unexplained pain, in knowingness, and with a lack of respect for themselves or others. Overall, they did not know what to be responsible for because they were not taught how.

Forgiveness is freedom from pain, shame, guilt, and even "dis-ease." First, be aware of where forgiveness is needed most. Looking at the heaviest emotion and breathing deeply without having to know what is needed to forgive, say to yourself, "I forgive you" and feel your body relax. When I look to myself first, I realize I am the last person I want to forgive. I was wrong in some way, and I should be punished, or this is my thinking. I felt I failed my mother. That somehow, I was supposed to heal her mental illness and anger. Since I could not heal her, I was somehow responsible for her actions and addictions and even her state of mind. It helped to know that we are only responsible for our healing; we can't force this on others, we can only live by example, and not all people wish to be healed. With the sexual abuse, three of the five served time, and two of the five blame me for how their life has turned out. Two of the five apologized, and one of the five took full responsibility with his actions of harm, and told me that I had no reason to be apologetic because he had taken advantage of me. With that statement, I felt a locked gate inside me open up, and I felt free.

What if the one who harmed never takes responsibility, is forgiveness still possible? Yes, of course. The secret to forgiveness is that it is not for them. Forgiveness is for you—by forgiving you are saying, "I no longer allow this person/people to harm me. I no longer let them harm me." Look at how you can be reconcilable, for in that you will find power. I am responsible for my anger, shame, guilt, disease, what I say to myself, and who I show the world I am. If I were an addict, it is *my* addiction; if I were anorexic it is *my* sickness. These are impacts of the abuse, yes, and the release of this disease is for me. The triggers that show up are also mine and how I choose to handle that is my way. Once I began to look at these areas and break them down, I found love and empathy for those who harmed me, and for all those who unknowingly failed me over the years. I forgive them as I also forgive myself. I now know who, when, and where not to be to cause myself further issue or disease, I also know how to create safety for myself. This all took time to allow myself to express what I had been suppressing. Forgiveness of yourself is the strongest place to start. What's possible after that is anything you wish. For me, it's the difference I am able to make in publicly speaking, being an author, hosting the Breakthrough & Thrive Summit, and being an empowerment coach, a wife, and a mother. I created my family and caused my friends. In all of this I follow my passions, and I am healing my body. What are your desires? What are your passions? Are they worth the effects and efforts of the forgiveness process?

What forgiveness is: Healing and freedom.
What forgiveness is not: Condoning, excusing, forgetting, allowing.
Does it mean the triggers will go away? In time, if you cause it, yes.
Lots of love and empathy on your healing path.

Stepping Into Your Sovereignty: Be The Queen Of Your Own Happiness
By Vanessa Johnston

Authenticity is paramount in my life. As a result, my career path has been circuitous in pursuit of what is genuinely rewarding. Early on, I incorporated mythologist Joseph Campbell's advice to "follow your bliss." While never predictable or easy, this course always feels right and true. It's a philosophy that some may consider glib, but it's served me well as a guiding mantra for a long time. I have faith that the alignment of thoughts and actions with what brings one joy and gratitude ultimately leads to the highest good for all. By shining your light, you become a beacon to the world.

I am an End of Life Doula. It's critical to establish emotional boundaries with clients and to protect your energy while doing such heavy heart-work. Grounding and centering are mandatory for successful service. This is something that anyone working in the palliative and/or hospice care industry knows from the outset. Burnout happens prematurely and often because these occupational hazards are real. To combat this risk, I focus on three main elements to cultivate happiness in my kingdom. I commit to meaningful practices, supportive connections, and intentional solitude regularly to step into my sovereignty.

Meaningful Practices

I value all the world's religious traditions as a Unitarian Universalist. Once, I taught a Sunday school class called "Neighboring Faiths," and spent several weeks exploring Islam with middle-schoolers. We were captivated by the tenet that requires adherents to pray five times a day, and wondered if that was something our class might be able to achieve. We set it as a goal, and endeavored to find prayers that were personally meaningful. I discovered this variation of the Metta Prayer of Lovingkindness from Buddhism, which resonated:

May all beings be peaceful.
May all beings be happy.
May all beings be safe.
May all beings awaken to the light of their true nature.
May all beings be free.

Though it may sound easy, I was unable to achieve the discipline required to say this prayer five times a day. My middle-schoolers fared no better in their attempts. However, I was able to commit to saying it sincerely once a day, upon awakening. Additionally, I soon realized this was an excellent way to start my morning, with a focus on benevolence for myself and others.

Other practices and rituals that have helped me focus on positive outcomes are: drawing daily affirmations from oracle decks, writing in a gratitude journal nightly, creating monthly intentions, and visualizing quarterly successes. Research has shown that deeper gratitude inevitably leads to a rise in happiness, so I incorporate actions of thankfulness whenever possible.

Reflection: If you were to say one silent prayer or empowering sentence every morning, what would it be? How could beginning your waking hours with this one thought improve the trajectory of your day?

Supportive Connections

As I've gotten older, I've come to appreciate the various networks of support I have created for myself. We are relational creatures, and the best way to resist our transactional culture is to place value on the connections we have with each other instead. This is how we care for one another long-term. The groups that sustain me are communities in harmony with my personal goals. Whether the collective in question is one that advocates for racial equity, or holds space for women and their struggles, or explores ways to be egoless in an egocentric world, I have sought out these groups as a way to reinforce my attempts at these worthy ambitions. When we share our struggles, we feel less alone. When we share our accomplishments, we feel happier.

After the 2016 election, I was fortunate to have direction and agency to pursue the social justice work I felt called to do. I became involved with the grassroots activist group, Indivisible, and met many like-minded and like-hearted individuals who shared the same desire to protect the most vulnerable among us. Because of this, I felt empowered to use my voice and was confident enough to meet with local legislators and bring my children with me to protest marches, rallies, and vigils. The political is always personal, but taking a stand as a group sends a much more powerful message to those representing us.

Reflection: If you were to join a Meet-Up group, what kind of group would it be? What hobbies or interests would you like to become more involved with?

Intentional Solitude

The third condition for planting seeds of self-contentment is to be comfortable with solitude. Once you become your best friend, you will crave solo ventures and relish the opportunity for quiet reflection. Daily meditation helps to still my always-racing mind, as does writing and journaling.

In addition, I've found the Japanese practice of *shinrin-yoku* to be calming, restorative, and rejuvenating. The term itself means "forest bathing" or "taking in the forest atmosphere." You purposefully walk through a forest of trees and tune in to your senses and all the beauty surrounding you. It is a simple and intuitive practice that connects one to the healing benefits of being in nature. It is an organic and natural way to lower your blood pressure, reduce your stress, and improve your mood. Whenever it's warm, I like to walk barefoot on the hard-packed dirt trails between the trees near my house and feel gratitude for the planet that sustains us all beneath my feet.

Reflection: Where is your favorite place to be in nature? If you were there right now, what would you see, hear, smell, touch, and taste?

It is my hope that these reflections will help you become a regal ruler of your true self. The key is to cultivate happiness and learn the practices that will encourage the growth and abundance of joy in your life. It is my belief that self-care is sacred, and by honoring ourselves, we may better serve each other.

Embracing The Takeaways
By Cindy J. Kaufman

One morning in January 2015, I awoke with a pressure headache. There was a winter storm approaching, and I assumed it was from the barometric pressure change. As the day progressed, so did the pressure in my head, followed by nausea and vomiting. I decided it must have been a virus and I would be well in a day or two. I was wrong on both counts.

As the days passed, the pressure headaches and illness continued. Other symptoms developed as well. I suffered from debilitating fatigue. My eyesight changed to blurry double vision. I noticed cognitive changes too, like getting to the end of a paragraph and not remembering what I had read. I had trouble with word recall. For example, I couldn't think of the word "chair" and would say "the thing you sit on" instead. My quality of life deteriorated quickly, and I was frightened. I didn't know what was happening to me, but I knew it was bad.

My primary care sent me to a neurologist and she did a full workup, including a cognitive exam. I began to cry when I couldn't do the simple math in my head or recall the short list of words I was asked to remember. Rather than showing concern for these symptoms, she said, "You seem to be anxious." I responded rather sharply, "I *am* anxious! Something is wrong with my brain, and I'm scared that I have dementia or a brain tumor!" She didn't think I had dementia, but she sent me for an MRI of my head which revealed a cyst in the center of my brain. I needed a second MRI to diagnose it. After that scan, I was told I had an 11-millimeter benign pineal cyst, but that it was not causing my symptoms; it was considered an incidental finding. "Then what is wrong with me?" I asked. "You have migraines," she responded, "and I will prescribe medications." I was dumbfounded. "But what about the other symptoms?" I asked. "The blurry double vision, the nausea and vomiting, the cognitive changes?" She claimed they could all be caused by migraines. I knew in my gut this was not right. I left and began researching everything I could about these benign tumors, and I sought more opinions. Three neurosurgeons also dismissed the pineal cyst as asymptomatic and referred me to pain management for migraines.

I did not give up. I persisted in the research like it was my job! I discovered a Facebook support group, and there I learned that only a handful of neurosurgeons in the world would remove the rare symptomatic pineal cyst. I visited one such surgeon in Houston, Texas who assured me it was indeed causing my symptoms, and ten months after that first headache, I had brain surgery to remove the pineal cystic tumor. The constant pressure headaches were gone, as were most of the other symptoms, except for the vision and cognitive issues due to the length of time the tumor was pressing on the structures around it. I was left with an acquired brain injury, but fortunately, time and therapy brought more improvement. I'm doing much better now, and I'm grateful for it.

A serious illness that threatens your life, or quality of life, comes with its challenges and lessons. I choose to focus not on what I lost, but instead to embrace the gifts, or what I like to call, the takeaways:

Takeaway #1: You must be your health advocate.

In your life, being your best advocate is paramount. No one looks out for you and champions for you like *you* do! It's the same with your health. Listen to your gut, do your research, and get multiple opinions. Doctors don't know everything, so educating yourself is sometimes necessary.

Takeaway #2: Don't compare one illness to another.

Someone said to me, "At least it wasn't malignant. You didn't have to get chemo or radiation." Yes, it was benign, but that doesn't negate the seriousness of it. It is insensitive and invalidating to minimize anyone's situation by comparing it to something else. This takeaway can apply to a lot of other situations in life as well.

Takeaway #3: Your friends will change, and that's okay.

Some friends will walk away when you are going through a serious illness. I don't know why. It could be her or his fear of mortality. Perhaps she can't handle the changes in you. Serious illness will change you (see Takeaway #4). Maybe she doesn't get the same benefit from the relation-ship since you became ill, meaning, she wasn't a true friend. I don't know for sure. What I do know is you will see who sticks around, and those are the friends you can count on. And guess what? You make new friends too! You will make new friends who can relate to you because they are going, or have gone, through the same thing. If you find yourself faced with serious illness, know there will be a change in your circle of friends.

Takeaway #4: Serious illness will change you, and that too is okay.

There was an awakening that occurred when I faced my mortality. I got clear about what mattered to me. I became restrictive about who and what I let into my life. I created a "no-drama, no-bullshit, no-stress, toxic-free zone" around me. I learned to say "No" to things I didn't want to do, without explanation or guilt. I ended relationships that were unhealthy. I went on a media-free diet. I rested and did self-care when I decided. I put my physical, emotional and mental health first. Those changes stuck going forward, and they made for a healthier, happier me!

Many of life's challenges come with the gifts of helpful takeaways. Coming through those challenges, we see with a new perspective, and we gain clarity on what matters most. Despite losses, takeaways can allow for more happiness and peace in our daily lives.

How My Father's Death
Improved Our Relationship
By Cindy J. Kaufman

When the phone call came, it felt like a heavy black cloak was draped around my shoulders. "I have lung cancer, and I have four to six months to live," he said. I don't remember what was said after that, except I know he said he loved me, and I said I loved him too. I had always loved my dad, even when I was estranged from him for my emotional well-being. That wasn't the first time he said he was dying, but it would be the last.

I was "daddy's girl" growing up, and I was proud of that title, but somewhere in my adolescent years my father became an alcoholic, and I became embarrassed to be daddy's girl. Later, I would come to understand that he was abusive to me in those years, verbally and emotionally abusive. The alcohol was like venom in his bloodstream. And things got worse. One time my father was assaulting my mother, and I forced myself between them so he would stop hitting her. That was my family's rock bottom.

My mother divorced my father when I was 17. After that he had no stability, moving from place to place, sleeping on the sofas of enablers. Long periods of time would pass without me knowing where he was. Twice he called me to a hospital to say a deathbed goodbye because of alcoholic hepatitis. The doctor said if he left the hospital and drank again he would die. And then he left the hospital and drank again, both times. This pattern felt like another form of abuse, so for years, I became estranged from my father.

For the last six years of his life, he found sobriety and I reunited with him, albeit cautiously. As a sober man, he was the loving dad I had missed, but his hard life had taken a toll, and he was disabled. Six months before his terminal diagnosis, he moved from Florida (where I also lived) to Ohio to be near his wife's family. That move made it impossible for me to see him; neither of us had the resources to travel.

After that phone call, I planned a trip to say a third and final deathbed goodbye. However, my father's impending death brought up issues of unresolved pain. I had stuffed it all down, allowed it to infect every area of my life, and told myself, "Someday I will deal with it." But that day never came, and time was running out. I wanted to bury the pain with him when he was buried. I wanted a future where I no longer perpetuated the abuse of my past on myself in the myriad of ways I was still doing that.

I sought counseling and was advised to write a letter to my father. In that letter, I would say everything I needed to say about the past and I would show him, and myself, forgiveness. Once written, I could choose to give it to him or not. If not, the pain would be out of me and onto that paper. I could destroy the letter by burning it, sending it out into the universe. Either way, it would be my release.

I wrote the letter, worked through the emotions with my therapist, and planned my trip to visit my father. I felt strong and resolved in my healing, ready for whatever would happen. On my last day, I handed my father the letter and explained what it was. I told him he could choose to read it and we could discuss it, or he could read it after I left, and we could talk over the phone. He chose the latter. We said our tearful goodbyes, for it would be the last time we saw one another. When I returned home, I called him. I waited for him to mention the letter, but he didn't. I asked if he had read it. He said he had. I asked if he wanted to talk about it. He replied, "No, except to say I understand." And that was it. I knew he was not capable of more. If he were, he would have said it.

My father died two months later, the heavy black cloak lifted, and the pain was gone. Three months after that he came to me like a dream in the night, surrounded by white light. He said not a word, but I understood. He was okay, and he would still be around me. That experience brought me further peace, and I felt nothing but love from and for my father.

The thing I hadn't expected is that my relationship with my father would improve upon his death. It's been 17 years now, and we have enjoyed a wonderful relationship! My memories of him are only good ones. My feelings about him are only loving ones. In my letter to my father, I told him I had always seen him as the father who failed me, but I came to accept him as the father he was; a flawed human being, just like me, who had his own pain and dealt with it the only way he knew how— by drinking. He could have been a better father to me, yes, but he wasn't, and I could not change that. What I could change was how I allowed that to affect me going forward. I granted him mercy for the pain he inflicted and mercy for myself for the pain I'd endured.

It is possible, if you want it, to have a better relationship after death with someone who harmed you in life. In my more than 20 years working in the field of death and dying, I've helped others achieve this as well. My dad still visits me all the time! Every time I look at the clock and it's 11:11 (which happens a lot), I know it's my dad saying, "Hello!" I smile and say, "Hi Dad! I love you!"

When The Wheels Came Off
By Susan Marie Kelley

I closed the door of the RV, hoping I hadn't forgotten anything for our five-week trip to the West Coast. Dave and I were excited about taking a trip anywhere in our little home, because it always spelled adventure.

We had just crossed the Indiana border when we heard an explosion. "Oh my God! What was that?" I shrieked. Because our RV is thirty-five feet long and weighs around 10,000 pounds, I get a little nervous when anything goes wrong—picturing us in a five-mile pile-up.

Looking disgusted, Dave said, "We blew a tire." This seemed incredible because we'd replaced the tires not too long ago.

"What can I do to help?" I asked, feeling surprisingly calm.

"Call a tire repair place," he said as he opened the door to get out. Watching him put on the spare brought warmth and gratitude to my heart. When you've been married for as long as we have (almost fifty years) "sexy" takes on a new meaning.

With a brand new tire, we were on the road again traveling to North Dakota and stopped to get gas. A man walked up and said to Dave, "Your rig looks like it's leaning, probably the suspension system." Then he disappeared.

Panic overtook me once again; I was sure the whole rig was going to collapse and leave us stranded on the highway.

Praying for a band of angels, ascended masters, and whoever else wanted to lend a hand, I asked for protection and divine intervention as we headed to a welding garage in some God-forsaken place with run-down buildings and trash strewn everywhere.

Early the next morning, with the sun low in the sky, we were on the road headed for Butte, Montana, and had to stop for gas. While waiting in line, I left Dave and went into the market to get him some lunch.

While holding a sandwich in one hand and trying to zip my purse shut with the other, a man with skin the color of coffee and cream walked past me and said something, but I couldn't hear him. "I'm sorry, what did you say?"

He stopped and looked at me, "I'm not trying to get in your purse." I pulled my purse closer to me. Then he spat out, "They treat you like animals, and I hate this. I hate myself." My fear faded into compassion. I felt so bad for him—I wanted to drop everything and give him a hug.

Praying for the right words, I looked into his sad, angry eyes and said, "There's a reason for all this. And remember, God loves you."

He smiled and said, "God bless you." Straight from heaven, that message was for me as well.

An hour later, we arrived at our campground in Butte. Dave is very particular about how level the camper is, so we backed up and went forward numerous times while watching many leveling bubbles to make sure we were not tipping too much to the left or right. On the third try, the rig got stubborn and decided not to back up. Every time Dave tried to move backward, the wheels locked. "Hold it," I yelled, standing at the back. "Something is wrong." We then drove forward around the campground a couple more times. It was on the third try, when we were nowhere near level and weary of going in circles that we proceeded to set up camp. Five hours later, the brakes, which had completely worn out, were fixed to the tune of twelve hundred dollars.

Our souls and our rig restored, we drove to pretty little Cascade Locks, which is in the heart of the Columbia River Gorge. Our campground was completely wooded with centuries-old pine trees. It was so quiet that Dave and I whispered to each other while setting up camp. As we lay peacefully in our bed, we heard the sound of a train storming up the tracks. When it blew its horn right outside our window, we sat straight up with hearts pounding. Every couple of hours and all through the night, a train rumbled past.

Bleary-eyed the next morning, Dave went to empty the holding tank, but it wouldn't drain. Neither one of us understood sewer systems, so again we called an RV repair place. Apparently, according to the nice young man who came over to fix the mess, we were doing everything wrong—

wrong toilet paper, wrong cleaner, and we were not keeping enough water in the tank. By this point, all the systems had failed.

Somewhere on the highway, while driving through miles of open land and big sky, we heard yet another tire explosion. If it weren't so terrifying, it would have been amusing.

Due to lack of sleep and with train horns still blaring in my head, I broke down and sobbed. There had been too many systems breaking down, too much stress because of the weight we were pulling, and too much feeling out of control. And in that enlightening moment, I got the message: *Let go and trust the process. The process is there to get you to your intention if you let it happen and don't block anything or let panic get in the way. Let go of the tons of baggage you are carrying and trust there is a loving force guiding everything.*

I realized that sometimes we have to go through a dark night of the soul. When everything starts breaking down, there hardly seems to be a reason to live. But there is a purpose. All experiences have a lesson, whether it's to teach kindness, patience, or compassion. If we just break down the barriers, love can enter in.

I began to understand that the only way for us to evolve is to let go of all the attachments, move through fear, and work on what you want, then the emotional freedom will come, and with it—peace.

The Dance of the Dragonflies: Dispelling the Myth of a One-Dimensional Person with a 'Disability'
By Amy King

"I don't know how you manage." Those words coming out of the old woman's mouth slapped me across the cheeks like the prickly cold of an icy snowstorm. As we moved in opposite directions, pushing our grocery carts through the market, I stopped for a moment and watched her labored gait, as she walked away. I was accustomed to receiving comments such as that and others that cut deeply. Still, it stung.

Disability isn't the challenge—the challenge is how society views disability, and the lack of access that able-bodied people take for granted. It's having no access to buildings with stairs, wondering if you can visit friends' homes and use the bathroom, comments like "you're too pretty to be in a wheelchair", and not "making it" because the only wheelchair-accessible stall is taken by a daft, able-bodied woman with a half-assed "sorry". I am not the four wheels and titanium that move me through the world. I would have relished an opportunity to sit down with the older woman and explain that my life has been filled with beauty, love, happiness, heartache, pain, fear, hope, and the mundane. All of the things that make this life beautiful.

Like so many of you, I was a Girl Scout, took piano and singing lessons, and played the clarinet in the junior high school band. I had water balloon fights in the heat of Sacramento summers and had to be in when streetlights shone. I babysat a lot! My parents got divorced when I was 13. Living in Japan briefly as a teen, I once ended up sitting in the snow in front of a bus stop with one broken crutch (the holes in the cement for snow drainage) and one intact. As if on cue, a bus pulled up and the people getting off stepped over me, shaking heads at the crazy carrot-topped foreigner (thanks, Summer Blonde). I graduated from high school and attended college, earning degrees and credentials. I worked in computer software development. I went to Africa and was able to experience life in a remote village and meet the King while breaking ground on a medical clinic. I've wept in front of the Mona Lisa and taken a tram to Mt. Fuji. I finished a 5k in 32 minutes 26 seconds, which took some serious training!

I became a teacher in Title I schools for a decade. I own a house and drive a car.

I longed for her to know that only the day before, I had returned from a solo trip to Hawaii, where I had a romantic connection with a beautiful man—one worth writing about. I played sled hockey on Olympic ice, won wake-crossing competitions, and I was a certified life coach. I have had true love and heartbreak, as well as beautiful, supportive friendships that have spanned decades. I say yes to what calls me, for the "yeses" get you to where you desire. However, life challenges are our best opportunities for growth and strength.

I was born with Spina bifida. After three surgeries and 60 days, I went home. The first five years of my life included many hospital stays. I spent my 30th birthday hospitalized, which turned into quite the celebration. And a decade later, my life was profoundly changed.

It was January 2011, I was preparing to return to my teaching position, after Winter break. I was living a happy life, owned a home, had an active social and dating life, and was happy in my career. I started feeling feverish. Ashen grey and feeling horrible, I returned to work.

The following day, I was in the emergency room with sepsis. I had a pressure wound that had tunneled ten centimeters to my left femur, giving me osteomyelitis. I spent four days in the hospital. I was released with a PICC line in my upper inner left arm for self-injections and a wound vacuum attached to my left butt cheek. Home health nurses would come every Monday, Wednesday, and Friday to change the wound vacuum dressings and measure the wound—shower days! Woohoo!! In March of that year, my mom was diagnosed with Amyotrophic Lateral Sclerosis (ALS/Lou Gehrig's disease). I had already lost my father and stepfather in the last four years, I would soon lose my mom. Things were dark, some days so dismal that I wasn't sure I'd make it. As the months wore on, healing slowly, I struggled to maintain a healthy mental attitude. My saving graces were friends who called daily and those who showed up occasionally with hugs, love, gossip, and food.

One morning, on a particularly emotionally raw day, I noticed something that changed me profoundly. I was lying listlessly in the living room on my hospital bed, and I looked out and saw the most beautiful thing. A swarm of about 50 dragonflies was dancing rhythmically. The light glistened off of their iridescence. I felt an overwhelming sense of connection to everything, tears rolling down my face. I realized that I was exactly where I was supposed to be in that moment. I began to pay attention to everything more acutely.

That was the beginning of a spiritual awakening which, over time, led me to a rewarding career in life coaching. In total, my physical healing took 317 days. Since then, I have become a life coach, and I have survived breast cancer. That's a story for another time.

I have learned some powerful lessons in this Earth suit:

You define yourself.

People will leave during hard times. Others will arrive just in time. Allow them to support you.

Challenges make us more compassionate.

Connect with nature, yourself, and with others daily.

Say yes when the universe pulls you, pay attention.

Sometimes we need to be stopped so that we can start again on the right path.

It's your right to have a phenomenal life.

Hiding With Bulimia
By Julie Lalande

Bulimia was my secret friend—a way to hide my feelings and deal with anxiety, fears, and disappointments. She was there through my divorce, motherhood, relationships, and deadlines. Bulimia gave me a sense of control over my feelings. During illness, I was convinced the trigger was the fear of being fat. I'd feel the rush of negative emotions then binge on comfort food to feel the high of indulgence and freedom. The recoil of guilt and shame would induce me to vomit, and I'd feel lightheaded and relieved. Every episode was my last time.

Sixteen years later, that pain surfaced, and I had to make a choice to get help. I sheepishly spoke to my doctor about treatment. I wasn't sure I could let my friend, Bulimia, go. My physician suggested an anti-depressant that would help my compulsions. I refused until she asked me, "If you were diabetic, would you take medication?" As a nurse, this information was reasonable, and I accepted treatment.

As long as I can remember, I was an introvert, constantly living in my thoughts. I would play in my sandbox imaging my role in the world. My loving parents didn't spoil my innocence. My earliest memory is of giggling while my father playfully hoisted me over his head until I grew too heavy for the game.

When school started, I was terrified. Shyness left me feeling paralyzed. I recall how my stomach churned at recess as I hoped no one would notice me. I would hold on to the teacher's hand for comfort. In grade two, a boy protested that he didn't want me on his team and I started to cry. I was horrified as the teacher yelled at the boy and gently excused me from the class to discuss bullying. Shame came over me, and I believed that I had gotten everyone in trouble because I cried. At that moment, I decided I would avoid pain by hiding my feelings.

Puberty created curves, and my height created a slimmer appearance. It was during an annual physical that the physician put his smoke pipe down and walked over to his assessment room where I followed. I bent down, unclothed, to touch my toes as he stood behind me, and told me he was assessing my posture to finalize the physical assessment. I got dressed humiliated and attentively sat across him. His conclusion was to share a statistic about the odds of having weight issues because I had overweight parents. It appeared I would have no control from becoming a statistic and gratefully accepted a referral to a dietitian. I handed over my prescription for a one thousand calorie diet to the dietician who read it and smugly said to me, "I am not making supermodels here." I was embarrassed.

High school introduced another awareness that my body was an instrument of attraction. Girls around me were trying to achieve hundred-pound benchmarks. The closer you achieved this, the more attention you would be certain to receive from your peers. My mother was afraid beauty would somehow scar my character and would always remark how internal beauty was more important than outside beauty whenever I asked her how I looked.

I attempted to show no signs that I cared; at least that's what I wanted to portray. At 21 years old, I entered a restaurant where an ex-boyfriend was on a date with a girl I knew. I felt betrayed by both of them. I was struck by her thinness and beauty, feeling certain that my ex-boyfriend preferred her appearance to mine. I smiled and said hello as my heart crumbled. That night when I got home, I binged and purged. From that day forward, it was a way to deal with emotions without expressing them to anyone.

Treatment involves disclosure to friends and family. Telling loved ones was difficult, and unexpectedly painful for them. I could not explain myself at that time except to ask, "What could you have done?" When bulimia is a secret, no one can stop the cycle except the bulimic person. Treatment didn't come without relapses, and to this day, I can still remember the release of anxiety from a binge. I also remind myself of the heartburn and esophageal pain and its endless grip on my life. Now I choose to feel and express myself. Although I allow myself the right to be hurt or indifferent, I still feel vulnerable and sometimes ashamed. Self-acceptance and self-love have been key. I am proud to be emotionally sensitive, aware and introspective. When I decided to close off and not share my feelings, I lost my voice. My voice may have told my mother how important her validation was or my dad how much I missed his attention. I may have told the doctor and the dietitian that they were not helpful. But instead, I choose to hide the hurt inside.

Bulimia, like other cycles of addiction, is chosen. Cycles of addiction solve an emotional problem immediately without the forethought of the pain that ensues. My fear of judgment mirrored my judgment of myself and made it easier not to address my pain. Shame and guilt come from darkened hollows in our lives and are not always obvious. Our decisions are influenced by our experiences, so looking into our past isn't to find blame, but to identify the alternative interpretation and rekindle our right to be ourselves. I acknowledge my pain was real and I allow those feelings to flow without any need to control them or judge them.

Experiences are different for everyone as well as our thoughts about them. Painful emotions can leave us blinded and neglectful of ourselves. The beauty is that we have the power to choose whether we will hide or be present. Pain is not calling on you for judgment; it has no expectations. Allowing painful emotions to flow allows you to recognize happiness when it comes.

Git-R-Done!
By Barbara Larrabee

Larry Whitney is known as "Larry, the Cable Guy," beloved by millions in redneck country comedy. He was my husband's favorite entertainer and provided us with hours of fun. Larry's catchphrase is *"Git-R-Done!"* It's common language everywhere. The Urban Dictionary says "complete a task, let's get this done."

Jim and I were married for 29 years before he passed in 2007. He was a diabetic with complications. It's a nasty disease that consumes your health, spirit, and finances. At this time, I was the breadwinner, the caregiver/nurse, cook, and the researcher. I became an excellent authority on alternative therapies. There were difficult decisions constantly. So many times, Jim would say, "Let's just *Git-R-Done!*"

He was always the brave one, not me. Every doctor and nurse loved him. He could be stubborn, opinionated, outspoken—oh, yeah! He was also caring, loving, vibrant, brilliant, the consummate entrepreneur. He was the funniest man I ever knew.

No matter how dire the circumstances, his humor reigned. When the doctor told him there was nothing more they could do, he said, "So, Doc, you're telling me I'm toast?" How brave and funny even then.

We had a sign that traveled from Jim's hospital room to his office, then back again as needed, *Git-R-Done!* It was his philosophy: assess the problem, face it head on, then just get it done.

I don't have a sign, but that saying has still been my inspiration to keep moving on in life. His memorial service was on a Saturday, and I was working again on Monday. I had to survive.

Grief and moving forward was my private journey.

I had to keep "getting things done." I sorted bills and looked at options. I shredded records of many years of business together, reliving memories with each piece of paper. I cleared out stuff—painfully—and I moved.

The day I moved was traumatic: miserable weather, pouring rain, problems. I was exhausted—had stayed up all night packing. I remember sitting down once bawling, then pulling it together and picking up the tape gun again.

At my new apartment, the ceiling was leaking. It was devastating! Did I make a mistake? Years later, my psychic friend told me that the water was tears of grief and a great cleansing. Eventually, *Git-R-Done!* morphed as my mantra from *mere survival* to creating my *new future*. Now I was on my own. It was scary but exciting!

Next—a car to replace the one I had with 250,000 miles. I had been driving junkers forever; always worrying about repairs, playing small. I took a bold, brave step and got a new car. This was a turning point for me and changed my outlook on life. My sparkling car's name is Misty because she's a misty blue. One night after a meeting, a friend and I were looking across the street, and a streetlight was shining down on Misty, spotlighting her in the dark. She magically glowed. Months later, I noticed that a similar car was on my vision board! Eight years later, I still talk to her and feel comforted when I get in.

By now, I was in my mid-60s. I wanted to have a more meaningful life and be the best version of Barbara I could be. No time to waste.

I took deliberate steps to change my job and create a new world.

On Oprah one day, they were talking about the Law of Attraction (LOA). I yelled out, "Where are these people? I want friends like this!" Within weeks my prayer was answered. I started going to a LOA Meetup group, a new circle of positive-thinking friends.

At Meetup.com, people join together with common interests. To start connecting with business people, I also found a business group I could do before I went to work. Today, I attend several each week. *Git-R-Done!*

I joined a professional organization teaching personal growth. A coach helped me design the vision of what my ideal life looks like. After recording it, I listened every day.

My best friend and I spent Friday nights with a glass of wine and Dr. Bradley Nelson's Emotion Code—a practice to release trapped emotions which can keep you stuck or cause illness. What a gift! Such incredible healing. Today, I still work on changing belief systems and DNA. Through most of this, I've been genuinely scared and usually second-guess myself, but kudos to me for being deliberate, tough, and relentless!

When I had a serious illness, a wellness product offered through a network marketing company restored my health. I thrived in that loving community of support, mentorship, inspiration, and leadership. My customers, my team, and my leaders are my family. Amazing, talented, beautiful people surround me. I'm in a new chapter with the richness of strong, caring, fun female relationships that I hadn't had before.

I've always been a nurturer, but I have big goals now. I want to help thousands of women create better physical health and financial health through the opportunities in network marketing. The average amount needed to fend off a bankruptcy is only $384 per month. Women need to have a Plan B. They give so much to the world, and need to stay healthy and wealthy. Of the people in network marketing who make over $100,000 a year, 82% are women. It is my passion to serve the world by inspiring and leading women and giving them this opportunity. Network marketing allowed me to quit my job, office at home, travel, and learn.

Recently I saw "Get 'er done!" on a highway billboard on the way to Austin, Texas! I still turn around in a store when I hear it. It's a reminder of my journey and personal power. Maybe it's even a special message.

Stuff happens in life and whether you have a *Git-R-Done!* sign or not, remember, *you've got this*. Keep moving, one foot in front of the other. You are tougher than you think. You *will Git-R-Done!*

The Accidental Entrepreneur:
In Three Acts
By Michelle LaRue

This is the tale of how I accidentally became an entrepreneur, just like my dad.

Act 1

My parents were South Dakota farm kids who married and moved to a little town where they ran a gas station together. They had known each other since childhood when they attended country school during the Depression, and it was common for children to end their formal education after eighth grade since the high schools were in town. Although my mom earned her diploma, my dad, as the oldest of seven, went to work instead of high school. His family couldn't afford to have him board in town or drive in. I can imagine he must have felt disappointed, but he never complained.

After the birth of my sisters a few years into their marriage, our parents grew concerned that the little town schools wouldn't provide a solid education. Our family moved to a college town, where my sisters (and eventually I) could go to school. Mechanically gifted, my dad went to work for the local John Deere dealership. Long hours, hard labor, and tight finances convinced my parents that white-collar employment would be a better life for their kids, and from our early years, it was assumed we would graduate from college.

Fast forward a few decades, and all three of their daughters had earned degrees in STEM fields—accounting, economics, and in my case, engineering.

I moved across the country and started my first job as an environmental engineer for a small consulting company. The timing was perfect. The start of my career coincided with the 1990 Amendments to the Clean Air Act. I was excited to be a "white hat" in Washington, DC, saving the planet. Consulting was a terrific experience for a generalist like me. During the 18 years of my tenure, I learned processes to manufacture cutting tools, ballpoint pen balls, airbags, nutritional supplements, cardboard boxes, toothpaste, automobiles, and more. Working for a small company allowed me to lead projects and manage clients while in my early twenties.

Act 2

When the son of the John Deere shop owner inherited the business, he laid off the senior mechanics to cut costs, my dad among them. I was too young to understand how this unexpected event blindsided my dad, but the hurt and anxiety in our home at the sense of betrayal after 19 years of loyal service was unmistakable. In his mid-forties, my dad was starting over.

Without a high school or college degree, his options were limited. He studied for his journeyman's license and became an apprentice to a plumber, 30 years into his work life. The change was positive. Seeing how a regular guy like his boss owned a business gave my dad the idea he could do that, too.

My path took a different route. I went from working at a small company to working at an international consulting firm. I had expected that the "green grass" at a larger company meant access to a wider variety of projects. Disappointingly, it meant more silos and more politics, as existing employees guarded their territory to preserve their utilization rates. Many companies jockey with their competition for desirable projects and billable staff hours; I didn't expect the hustle to be internal. More than once, I worked on proposals to boost my workload, only to see the projects reassigned to younger (read: cheaper) staff. Although I worked with some terrific people, I found that the corporate machine is not kind to mid-career types who are not senior management. Experience costs money, and in the last decade, the trend in corporate America has been sacrificing institutional knowledge to cut costs.

Act 3

My dad found his second act in his mid-forties, and then went on to a third. After becoming a plumber, he decided he wanted to own and operate a business. Combining his skills and experience with his ability to diagnose and fix nearly anything, he became a handyman. When people needed someone to install appliances, furnaces, air conditioners, fences, windows, and doors, he was the go-to guy. My mom kept the books and helped him manage projects.

My teenage self sometimes wished he had a "normal" job, but the change in my dad was unmistakably good. He still worked long hours, but on his schedule, and to the benefit of his bank account, not an employer's. The autonomy he gained was worth the risk of running his business. I'd never seen him happier.

My third act began when my job became one of many eliminated from my global employer. In my mid-forties and a single parent to a young child, the least risky decision would be to take a job at another company. Or was it?

The thought of climbing into my car every day, sitting for hours in city traffic, racing to an office, and racing home to spend a few hours with my daughter was not appealing. I had gone to a larger company to have options and job security; in reality, the security of being at a larger company was an illusion. Friends told me I was brave to go out independently, without the security of a steady paycheck. After seeing so many other mid-career friends suddenly out of a job, the corporate option now appears riskier to me.

Five years into starting my company, I haven't regretted the decision. In an interesting plot twist, my career has evolved from environmental engineering to social media marketing. They're not so different. There are topics to learn, problems to analyze, and strategies to develop. Success depends on effective communication and consistent action.

Best of all, my flexible schedule means I get to be there for my teen daughter, while she sees me build a business that delights and fulfills me. I hope that someday she is as inspired by me as I am by my dad.

Heaven Is Here On Earth And Angels Surround Us
By E. Chloe Lauer

In the age of the #MeToo movement, when men's credibility and honor interacting with women are often questioned (and rightly so), travel coach, speaker, and author, Chloé Lauer, shares two stories of men coming to her aide during solo adventures in Greece and Argentina. Men can be our angels, too.

Greece

I could barely urge myself out of bed to leave the tiny studio apartment near Santorini's black sand beach. I hadn't eaten all day, and I felt weak with fever. The food poisoning had started the previous night, and between the stomach pains and anxiety about catching a 6:00 a.m. ferry from Athens, I hadn't slept more than a few short stretches. Though the ferry journey was objectively beautiful, I had a difficult time appreciating the grandeur of the scenery in my feeble state. And I was simply grateful to have landed in this quiet guest house with a mini kitchen. I planned to find a market, pick up some ingredients, and make a healing pot of chicken soup. I'd rest until I felt better, and then I'd venture around the island.

When I finally made it outside, I was struck by the crisp breeze and bright blue skies of the early May day. It was time for all of the islands' establishments to freshen up for summer's high season, only a few weeks away. Leaving my guest house, I turned right, inhaling the scent of fresh paint. It was fun to be here during this in between time. While the weather was not yet ideal for sunbathing and beach fun, the locals were out and about, and tourists were starting to arrive.

Not finding a market in that direction, I retraced my steps, wondering how I would manage to make my soup! At that moment, a little car with windows wide open, framing two gregarious men, approached me and slowed down. One of the men leaned out and asked if I needed assistance. I inquired about a market, and he pointed away from the ocean, "Oh, about a kilometer that way." I thanked him. Our conversation continued for a bit, and I must have mentioned I wasn't feeling well. They immediately expressed concern and offered me a ride to the store. I hopped in, thankful for my good fortune. Help always arrives when I need it most!

When we arrived, I expected them to say good-bye and drive off. Instead, these kind souls offered to wait as I did my shopping and then drive me back to my guest house. I felt so supported and loved. This extra care was exactly what I needed! In my weakened condition, walking even a kilometer with heavy groceries would have been quite taxing, especially under the midday sun.

Indeed, when I exited the market, there they were, happily waiting for me. They drove me home, and I thanked them from the bottom of my heart. True angels, here on earth.

Argentina

Spring rains had come early to San Carlos de Bariloche in Patagonia. Instead of catching the end of ski season, it looked like I'd be hanging out in the hostel's common room, studying Spanish and writing postcards. I wasn't upset. After eight months on the road, a quiet week was welcome.

What I wasn't so happy about were the fever and chills that had plagued me the night before. After that first night, the women in the room checked out, and a new crew showed up -- a group of four guys who had also hoped to ski. They lived in Buenos Aires, spoke fluent English, and enjoyed an annual "guy's ski trip" tradition, having been friends since university days.

I shared about my journey around the world, and how I'd started studying Spanish. They were kind enough to help me learn how to conjugate verbs—an important skill that I hadn't yet acquired in my two weeks of study. One of the men went so far as to make flash cards for me!

Unwell, I went to bed early and felt worse the next morning. As I approached the front desk to ask for a recommendation for a doctor open on a Sunday, my new acquaintances were also there, wondering what they would do on this rainy day. They overheard my conversation with the hostel employee, and offered to drive me to the doctor. Given that it was raining heavily and I was ill, I gratefully accepted their offer.

What unfolded was a bit of a wild goose chase, and they were with me every step of the way! First, we went to the local hospital, where they worried I'd have to wait too long. So they asked around for other clinics and found one, which was closed, and then another, which was open. One of the four accompanied me to help with translation, while the others waited in the car. I felt thoroughly provided for.

The doctor gave me a prescription, so we went to the pharmacy, and my friends insisted on paying for the medicine. Kindness upon kindness. I did my best to make room to receive everything they were sharing with me.

Finally, with the medical errands behind us, the crew invited me to join them on a drive to a beautiful hotel in the hills where we could sit by the fire, have some tea, and stay out of the storm. I said, yes.

The place was cozy and elegant, and the views were magical. I fell asleep on the couch, and then my new friends took me home and made dinner for me. After a restful night, I felt like myself again. That next day, I purchased ingredients to make a pear galette as a gesture of thanks to my new friends. We had so much fun—making the most of illness and inclement weather by joining together in community. They accepted me—a stranger—into their circle. They will always be angels in my book.

Why We Exist
By Kenneth Laws II

P at was a local restaurant owner who I became friends with because I regularly ate lunch at his establishment. While eating there, I always had a book in my hands and, as I recall, he became curious about what I was reading. I began to share not only what I was reading that day, but parts of my life with him—mostly in passing. Eventually, the days came when he was able to sit down and have lunch with me. During these times, I began to share my life, my joy, and my pain surviving the loss of a loved one, and he reciprocated with stories of his amazing and wonderful life.

I began to share the lessons I had learned along the way from my life, and as I was not always the person that I am today, I shared my humanness as well. I cannot tell you why I shared what I did other than I was guided and felt compelled to do so. Here was a man I didn't know much about, other than he was a dedicated businessman, father, and husband, who absolutely adored his wife. I told him of things one does not typically share even with family, let alone other people. Pat and I were not exceptionally close, but I know despite what he knew of me, he did not judge me and showed kindness and a mutual level of respect towards me.

A couple of years had gone by, and I still saw him occasionally during my lunches, generally sharing my life or the most recent book I was reading, with Pat sharing his latest adventure. I happened upon a post on social media that described the sudden death of a man's wife after complications from elective surgery. It was Pat's wife. I wept in pain because I knew exactly how he felt and what he was going through. My heart broke for Pat that day.

I drove by his establishment for about two months before I could bring myself to make it to the front doors. Every time I tried, I could feel the tears and emotion welling up inside of me. When I finally did make it through the doors, I mumbled my order with tears running down my face. Pat knew why I was there, and when he was finally able to sit down with me, our visit went as one might not expect, two grown men eating lunch and crying together. My first words I could muster were, "It's my time to give back." I felt and shared his pain. Pat was already well-versed of my journey.

Pat began to share the tragic story of the death of his wife, one in which I knew all too well. All I could do was sit and cry with him while he did this. At some point in the conversation, I recall saying that despite all that I have been through in life, it has taken all of it to become the person I am today. I had to be grateful for all of it. Difficult to hear and sometimes harder to understand, Pat knew that it came from a place of love. The time spent with Pat that day was one of utter vulnerability, compassion, and love. I knew that his life would change drastically and would be forever altered from that day forward. I also knew on a much deeper level that his entire purpose in life, as well as his path, would change. Death, especially when unexpected, has a way of completely altering our entire outlook on life, if not completely altering who we are as people.

We can never know the impact our words can have on another; they may save their life, or help someone through pain and grief. Either way, when we choose to be genuine and authentic and speak from a place of love and kindness, we help others in ways we cannot possibly imagine. When this is done, we, in turn, help ourselves in the process.

Knowing what I know today, I do believe in my heart that our conversations helped Pat. I always spoke of the significance of love and kindness, and how important it was to always do our best to always show it, even when it is difficult. I think he gained a greater appreciation not only of life after death but for truly being present in each moment of every day. I always spoke of living in the now and being fully present and immersed in it. It is then when life begins to reveal its magic in the simplest of ways. We become grateful not only for those in our lives, but the little things in life. That's where life takes a turn, and we begin to live it, one moment at a time.

At some point in time, I think most people will eventually question their existence. So, to anyone, or more appropriately, any one of *us*, who has ever questioned their worth, their existence on this planet, and who has ever wondered if they matter, this is for you. *We all matter.* Everything we say and do matters. We matter in ways we do not always understand.

I can say that without the willingness and presence of mind to be genuine and authentic with another person, this opportunity would not have presented itself. Our daily interactions, which can be seemingly meaningless at the time, can ultimately have the most profound effect on another person. It not only affects other people, but also affects us in ways that force us to open our eyes, our minds, and our hearts just a little bit wider. It may not happen in that instant, but it will. This will always return to us in the form of love, meaning, and a passion for life that exceeds our wildest expectations.

Inspiration Found in Unexpected Spaces
By Anne Mackie Morelli

Inspiration can be found in the hard spaces and in the overcoming; where a trial is bravely confronted and tenaciously wrestled through. And, through the vicarious witnessing of how the battle is waged, wisdom can be gleaned and harvested. These battles can be played out on the world stage or in the intimate arenas of our lives.

My mother was 90 years old when her health took a rapid downturn. She started to experience difficulty when she was walking or doing simple tasks like getting dressed and rising out of her chair. There was a constant frustration written on her face as these once easily accomplished tasks became formidable. Even the most basic actions required her focused concentration and effort.

The hallways in our family home that she once dashed down on her way out to the theatre, to Scottish country dancing, or to the sports club were now painstakingly navigated with her walker and her tentative, shuffling gait.

I found it challenging to observe her morphing from vibrancy and athleticism into frailty and uncertainty. Thankfully, there were moments where her blue eyes sparkled with delight as she engaged in a stimulating discussion or as we laughed about the absurd sides of life and aging.

At moments my grief was overwhelming, where raw emotions pummeled my heart. I would weep, overcome by the mere thought of a world without her.

We shared tender moments, such as when I knelt by her bed so I could gently rub the cream over her crooked toes and worn, knobbly feet, or when vulnerability was forced upon us as I helped her bathe. It was so unbearably poignant to help her slowly undress and then, as she leaned into me, to maneuver her onto her shower seat.

I had moments of deep gratitude as I watched her highly skilled and compassionate caregivers assist her with daily tasks.

I noticed our conversations gradually changed. She had never been one to share her feelings. But, there were moments where she became more revealing about the matters of her heart. She reminisced about her life and shared her worries about the future. She disclosed how she wished that this final leg of her journey could have been easier. There was also a greater immediacy to share my heart, to vocalize my innermost thoughts and feelings, and give them space to breathe before it was too late.

As I walked alongside my mother in her final winter season, I reflected on what it revealed about how best to traverse our inevitable journey through aging. I can't say that I have it all figured out. But at least I had begun to grasp the complicated, thorny language of loss and grief, and to prepare for my personal inevitable winter season.

I learned the necessity of genuine, loving companionship, free to both weep and laugh with each other, to reminisce and look ahead, to express fears and to lament. The companionship where we can authentically and transparently grieve the cruelties and challenges of growing old.

We drew strength and resiliency and courage from each other. We became comfortable with vulnerability, more willing to enter into the hard spaces of grief. We grew in our capacity to both engage in intimate conversations or with being able to sit in companionable silence.

As I watched her health decline and a corresponding need for assistance intensify, I learned the importance of being willing to ask for and to accept help. While having to receive help can be humbling, it also cracks open fertile spaces where others can both demonstrate and grow in their capacity to extend compassion and care.

No one has any idea what the next day or even the next moment holds. Life will always be interrupted with twists and turns, the unexpected and unwanted. So, I learned to appreciate the gift of each breath and to find delight in however my days unfold. I learned to slow down, breathe deeply, and take time to look around and marvel at the intricate splendors in creation, appreciating the symphony that constantly plays all around us. Or alternatively, taking time to pause, to savor stillness and silence.

I now try to notice the truly important, and hold the things of this world more loosely. I am growing in the certainty that there is a plan for my life, and that no matter how hard I try to exert control, it will always surprise me with the unpredictable and the unforeseen.

I now celebrate what is still possible for me to do. I find gratitude for the blessings found in each day. Seeking the small pleasures that bring delight. Being curious. Holding wonder.

I learned that even in the hard spaces of grief, it is possible to find joy. I merely have to look for it and to grow in the acceptance that we can simultaneously hold both sorrow and joy.

So, instead of avoiding the grueling experiences of life and endeavoring to remain untouched and unaffected by trials, we are called to courageously step into each other's stories, not only because these hard chapters are lonely to navigate by ourselves, but because we are transformed through sharing our journeys.

Like most mother and daughter relationships, ours was not perfect. It had its challenging moments. But, as I accompanied her on the most challenging leg of her journey, I felt privileged to be her final traveling companion.

As we stumbled forward, we were never completely sure about how best to approach the next steps. Yet, we did find our way forward, though I desperately wanted to change the direction we were traveling and keep her with me. I grew to understand that it was not possible. Instead, my role was to support and encourage her as she inexorably traveled to a place where I am not yet called.

The Transformative Power Of Forgiveness
By Anne Mackie Morelli

She was now an elderly, dignified woman, but a warmth and gentleness emanated from her coffee-colored eyes and sweet smile.

Twenty years ago, on what started as a typical day, Esther and one of her sons traveled to a small neighboring community to conduct some business. She ran a small but prosperous home enterprise where she made and sold homemade crafts.

They both arrived home to an empty house and to a community that refused to speak about the horrors that had transpired in their absence. Her family members were victims of a genocide where an estimated one million Tutsi and moderate Hutu in Rwanda were slaughtered during the Rwandan Civil War from April 7, 1994, to July 15, 1994.

As Esther and her son contemplated how they were going to recover from the devastating loss of their family, Rwanda as a whole collectively decided that revenge and retribution were not the answer. The Rwandans were wise enough to recognize that healing and moving forward was only possible if the wounded did not seek revenge. Killing all the offenders as retribution would only contribute to a never-ending cycle of violence.

As a nation and as individuals, they rationally concluded that there was only one way to emerge from this horrific period in their nation's history. So, while the nation and each individual mourned and began to process the unfathomable and their profound grief, ultimately the only clear avenue forward was going to be through forgiveness. It was the only conceivable strategy to amend their history and to forge a new destiny.

Although Esther had no idea who had brutally massacred her family members, over time, she gradually found it in her heart to forgive. Yet, almost daily, she studied her community and speculated about who might be responsible. Wondering whether it was him, or her, or that group? Every time she interacted with someone, she wondered whether they could be trusted, what they might know about what had happened to her family but were refusing to tell her. Most days, the grief was so debilitating that she primarily focused on putting one foot in front of the other.

She persisted in her quest to find forgiveness. Every day she continued to make the choice to reject the anger, grief, fear, and desire for revenge, choosing instead, forgiveness and mercy. Gradually, as she processed her grief and committed to forgive, the overwhelming weight of her heartache began to lift.

She began to experience the first whispers of joy and hope—mere hints at first—but which eventually gained the power and momentum to wrestle back the desolation. Then one day, one of her employees approached her and confessed that he was one of the people who were responsible for killing her family.

He confided that he had become consumed with suffocating guilt and distress. The consequences of what he had done had become so unbearable that he had become utterly indifferent to what might happen to him should he confess. He asserted that she should tell her one surviving son so that if he wanted, he could now seek retribution.

She listened, and considered his confession.

But in the end, she elected never to tell her son. She was apprehensive that he might decide to seek revenge as a way to right the brutality committed against their family. So, she remained silent and buried the truth of what he told her deep in her heart. Instead, she chose to look directly into his eyes as she forgave him.

Later, it was pressed on her heart that not only should she forgive him, but she must go one step further. She felt compelled to bless him. She sought him out, and as she stood before him, she gently touched his arm, and said, "I forgive you and I bless you."

Her grace and compassion helped release the heavy burden of remorse and the crippling weight of shame that he'd been carrying and that had been progressively stealing his life. Suddenly, a new life cracked wide open for him—a life that could now be re-written and transformed because of forgiveness. A new future that pulsed with infinite possibility and a sense of hope.

Esther would never be the same either. The tragic loss of her family had utterly shattered her heart and drastically shifted the trajectory of her life. But, her noble decision to forgive and to show mercy had the power to dissolve the bonds of anger, bitterness, and despair that otherwise would have enslaved her. Forgiveness and benevolent mercy freed her, opening the way for her to find inner peace and to restore her life.

It took time for each of them to write new storylines and lean into their altered destinies. But, in due time, they shuffled out of the darkness and stepped back into the light. While Esther's story is arduous and heartbreaking, it is also a narrative that edifies and inspires. She exemplifies grace.

She demonstrates the better path to walk when we have been wounded by others. It is the avenue that has the utmost power to heal and to transform both the wounded and the offender. It is a path that leads us into and through the pain, and beyond forgiveness into reconciliation, healing, and hope.

Arriving At Acceptance
By Sarah McArthur

I look into her eyes, and she looks back into mine. I realize, I no longer hate her. I smile at her, and she smiles back. I have hated her for so many years, I can't think of a time when I didn't feel some level of hatred for her. In my mind, hate is such a strong feeling. It's a feeling I don't feel often and one I try to hide when I do. I exhale now as I look at her smiling back at me in the mirror and I realize, I accept her. I think about the journey to acceptance; it was a long hard road, and yet somehow, I know this is a new season in my life—a new chapter, a new space—and my smile grows wider. I exhale.

You see, as far as I can remember, I believed I was not loveable. It was a core belief that somehow found cycles of life experiences that continued to repeat the message, "No one loves you, you're not worthy of love, if people loved you they wouldn't have hurt you so bad, there must be something wrong with you." This message played so frequently in my mind that I became a believer. I lived it constantly, and the more I believed it, the more I hated myself. I believed I was broken. It wasn't always a conscious hatred, and often I denied that it existed, but others could see it. If I am honest, I knew it was always there, lurking in the shadows of my mind and heart waiting for an experience that would give it a voice to say, "See, I told you so." Do you ever get tired of that inner voice that tells you, "You are never enough?" It was only in the past year that I became self-aware enough to listen to what my mind had to say to me. I slowed down enough to listen. I became present enough to hear. What I heard reflected my extremely deep, extremely real self-hate.

About a year ago, I was at a crossroad—I could continue to deny and ignore the truth, or I could look truth in the eyes and find a path of acceptance. I chose acceptance. I turn 39 in August, and it's bizarre to think I have been on my path to healing for 20 years. I made a profound choice at 19 that I had to find a way to fix myself to be functional and acceptable. At that time, I believed that if I did all the right things to find healing, I could finally be fixed as if nothing bad had ever happened. Twenty years later, my paradigm has shifted from being fixed to accepting myself where I am on my journey. I have found that when I have an expectation of a certain healing outcome for myself that hasn't come to pass, I become frustrated with myself, believing that "I should be further along" or "My past shouldn't affect me this way anymore." When my PTSD is triggered, I begin to think that I have not healed at all and that I truly haven't experienced any growth in my healing. I have come to realize this is not true, so I am learning to give myself credit for the ways I have and am growing—both small and large.

I am a survivor of childhood abuse and sexual assault. I was severely bullied in school, and I have experienced other traumas that left me with PTSD. I am an adult diagnosed with ADHD and anxiety. I have not lived an easy life, and more than once I have found myself exhausted to my core—*soul exhausted* is what I call it. When I found myself only focusing on all the ways I felt broken or not good enough, the exhaustion intensified. Sometimes I felt stuck, other times I felt so weak that I was not sure I had another step inside of me. It is at these times that I realize how grateful I am for the people in my life and the choices I have made along my journey that returned my power to me. These choices fueled and empowered me. I share them knowing that they may not be the same choices you would make for yourself, but perhaps they can still provide hope along your journey.

Faith has played a big part in my healing. Both talk therapy and group therapy helped in many ways, but they were not the end all be all for me. Nine years ago, I realized that fear was paralyzing me from living my life, so I took an empowerment-based self-defense class. It gave me tools to feel empowered and confident in the face of fear, which was life-changing for me. It has been an integral part of my journey, and I am still very involved with the program today.

About four years ago, I began incorporating essential oils into my daily wellness, and they helped me to relax and feel calmer. One year ago, I became certified in Aroma Freedom, which is a healing modality that uses essential oils to break through negative thoughts and feelings. This is how I became self-aware. It has been through this modality that I began releasing those voices that told me, "I am not enough, I am not loveable, I am broken." It has brought me closer to my path of self-love; I have arrived at acceptance. Acceptance has let me release much of my self-hate, and has allowed me to make peace with where I am in my journey and who I am right now. Acceptance gives me permission to know that where I am is okay. I am honored that I now help others find acceptance. I encourage you to explore your healing, find what works for you, and know that where you are on your journey is okay.

Perfect Imperfection
By Ghene't Lee-Yong McCormick

T he tree rose before me tall and wide. Its trunk twisted and bent, the dark bark straining with each turn as it rose higher and higher into the air. The trunk was unnaturally bent at the base forming a sort of 'L' shape. It seemed to me that this tree should not exist. Or at least it should be unhealthy, not grown and aged one hundred years or more. I was compelled to stop and just gaze at this tree. I did. I was two miles into my weekly hike of Mossy Ridge Trail, and I had been making good time. I had my earbuds in with music playing, trying to drown out the endless thoughts going through my head. Thoughts of being overweight and unappreciated. Thoughts of lack of worth because I was not the most important thing in my husband's life. Thoughts of financial instability because the money was going out faster than it was coming in. These thoughts were powerful, and I knew enough not to wallow in them, but to work them out in any way I could. Hence, the four-mile hike every weekend.

Yet, this tree forced those thoughts away in an instant, and I was focused only on it. Was this an anomaly when it was growing, was it done on purpose by earlier humans? Or maybe it was born that way, engrained in its DNA an imperfection that altered the shape of the tree. I was struck by its beauty, its height, and its color. I reached out and touched the bark. Hard and rough beneath my hands—and something else. I felt strength. It was warm in my palm and pulsing. I pulled back, not sure what had happened. Again, I was struck by how beautiful it was. A couple trail running brought me out of my reverie, and I continued hiking. However, my hike was not the same after this moment.

I began to see other trees. Imperfect. Bent, lightning struck, burnt, or twisted. Some were covered in poison ivy vines, others by euonymus. Some trees, different species entirely, seemed to sprout from one trunk. I listened to the creak of a tree that was soon to fall. A call reaching from crust to sky, echoed in the air, bouncing off the other trees in the area and leaving its mournful cry to linger in my heart. At the end of its life, this tree was calling out and leaving its voice to any who would hear, any who would listen and care. These experiences were not a part of the movies about singing princesses skipping through the forest. These were the realities of the real forest, the real nature. It was not perfect by any means.

It was wild, imperfect, and untamed. Yet, it was still beautiful. Then it struck me—that life was also like this forest with its twisty trees, strangling euonymus, and poison ivy. Beautiful, uncomfortable, and, yes, imperfect.

My life was like this; I was like this. If I could accept the beauty in the imperfection of nature, maybe I could accept the beauty in the imperfection that was my life, which was me. I realized that there was never going to be a perfect life. A time when everything went exactly as I planned it. There was never going be a person who would treat me exactly the way I needed to be treated in any given moment. People are imperfect, and life is riddled with the consequences of people's choices bumping into each other. How was I to think that I could somehow escape this? I couldn't. If I accepted the humanness of the people and circumstances around me, I had to accept their imperfections and see the beauty in that. If I was to grow in loving and caring for myself, I had to see me as imperfect, yet beautiful as well. I left the trail that day feeling light and loved. I knew that I had discovered something profound. I had a purpose and place even in my crazy, messed up, imperfect life. Even if that purpose was to show others that they, too, could find self-love and happiness in their imperfection and chaos. Creation always holds lessons for life if we are willing to slow down, observe, and listen.

Nature Immersion Activity for Self-Care

Find a comfortable place to walk. Bring water and apply insect spray and sunscreen, if necessary. Bring a small journal or notepad and paper. Set an intention before you start on the path or trail.

Affirmation:
I walk to listen
I walk to see
All the beauty without
All the beauty within

Walk your trail slowly. Make sure to pay attention to trees, wildlife, the grasses or soil, even the sky as you walk. Feel how the air touches your skin, moves your clothes, ruffles your hair. Listen to sounds around you. Are there cars nearby or children? Do you hear birds or squirrels? Listen and accept their presence. Where you can, physically connect to nature objects such as stone, bark, sticks, and leaves. Take in their textures. Enjoy your time on the path. Either after or sometime during your walk, write down thoughts that came to you while walking, whatever they were. Do not shy away from thoughts about work or chores or spouses or children. These thoughts came to you for a reason. Reflect on your writing after a few hours or even a day. Meditate. See what comes up for you. Find the beauty that comes from being able to freely and honestly write and observe your thoughts. Eventually, clarity will come to you, and you will begin to understand and love yourself more.

You can repeat this activity as often as you want.

The Lessons That Shaped Me
By Stacey Moore McGown

M om, you're the strongest person I know. You have inspired me to be the person I am today.

Thank you for letting me grow, learn, make mistakes, and build self-confidence so that I could become who I am today. You pushed me to undertake tasks autonomously, to be an independent thinker, and to be responsible for myself. You allowed me to use my imagination and creativity. You gave me the freedom to learn and explore independently. You were always there when I needed you. You were there to guide and teach, as you still do today. You knew when I was ready to tackle things without my hand needing to be held. What a privilege to have the opportunity to take risks, knowing you were there to rescue me if needed. I fear that this is something that a lot of kids these days don't get to experience. Thank you, Mom.

Thank you for showing me how to be brave, face challenges, and make sacrifices. When I was in pre-school, we left Dallas and moved to a small town in East Texas. I know it was an adjustment for you. You grew up in the city, where you had friends, family, and access to entertainment, cultural events, and shopping. You ended up in a rural town, knowing few people and taking care of three small kids while daddy worked. You adjusted to your new life, and I can imagine that it wasn't easy, although you never complained. I feel like people in today's environment might think that someone in your position should not have moved. They would be wrong. I think you were brave. You were willing to face new challenges and sacrifices because you loved your family more. You believed in and trusted the decisions that you and Daddy made together. You had faith that everything would not only work out but that we would flourish as well. You were right.

Thank you for showing me how to be compassionate and embrace differences in others. When I got a little older, you jumped back into what you loved, teaching. I was in elementary school when you became a special education counselor with the school district. I didn't have any idea what you did all day. What I grew to understand through the years, was that you loved your work and gave 110% to the kids and families you worked with. You visited their homes and provided food and clothing when needed. You participated in Special Olympics and field trips. It was obvious that you loved these kids and demonstrated that love with patience, understanding, and compassion. Every year, you gathered up prom dresses for the girls so that they could enjoy their special night. You took phone calls at home from parents and, sometimes, the students. A couple of special kids even spent time at our house.

Thank you for showing me how to put family first. Over the years, you worked hard and eventually became the special education director for the school district. On top of all that, you took care of three kids. You cooked dinner almost every night and hauled us around to all our activities. We didn't make it easy. We all chose totally different activities. When my Girl Scout troop had no leader, you stepped up and took over. Not only did you become the leader, but you were determined to give us the full scouting experiences; backpacking, hiking, camping, building fires, arts and crafts, cooking, observing wildlife, and teamwork. With everything you were doing and all the people that you were helping, one of the most important things you accomplished was the ability to put our family and spending time together as priority number one. We always came first, and you made sure that we knew that.

Most importantly, thank you for your examples of unconditional love. I made plenty of bad decisions and mistakes, and still do, I suppose. You got frustrated and upset, but you never made me feel stupid or inadequate. You helped me to understand my errors and set me free to try again. You have the same love and relationship with your grandkids. They are so blessed to have you. You are patient, understanding, and supportive. You set the example of unconditional love in your marriage as well. I never heard you and Daddy fight. I'm sure that, like any married couple, you two had moments when you were annoyed with each other or disagreed on something, but you had the ability to communicate and get through whatever it was. As a kid, I didn't know that. I didn't know that you were normal people with normal issues. I never worried about divorce or someone leaving. Thank you for that. Growing up is hard enough without having to worry about your parents. After 50 years of marriage, you continue to love and take care of each other.

Mom, you inspired me to be the best mom and woman I can be. I know I have a lot to live up to, and I'm sure you did it better. Without your examples of bravery, unconditional love, sacrifice, compassion, patience, and faith, I could not have raised my two kids to be the exceptional humans they have become. I am blessed to have had such a wonderful role model, and to have been given the opportunity to practice your examples.

I love you.

A Reluctant Widow's Grateful Journey
By Paula Meyer

I became a widow on June 1, 2018, at age 54. I knew it was coming. My husband Gary, 62, was winding down a courageous battle with throat cancer, yet his death was still a shock. I hadn't planned for this. I assumed we would live into a long retirement with travel, grandchildren, and good times. We did do some traveling while Gary was still able. We didn't have grandchildren yet, so if my children grace me with any, I'll be a grandma without a grandpa. And good times? Well, life is rough when you lose your partner of 21 years. Two days after Gary died, my children's father (my ex-husband, Brad) died unexpectedly. We had time to say goodbye to Gary, but not to Brad.

Gary was no stranger to major health challenges. In the 1980s, he broke his back and had stainless steel rods implanted in his spine. He embarked on a healing adventure and met many healers along the way. In the end, he healed his back and had the rods removed. When we met years later, I was amazed by his story and found the long scar down his spine sexy! I learned about the divine light in all of us and the power we all have to heal ourselves and others.

When Gary was diagnosed with cancer in 2014, he was confident he could heal himself again. He tried non-traditional methods and did well, but when the cancer returned in early 2017, he reluctantly agreed to traditional therapy. As the tumor grew, Gary needed a feeding tube as well as a tracheostomy. He endured chemo, immunotherapy, and radiation. Nothing worked. When he asked a psychic friend for guidance, she told him spirit said he had healed himself in so many lifetimes that he'd mastered that, and now it was time to move on. He resigned himself to the fact that he was not going to pull off another miracle.

When Gary's pain became totally debilitating, I told him I wanted him to be free and happy—he had suffered enough. In May 2018, I was headed to Berlin for work, but he asked me to stay instead while he transitioned. It was a gut-wrenching moment for us both.

In preparing paperwork, we discovered Gary's retirement annuity included a life insurance policy that would pay out a small, but still significant amount. In the last few weeks, as we discussed the things that we needed to address, and expressed our love and appreciation for our life together, I asked my husband to send me signs from the other side that he was okay. I promised to look for them.

Memorial Day 2018 was bittersweet. Gary's family came, as the original plan was for them to stay with him while I went to Berlin. As a surprise, I flew our children in and invited other family and friends. Even though Gary was at his sickest, I knew inviting people into our home to celebrate him was important. He was mad at first. He didn't want to be remembered as a shell of the man he once was. But he quickly got over it. His energy severely sapped, he could visit only in short intervals, yet he kept coming outside to join us. One of the greatest gifts of his illness, he told me, was receiving so much love.

Friends from Holland came to hold the space for Gary and me in his last week. Another friend connected with those waiting for him on the other side. She assured him they were ready to welcome him home whenever he was ready. Knowing that, and that so many people would love me in his place, allowed Gary to make peace with dying.

Two days after he passed, I drove to a massage appointment. While driving, I got a message in my head saying, *You need to connect with TG*, Gary's daughter, who Gary had sadly lost touch with years before. I decided to connect with her as soon as my massage was finished, and guess who messaged me during my massage? TG! Gary had reached out to her, too. He couldn't voice his love here, and she couldn't hear him here, yet he was able to connect once he passed! And she was ready to listen.

The day she told me, "I think we can fix this, now that he's on the other side," was so profound. For me, this answered the question of why Gary couldn't heal himself. The sacrifice that we had to make with his death was worth it for him and his daughter to be united again. Now I have another beautiful daughter in my life, my children have a wonderful older sister, and my mom has another granddaughter!

And about that gift of the life insurance policy? That enabled me to retire early, which is what Gary had wanted for me. Now I have the space to figure out who I am again. I encouraged my mom to retire with me, and 2019 is our travel year—and my year to step into my new life.

If you've lost a loved one:

- Love yourself.
- Find a grief coach who has experienced the same loss.
- Let people help you.
- Let friends know it is okay to talk about their spouses and families. Life goes on, stay connected.
- Educate yourself about your financial situation.
- Take self-development courses.
- Listen to your inner voice.
- Watch for signs that may come as thoughts, animals, songs, books, or even people who suddenly get your attention.

If you hear an estranged loved one has passed:

Whether you were right or wrong, connect with their closest kin. The estrangement may weigh heavily on their heart, so reaching out is a simple act of kindness that can ease that burden. Saying, "I'm sorry I was not able to rise above my anger and send them off with love. I'm sorry I didn't allow their voice to be heard" is enough.

The Best Is Truly Yet To Come
By Tina Miller

I grew up on a large lot on Muscatel owned by my grandparents, with the main house and three other houses all sharing a common yard that stretched the full length of the property. Beautiful citrus, walnut, and shade trees dotted the grass. It was the perfect place to be, and some of my best childhood memories included running from one end of the property to the other—hair flying in the breeze, fully present in the moment, just being a kid. Total joy!

Those innocent, joyous moments were at odds with another truth I felt but could not put to words until much later in life. You see, before I lived on Muscatel—before I was even born—I was adopted. I always knew I was adopted. Unwanted by my first family and unable to fit in with my second, I found myself stumbling all the way through my teen years and early adulthood. The dysfunction of my second family became increasingly obvious as I suffered through the messes created by the adults around me.

By the time I was 30 years old, I had repeated a lot of their toxic patterns. I had repeated scores of their mistakes, and even added a few of mine. Those life choices—and their far-reaching consequences—brought about severe self-loathing and shame, which I always hid beneath the surface. I continued to stumble, clinging to the hope—no, the *knowing*-—that there was something more. With a faith fueled by fleeting moments of joy, I got back up each time I fell down. But I was heavier each time, burdened by new guilt and shame.

I never completed anything. I would try hard for a while, and then the eventual meltdown would hit, and I would leave whatever I had invested my all into. School, a new job, a project, a side business, it didn't matter. And my arms would be heavier with the self-loathing and shame.

I read countless self-help books, went to church, counseling. No one could see what I saw when I looked in the mirror. A monster. No one could reach inside and touch the place I was hurt. I continued to cover her and convince myself everything was okay, but then she would resurface. This continued for twenty years. There were a lot more messes, sprinkled with a lot more moments of joy.

I woke up one morning after turning 50 years old, wanting and *needing* to rediscover that little girl with the wind in her hair who was so full of joy even though things weren't perfect. That was where the real work began. I began to read books and listened to people speak, exploring my inner and outer worlds with a curiosity I hadn't felt in years! My family was instrumental in pointing out changes that needed to be made. At some point, I stopped feeling defensive and started listening, making those changes. I learned to get still.

It was then that the real me spoke, and I heard her. From that moment forward, everything was a choice. I was no longer a victim. I was going to make a difference, if only for myself. Then I noticed something incredible. As I changed, it spread out around me and touched others. I was finally sharing something good! I was having a *positive* impact rather than a negative one.

In shifting my thinking and reevaluating my life, getting rid of what no longer served me, I searched for the things I could use to keep moving forward and came across an invaluable realization. Everything that had ever happened to me or because of me had become the framework for who I am and what I do today, to be of service and help others, but I always felt like a hypocrite. I released that fear when I realized that it was precisely all of the reasons that I deemed myself unworthy that made me useful.

At 60 years old, I have decided it is okay to be me. I am okay. I think differently, and my actions reflect that. I have found a way to forgive myself for my mistakes and allow myself to make many more as a way to grow.

My practice was founded upon a promise to myself—I would step beyond myself and do what it took to make it work. I had a couple of false starts, as I had in the past. For a while, I could not trust myself. But I kept my promise to myself and stepped through my fear of not being good enough. Now almost three years into my practice, I still have a lot to learn. But I learn every day. Each day is a new adventure. Not only is there joy in my heart, but I cultivate joy all around me.

There is joy to be found in the process of life. The ever-changing, the tearing down and rebuilding—that is my new normal. I provide a space for people to experience that kind of expansion; to tear themselves down and rebuild themselves as many times as they need to. Where they can heal and *just be*.

I am inspired by all those who come to me and allow me to hold sacred space for them. I am inspired by every person I meet who didn't want to get up in the morning but did. By those who don't let what someone thinks of them define them. By those who don't let what they think of themselves defeat them. I am inspired by those who have done things some of us cannot imagine and are trying to do good things. They inspire me because I recognize myself in them, and we are able to hug ourselves and say, "Good job."

The Invisible Work
By Meaghan Miller Lopez

The question asked by no one was how many times I was going to crash the car.

I t's true back then I was distracted by the sense that something beyond "reality" was taking place behind the scenes. The way I remember it, though, it was more like the cars were crashing themselves.

But before all the crashing was the breaking down. I'd been taking frequent drives into the city, every part of me repelled by the blank sameness of the suburban town I'd landed in, believing proximity to him would seal our fate. I hadn't known that the breaking would happen before I had unpacked my bags, nor that the wreckage would take up so much space, or take so long to clear.

At least in the city, I could fall into the arms of artists and musicians, attend their nightly carnival, throw a tapestry over my restless longing. By drinking in their essence I became one of them. I learned to weave magic into washing dishes, chopping vegetables, crossing the street. My determination to have life emerge beautifully from the boring routine that was expected of me jolted me awake every day.

So even though I knew the car wasn't fit to drive so far and often, I couldn't resist the magnetism of the transformation pulling me to the city. The day the power disappeared on the way home, the full weight of the dying thing fell into me. I remember almost laughing as I aimed for the side of the freeway. Of course this was happening.

"Seized up," the tow-truck driver said, describing how the moving metal parts of the engine had melted into one. As the car was dragged away, I couldn't help remembering the night we'd gone looking for beauty, not wanting to admit we were gazing at the gas refinery.

We didn't know then that the path ahead had been designed to break both our hearts.

"Do it now," they insisted, "Break it. It's time."

Over seven years I waited for every cell that made me up to be replaced by something new. I spent the time yearning to find anything I could love nearly as much. The crashes happened on the way to the coast; the edges called to me. Somehow I always survived. Why?

All I'd found after years of wandering the shore were the tiniest pieces of my soul. I collected them one by one. They were visible only during the lowest of tides, each a tiny sparkle, almost nothing on their own. One day I poured them all out on the bed. At last there was enough to dot the faintest outline of a whole self.

After that I started working at the station.

At the station we recorded the last farewells, documenting unexpected exits from the earthly plane. The characters came falling out of fantasies, tumbling down mountains, hurtling over cliffs, smashing into trees, always by surprise and with velocity. People would come to the door to tell you the news. We hadn't forgotten yet that we were human.

From the beginning we were setting up the systems; she working on one side and me on the other. We spent those days doing the invisible work that no one cared about, the kind that doesn't make the gratitude list.

Nobody cared until they needed the thing we couldn't stop ourselves from making. When news got out about it once, the crowd became unmanageable. We learned we couldn't tell them how to find it. We had to wait until they asked, which was rare, as they didn't want to know.

It all goes on without you.

Who wants to know that?

If I left the station idle the whole thing would fall apart, so I learned to stay nearby. But when the tide descended I still liked to visit the shore. It wasn't far; I didn't need to drive anymore. I posted the sign so they knew I hadn't left forever.

She was there when I returned from a wandering. I recognized her from the first time. She'd been so little then, standing near the tracks, suitcase in hand. The world was rushing at her, whirring and loud, overcoats bustling against her small body, her gaze softly focused, familiar. I wondered if she knew yet who she was. Would the gifts she carried with her be of value? Would anyone pause the chaos to find out?

No one stopped.

Eventually, I saw her board the train. At her destination, she was met by smiling people who sang while making sandwiches. They took her to the creek, amusing each other in the afternoon breeze, telling ancestral tales of folly, madness, and betrayal.

After the picnic, they showed her the cage where they kept the tiny birds. The birds drank colored water that filtered through their feathers, producing a fluttering rainbow behind the metal grid. The cage seemed large to the little girl, but she could sense the birds felt differently.

Years later the suitcase was finally emptied, and the smiling people passed away. She gathered the memories they'd left for her, released the birds into the sky and returned to the station, grown.

I welcomed her in, passed her the painted teacup and asked her to fill it up. When it was full, I showed her to the room where we kept the edge. She moved towards it, found her center, and closed her eyes. I pulled back the veils, opened the port and poured in the salty waters.

Then I plugged her in and let the thing do what it does.

I saw her body shimmer when she got the thing she'd come for, and again when she saw who'd bought her ticket. Then she was gone. I remembered her eyes, dense with recognition, and felt the whispering of silvery words.

Our work is done.
We will not meet again.
Here's all the love I made for you.
Take it with you now.
You're free to go.
You're free.

Bobbie Blue Eyes
By Roseann Minafo

This is a story about a young girl, a teenage girl with stunning blue eyes, blond hair and a contagious need to have fun. It is a story of my mom's last two months of her life. She was 78 when she died, but she regressed to her teenage years after my father's death. When I say "teenage girl," I mean "set me free, teenage girl!"

Bobbie, my mother, was born in San Francisco's Mission District in 1938 as Barbara Joyce Sanchez, the second daughter of a Spanish immigrant. Her father was as handsome as a movie star, and her Italian immigrant mother oozed love from her heart down to the tip of every finger. When Bobbie was 15 years old, she and her sister were put into a girl's home in SF, above the Castro District's high hills because her sweet, petite mother had broken her back and her father was entirely too popular and socially busy to take proper care of his two daughters. Bobbie would never eat another egg again after this stay as she was forced to eat raw eggs every morning, thus fueling her need to escape! After a short time, Bobbie decided to run away from the shelter and marry a traditional Sicilian man, named Joe. My father, Joe, was 21 and Bobbie was 16. Now remember, this was 1954. The easiest way to consummate a marriage was to get married quickly in Reno, Nevada, a dirty little town just over the Nevada line. They filled up the Chevy with gas, and there they went.

As the years passed, Bobbie led a pretty traditional life for a wife in the 1960s. Her perfect image was completed by a French twist in her hair, lipstick, a clean house, and nightly cocktails. Along with meeting her husband's every need, Bobbie was forced to put her unfinished childhood behind her to be a wife and mom. After two miscarriages and then two kids (my brother and me) the years went on, plagued by horrible domestic violence.

When I was about 10 years old, my mom was able to work at a bank, and there she met a few girlfriends and began her 45-year smoking career. My father did not allow her very much freedom and was waiting outside for her every night after she balanced her till.

I want to bring this story into the more beautiful part, the reason I am sharing it with you. My father died in 2012. Bobbie had been sad, mad, confused, and mostly regressed into the childhood she missed. I noticed how thin she was getting and it startled me. She always tried to lose weight, but experienced insignificant results. Shortly after that, she went to the ER with pain in her right side. She was diagnosed with stage four breast cancer which had metastasized into her liver. It seems Bobbie was not caring for herself by regular breast exams as she always put my father first.

My mom acted out as a teenager at this time by getting a tattoo on her butt, no less, spending money without restraint, and taking trips by herself at whim. She was very difficult to reason with. She wanted us to leave, she wanted money and more money, and then she would give it away. She would be jealous of me and say she hated me. She began smoking again. We tried to love her through it. Every day, we tried. By saying "love her through it," I mean forget the nasty letter she wrote to me and put in the drawer, and simply take care of her. It's as if she knew she was making up for lost time and it was at the expense of the people closest to her. She refused counseling and merely wanted to have fun.

There came a day when I found it more difficult to be at work than to be at home. Luckily, my husband of four years was retired and able to be there for her. We all lived together, Bobbie upstairs in her flat and my husband, my daughter and me downstairs. One day, I came home and said, "Mom, let's stay home and watch movies like we did when I was a kid."

My mom was overjoyed. We set up a bed in the living room, complete with bright sheets, blankets, pillows and her fluffy white dog, Billie. We watched movies, ate yogurt, jello, ice cream and had guests in and out all day. I eventually had to keep a calendar to find time slots for all her friends. Each day she got weaker but thrived on being the center of attention and action. Things were cheery for her. She was afraid to die like a child is scared of a needle.

I was inspired by this woman. I was inspired to love her through her mean times, her selfish times and inspired to dig deep to go where the love was. She was loved and she loved us. She died the day before my birthday. When I said to her, "It's my birthday," what do you think she said? She replied, "I wish I could take you to dinner, honey." My mom died with my husband, my brother and me around her. It took her eight hours of labored breathing. It was no doubt a rebirth in my mind. My husband said to me that it takes hands to bring you into the world and hands to take you out of it. Well, that's exactly what happened when she took her final breath. I felt like I had done one of the most amazing things in my life. I loved her and was able to let the bad go and seek the kindness. I'm so glad I did.

Sometimes, What We Want the Least Is
What We Need the Most
By Aerin Morgan

To anyone on the outside, my life looks pretty good. I grew up in a wonderful family, got a great education, and have been blessed with surprisingly good health. I live in a cozy home in a prosperous neighborhood, have terrific friends, and even met the man of my dreams while living on an island in the Caribbean.

Who wouldn't be happy with that? Me. What was I missing? My career.

I've never been what most consider a *normal* girl. From day one, I had a single-minded focus and knew exactly what I wanted to do when I grew up. I studied hard, went to college, and set about fulfilling my dreams. While most of my friends were chasing boys, I was dreaming about how I'd run my business. When my friends were searching for mates, planning weddings, and having babies, I was focused on my career. My profession wasn't only a job—it was the thing that most inspired me, fulfilled me, and defined me. My career came first, before anything else. Period.

Over the years, my line of work changed, and I started down a different but similar path. Advances in technology forced changes in my industry, and I gradually found myself feeling like a prisoner to something I no longer enjoyed. My career had always meant freedom, excitement, and the ability to create. I now found my days reduced to robotic repetition, creativity replaced with a need for rapid and mediocre output.

I gradually went from being double-booked to working 100 days a year. With every lost client, my sense of purpose withered away. As my work continued to decrease, my feelings of worthlessness increased, and a deep sense of panic crept into my life.

I tried to put on a brave face, acting like I was thrilled with the situation. I was getting older, my husband was making great money, so I could finally slow down and do other things.

Unbeknownst to those around me, my panic had transformed into an unwavering depression, and I had secretly begun searching (and praying) for something to give my life meaning—something to live for.

When I got a text from a friend who runs an animal rescue organization, my heart sank.

"Aerin – this is Kim. Is there any way you would consider fostering this little guy (we're calling him Jethro)? The shelter is at 99 percent capacity, and I'd love to get him out. All my current fosters are full, we could sure use your help. We'll take care of all vet bills, food, meds, but we need someone to give him a temporary home."

Kim is an amazing human. She runs a rescue organization, and in 2003, she brought Bella into our lives. When I say Bella was the most kick-ass dog in the world, that's not an exaggeration. She was *amazing*! In 2017, we had to say goodbye to Bella. Watching her die was the hardest thing I've ever had to do. She was never *just* our dog—she was a member of our family. In her final days, we'd take turns sleeping in the living room with her. Her body was failing, and she found it increasingly difficult to move from room to room. I'd curl up next to her at night and whisper lovingly in her ear, "I adore you, you're perfect in every way." In those quiet moments, my heart was filled with the purest and most all-encompassing love I could imagine. When she died, a piece of me died too. I swore I'd never adopt another dog. My soul wasn't strong enough to endure that kind of pain again.

My husband had recently been longing for another dog, and fostering equaled no long-term commitment, so this seemed like the perfect solution. I reluctantly agreed to the situation, and five days later, a scared, skinny, and unbelievably stinky coonhound arrived at our front door. The sum of his existence had been spent chained to a tree. He wouldn't make eye contact, jumped at the slightest sound, and cowered whenever anyone tried to touch him. It became glaringly evident that he had suffered not only neglect, but also abuse. Based on past experiences, he had every right to hate humans and every possible reason to distrust us. I quickly began to fear that we weren't properly equipped to handle his needs.

We have a huge portrait of Bella that hangs in our living room; I looked up at it and thought, "Bella, please help me. What am I going to do with this dog?" One sentence immediately, but gently, popped into my head, "Just love him, like you loved me." I looked down at Jethro, took a deep breath, and said, "It's okay, you're safe now. No one in this house will ever hurt you, and we're going to do whatever we can to make you happy."

As we had done before, we set up an air mattress in the living room, and my husband and I took turns sleeping with him. This arrangement ensured that we'd be closer to the backyard in case Jethro needed to go out during the night, and, more importantly, so he wouldn't feel alone in his new home.

Having never lived inside, he spent the first several nights pacing back and forth, completely unsure of what to do. On the fourth night, he cautiously stepped onto the wobbly mattress and squeezed himself into a tight little ball next to me. I gently wrapped my arms around him and whispered, "I love you with all my heart and soul, and I'm so happy you came to live here." He let out a big hound-ish sigh, and I once again felt an overwhelming sense of love. I knew that I'd found what I'd been searching for.

Sometimes, what people want the least, is what they need the most. Jethro is now a forever member of our pack.

Never Stop Learning
By Luann Morris Morton

It was a beautiful sunny day in my small town of Archer City, Texas, but I was mournful. My beloved mother and father had passed within three years of each other. With no siblings, I was alone. The loss weighed me down like being underwater. In July 1978, I decided to visit my cherished friend, Mitchell, and his mother, Gussie.

Mitchell and I had been friends since 1968. After his cancer diagnosis in 1972, he bravely ran off all of his friends. He felt that if we hung around as he was dying, we would be wasting our time instead of living. His mother was his sole caregiver. To give Gussie time away from home, I learned the ropes of Mitchell's daily routine. Caring for Mitchell seemed second nature to me, *except* when it came to giving injections. Mitchell received injectable morphine in his buttocks for his pain. The first time giving his injection, my hand appeared to have a mind of its own. The violent shaking back and forth of the needle was almost comical. Mitchell asked, "What's going on back there?" I exclaimed, "Give me a minute!" After three attempts, I was able to regain control of my hand and give him a perfect stick. He said, "Finally!" Lots of laughing followed!

Despite the fact that Gussie was taking care of her dying son, she began to prod me to attend nursing school. She recognized my ability to be nurturing, giving, and adaptive when I did not. She was my role model and inspiration. For 20 years, she had worked tirelessly as a pediatric nurse while taking care of her family of five. As I was starting school, she asked me to move in with them. She gave me plenty of time to study, painstakingly cared for my uniforms, and fed me delicious meals, all while caring for Mitchell. What she asked for in return was that I excel at learning. I agreed, but only if she would allow me to help with Mitchell's care.

In 1980, while I was in school, Mitchell developed an open sore over his tailbone. Nothing the doctor prescribed seemed to work to heal this open sore. Gussie asked me to find some alternative to help it heal. Since this was before Google, research was difficult. However, I found a powder called *karaya* to apply to his wound. This powder was the solution to his healing. This accomplishment led me to continue to search for alternative solutions to enhance modern medicine. Sadly, to our loss, Mitchell passed as a consequence of his cancer that same year.

As I graduated from nursing school in January 1981, Gussie was there front and center. She said it was one of the proudest moments she had ever had. I spent 13 years working at various hospitals in the operating room. Concurrently, I got married and was raising two active, precocious boys. The need to acquire more education pushed me to return to college for an Associate's Degree in Science. In my first science class, I met the Dean of Biology. She asked me to work in the Biology lab as a student assistant. The reason I loved this job was that it gave me more time with my kids. When I graduated in 1994, the Dean asked me to stay on as a Biology Lab Manager. This work kept me up to date in science and medicine. I continued this position until my retirement in 2018.

In 2008, after a long-existing surgical infection in my shoulder, and months of traditional antibiotics, I began to search for alternative therapies to help me regain optimum health. With the advent of the internet, research was easier. Current information, books, and recipes were more accessible than ever. To help control the pain in my frozen shoulder, I learned to make a tea with turmeric and ginger. Because sleep eluded me most nights, I made an herbal tincture of valerian and passionflower. My discovery of essential oils helped my seasonal allergies by using peppermint oil to open my sinuses. These natural medicines are not a cure, but palliative agents to use instead of manufactured solutions with additives and preservatives.

Word gets around when you are using alternatives to prescription drugs. Some people are curious, but some truly want to know how they can use natural remedies. It was amusing how co-workers thought I was an expert. Most of the time, I looked things up just like they could. Finally, in 2014, I was smacked with the proverbial plywood plank, "Why don't you get certified as a master herbalist?" I talked with my favorite "cheerleader," Gussie. At 92 years, she was encouraging as ever. "Never stop learning!" she exclaimed.

Where do you go to be a certified herbalist? I started with the American Herbalist Guild then advanced to investigating where herbalists in my area received their certifications. There are numerous ways to achieve your goal—traditional college courses, online courses, and online self-study, to name a few. Because there is no board or body that governs herbalists, how you learn and get certified is up to you. As an herbalist, remember that you must not diagnose, otherwise law enforcement can accuse you of practicing medicine without a license—a felony! A certified herbalist can also work with physicians (M.D. or D.O.) interested in offering their patients natural alternatives in addition to standard care.

Regardless of how you decide to practice, now is the opportune time to be an herbalist. Society is moving toward natural organic ingredients with no artificial preservatives and no pesticides. This is what I offer to my clients. Concentrating on tinctures, syrups, and teas as remedies. Client education is essential. You cannot offer these remedies to clients willy-nilly without knowing the whole story of an herb or essential oil. To do this, you need experience and education. So, as my inspiration, Gussie, would say, "Get that education now!"

DohDoh
By Kiauna Skye Murphy-Ballard

S ometimes, what you wish for can show up at the most unexpected times. It was Wednesday, at 3:25 p.m., when my dad picked me up from school. I was nine years old, in the third grade. I got in the car, and my dad told me my mom was going to stop by to give me a comforter. We waited a couple minutes for my mom. Once she parked, Mom grabbed a box out of the front seat of the car. She had a look in her eyes that told me something was up; I thought maybe there was something else in there. Mom told me to open the box.

But first, I'd like to tell you a story about my dog, DohDoh. It will give you a clue about the importance of what's in the box.

My mom and I were living alone in a home not far from the city. There was more crime than normal at that time, and we got scared sometimes, being home alone. We were most frightened when there was a murder a few blocks away, and the police had to come and inspect all the homes nearby. That was when we decided to get more protection and look into home safety. My mom asked the police if we should get a security system, and they said we should get a dog. The best way to keep intruders out of our house was to have a dog that would bark and warn them to leave. They said most criminals don't want to deal with a dog in the home.

We looked online for rescue dogs that needed a home. We narrowed it down to two—a Chihuahua and a Rottweiler. We went to visit a woman who fostered all kinds of dogs for the shelters, to give them as many extra days as possible before they were put down. This is where we found DohDoh. He was on the list to be put down in two days, so we decided to adopt him right away! In his first home, he was abused. The kids who owned him shaved his head. He was kept in a kennel for so long that his claws were curled into the pads of his paws and had to be surgically removed. Thirty-eight rotten teeth were removed from his mouth, and his eyes were white with cataracts. The foster lady said he almost starved to death and we needed to feed him as much as possible! We knew he was not the best dog for protection, but we fell in love with him, and he fell in love with us. From the moment we met, we were inseparable. His name was Dos Equis, but we called him DohDoh.

As we got to know DohDoh, we discovered he was a master at escaping, but we always found him. He was like a cat with nine lives! In his short life, he had been starved, abused, ran away, hit by a car, hospitalized from eating elk poop, and even slid on ice and fell into a river. The longest he was gone was when he was dognapped from our yard.

One afternoon, mom and I returned home from the store. We went to get DohDoh from the backyard, but he was not there and the back gate was wide open! We were freaking out and checking everywhere for him. My mom posted on social media and lost pet sites, and searched the neighborhood. Nobody put any found posters on stop signs or signposts. We had almost lost hope when 11 days later, we got a call from a man who saw our Craigslist ad. He was a handyman working on a woman's home nearby. He said he had overheard her talking about how they had stolen a dog, and were about to take him to Kansas as a gift for their son! He was curious if the dog was indeed stolen, and checked Craigslist lost dog ads and found ours. The man was certain that it was our dog. He said to hurry because they were about to leave town. The man gave my mom the address, and mom drove straight there.

When she arrived, she saw a woman walking out of the house with a cooler and a blanket sticking out of it. Mom asked the lady if she had seen this dog, pointing to the Lost Dog poster we had made. The lady acted scared and said, "No!" before running to her car and driving off.

My mom had a weird feeling, and had heard a dog-like noise coming from the cooler. She dashed to her car and followed her. The lady pulled into a parking lot at a nearby Safeway. She saw that mom was getting on the phone to call the police and panicked. She got out of the car and admitted the whole thing—they did have our dog. When we got DohDoh back, he had a brand-new name on his tag—Frito!

That was the day my dad picked me up from school, and my mom brought the box with the comforter picture on it. When I opened it, I could not believe my eyes. Inside was not a comforter but an old blanket with DohDoh inside! I was happy to see him because I hadn't seen him in almost two weeks! Even though I was worried he was dead, I always believed in my heart he would come back home. Every day while he was gone, I imagined him snuggled in bed with me at night and running to the door when I got home. I know when you use your imagination and emotions together, it creates miracles and surprises can show up in unimaginable ways!

My mom asked me what I did to cope with the fear and sadness while he was gone, I told her, "Don't give up, stay calm during hard situations, and have faith. Solutions can appear in the most unexpected ways. Keep believing even when it seems like it could never happen." If my dog can live such a tragic life, with so many obstacles and hard times, and still end up back with the people who loved him most, then anything is possible! The hard times teach us to believe more and love stronger. DohDoh is still alive and happy at the old age of 18. He is blind and deaf, with no teeth, but is still happy and enjoying life cuddled up in his blankets most of the day.

The Ripple Effect
By Georgia Nagel

I had watched that black and white dog while doing my noon dog-stop across the railroad tracks for over two months. The dog seemed to be well-behaved, seldom barked, and stayed with whom I assumed was his owner. The owner, as far as I could tell, was a rough-looking male, and obviously homeless, since they were living under the highway bridge next to the railroad tracks.

On this August day, I decided to approach them, as my curiosity and concern for the dog was getting the best of me. Besides how bad could he be? He owned a dog. As I crossed the railroad tracks, I yelled out to them. The dog heard me and barked while tugging at his rope to come over to meet me, his owner following behind him. I introduced myself and said that I just wanted to meet his dog and see if they needed anything. The man was shy, and while I was talking to him, I checked out his dog. The dog appeared to be in good condition for being on the road, and I could tell the dog meant everything to the man.

Now I had never talked to a homeless person before, and this was a new experience. I was not sure what to ask him. I again asked if he needed anything, and he told me he did not take charity, to which I replied, "I'm not offering charity; I'm asking if your dog needs anything, not you." He looked at me for a few seconds, then grinned and said, "You're okay." I explained that one of my pet sitting clients had put his dog down that morning, and he had asked me to come and get some dog items to donate to someone who could use them. I had a new bag of dog food and treats for his dog if he would take them. He looked at his dog and pondered for a minute, then agreed to take the food.

As I walked to my vehicle to get the food and treats for his dog, I remembered I had three raincoats in my vehicle, and that I only could wear one at a time, so I grabbed one of them and walked back across the railroad tracks to where they were sitting under the bridge. I set the dog food down along with the dog treats, and then handed him the raincoat. He looked at me and I said, "The coat is not for you, it's to help keep your dog dry." He smiled and took the coat.

I left there and continued along my pet sitting route, and at my next stop, I checked my phone and saw that the man whose dog had died had posted something about his dog. I commented on his post that the items he had given me had gone to good use—to a dog and homeless man living under the highway bridge. This is where the ripple effect started and would continue throughout this story, and continues today.

The next day I received a call from a young gal at the newspaper office; her co-worker had seen my post on Facebook and suggested she investigate it. She asked me if I would take her to meet this man and his dog. I said I would, but could not promise he would talk to her. I also suggested she not give anything to him, only to his dog, because he didn't take charity. On that note, we agreed to meet mid-afternoon. We met as planned, and both walked across the tracks. I could see the dog watching us from his perch, and he barked as we approached, his tail wagging. His owner got up as I greeted him, and I introduced the young gal. She explained she would like to get his story for an article she was writing for the local paper if he was interested. To my surprise, he said yes, and when the interview was over, she handed him a sleeping bag—for his dog. The man was smiling and shaking his head as we walked away. During the interview, we found out that his birthday would be in two days, and he would be turning thirty-five. He had been on the road for seven years, and his dog had been with him for four years—they had been together since he was a puppy. Why he ended up in our town is the mysterious way the universe works. The interview came out the next week, and that was the beginning of change for him and his dog.

The article in the paper went statewide, on public radio and social media. Everyone was willing to help. He was getting stopped on the street, and I was getting calls and texts from people wanting to help in all ways. There was a Go Fund Me account set up for him, and within three days, there were over five thousand dollars in it. He qualified for a housing program, and he got help getting his I.D., birth certificate, medical, and medications. There were some ups and downs, but he has been sober for five months and is working in an employment program. He has been in contact with his sister, who thought he had died on the road and was possibly a John Doe in a morgue somewhere.

After the article came out, church groups and organizations got together and started addressing the situation with the homeless teens in the area. Many people had been unaware of this situation until others started talking about it. It only takes one person to step up, and it can create a ripple effect that keeps moving and spreading like a stone tossed in the water. Will you be that person?

The Joys Of Working With
Autistic Teens
By Barbara Nersesian

In 2018, the Center for Disease Control determined that one in fifty-nine children is diagnosed with an autism spectrum disorder. Autism affects all ethnic and socioeconomic groups.

I'm a teacher who has taught middle and high school students, and I was ready for a new challenge. I had never met or worked with autistic children during my career as a teacher. I never realized how my limited experience affected my life.

One day I was in the principal's office, and she asked me if I would consider teaching something different. She told me that they needed a teacher in the Autistic Teens program. As we talked, the principal let me know that those teachers who worked with the autistic students told her how much satisfaction they got from doing so.

During my meeting with the principal, I learned that the teens were placed into functioning or non-functioning non-verbal groups. It was in the non-functioning non-verbal group where they had the need. It would be one teacher to one child. I told her I would take the position. This powerful experience changed my life and gave me a new perspective on the world.

What stood out, when I entered the room on the first day that I observed these children, was that each one of them had a unique personality. I also noticed that each one had a special talent, for instance, two boys with varying degrees of autism, limited communication skills and impaired social interactions. Since then, both boys have had a profound and lasting impact on my life. Every morning I was grateful and looked forward to improving their life skills.

The first time I met Jake, a fifteen-year-old boy, I realized how limited his communication skills were. He would repeat whatever I said to him. Every morning, I'd come in and say, "Good morning, Jake." Jake would put up his hand, giving me a high five sign and say, "Good morning Jake." He was a happy kid; he always had a smile. Jake's special talent was coloring in his coloring book. He was focused and could keep within the lines perfectly, and he chose beautiful color combinations. One day I decided to bring him tracing paper and had him trace the picture from the book and color it in, making his own drawing. He loved it. Every day, I brought him tracing paper. One morning I came in and he said to me, "Tracing paper for me." My heart glowed. He was communicating to me for the first time. Who would have thought a small thing like tracing paper would make such a strong difference in Jake's life? Imagine that! I will always remember Jake as the outstanding artist he became.

Meeting Edgar gave me an appreciation for using my imagination and innovation. Edgar was a seventeen-year-old boy who spoke very little. He was always smiling and happy. Every day his parents made sure he was well-dressed and well-groomed. He was insecure and always had a little blanket covering his head. I asked the other teachers what we could do to have him discard the blanket, and we came up with the idea of giving him a hat, which might do the trick. I gave him the hat, which he loved, and he put it on—and then he put the blanket over the hat. Most mornings, we took the kids for a walk around the football track for exercise, and Edgar would grab onto my arm and not let go. I came up with a plan to help Edgar feel independent and still allow him to be himself. I told him we would march around the track. As we marched, I said, "Left, right, left, right, left, right." For two weeks, we could be seen marching around the track. Then, one day, a miracle happened—Edgar let go of my arm. Oh, the joy in my heart was overwhelming, just knowing that Edgar was becoming independent!

Gratitude had an amazing effect on me. It opened me up to new things, improved my body language, and made it easier for me to relax. I was doing what I loved and experiencing a sense of peace with the world. I had it all, love and gratitude—the two highest emotions we can feel as human beings. For the first time in many years, I was energized and connected.

In reflection, the joys of working with autistic teens have changed me in ways I could never have imagined. They have definitely made me a better person; I'm more compassionate, empathetic, and understanding. When I was working with these autistic children, I felt I was facing an impossible situation. I changed my mindset and unlocked the door with love, patience, and compassion. They changed my life and I changed theirs.

Are you facing a challenging situation in your life? Unlock your door with love and gratitude and the solutions will find you. These students taught me the way to happiness. It's amazing how many small moments of joy occur when working with autistic teens. I totally fell in love with these kids! I came to realize that these children are on this planet for a very special reason, even though we may not know what that reason is. I turned my everyday life into an example of how being happy with who you are can make you a champion who inspires others. These students are my champions!

Happy Valentine's Day
By Nicole Newsom-James

My four year, four-month relationship had broken up, and I was moving things out of our home to start a new single lifestyle. I was staying at a mutual friend's home, where I was able to move a few things into an unused room. During one of my trips back to our home, I arrived at around 8:00 a.m. I noticed a white car parked out front which looked like my ex's best friend's car, so I knocked rather than entering the front door, as I didn't desire to walk in on their conversation. I knocked again. Waited. Knocked again. No answer. So I went to open the front door. Locked. Strange. So, I used my key and walked in. No one was in the living room or kitchen.

Then it hit me like a ton of bricks, as my ex comes dashing out of our bedroom in a robe with a surprised look across her face. I asked her if Deb was here. She relaxed and had a devilish smile. Something was off. I walked towards our bedroom, and she blocked me. I demanded to know who was in there. I registered that it wasn't Deborah. Then, I realized that my ex was wearing a robe, but she didn't own a robe, and there was nothing underneath it either. I cannot explain all the feelings that bubbled up and streamed throughout my body at the realization that we didn't break up because of her being fired three years earlier by her police chief, or the fact that she hadn't worked for the past three years while I supported her. She broke up with me because I started holding her accountable for her recovery. After she was fired for fraud, she was unable to get another job in her chosen career as a police officer. Fraud was unforgivable, and any honest police force would have to refuse to hire her. But all of this had been unknown to me as my ex had told me she had a personality conflict with the new police chief. I believed her story.

It wasn't until years later that I would find out that accusation of fraud was actually why she stayed in a depressed state for three years. And why, ten years after her firing, I was in a deposition giving testimony that I wasn't even in Texas when someone forged my signature on a deed transferring my name off of our joint home and solely into my ex's name. A couple of months after the forged deed was signed, the property was sold and all monies pocketed by my ex. Now in the deposition, I testified that I was in Oklahoma at the time the deed was signed and notarized by someone other than myself in Texas.

The next to be deposed was Dozy, the notary of the forged deed. During Dozy's testimony, it came out that she worked closely with a lover of my ex. This lover was vice president of the company Dozy worked for, her name was Carol. Dozy basically testified that she trusted Carol, and didn't check the signature on the deed transferring the property into my ex's name, nor where Carol signed it in Dozy's notary's book.

The woman who was in bed that last day I walked into our home, and the next to be deposed, was my ex's wife, Juanita. I couldn't help but like Juanita. She was a healer like me. She taught students how to heal others like I did, and she even had the same hairstyle and hair color as I did when I first met my ex. Basically, she was me, just a ten years younger version. I thought women dating women was going to be different than men dating women. My ex proved me wrong. She was like the stereotypical guy, dumping his wife for a younger, newer model.

Juanita testified that my ex knew that Carol had taken care of removing my name from the property, but she understood that Carol had talked to me and I had just signed over the property. Juanita had no clue it was fraud. Truth be known, Juanita had no love loss for Carol, as she believed Carol and my ex were having an affair during their marriage.

The last deposition to be taken was that of my ex. She was so pumped full of medications to keep her calm that her testimony made no sense, and her attorney, in an attempt to protect her, objected to almost every question asked of her. My ex, even heavily medicated, could not stay calm and walked out of the deposition. Unknown to her, my wife was sitting in the lobby when she burst through the door and said, "I'm done." And she was right.

Six weeks before the notarization of the forged deed, Trish, my partner of four years, decided it was time to make me an honest woman. So she set up our wedding in Oklahoma City at a beautiful little chapel where we eloped. We decided to use both of our family's last names from our birth certificates as a symbol of joining two families. Newsom was my last name, and James was hers. This reminded me of when I was baptized as an adult; I changed my name as a symbol of my new life in Christ. I now wanted to honor my new life as a married woman, so I dropped my middle name, and legally changed it from Nicole Kathleen Newsom to Nicole Newsom-James.

Believe it or not, this is what made the title company settle with me. The person who forged my name on the deed signed the wrong name. So, because of my marriage on February 14, 2017, not only did I receive a beautiful new wife, a new name joining our families, but also, compensation from my previous home which enabled us to build our dream home. Happy Valentine's Day to me!

A Call To Love
By Peggy O'Neal

"My worst nightmare has come true! I am 55 years old, divorced with no children, and going back to live with my 83-year-old mother." My lunching buddy added, "All you need now is a bunch of cats." We had a good laugh.

My work in Singapore was complete, and I was moving back to Fort Smith, Arkansas. I wasn't looking forward to living with my mom (my dad had died two years before), but I was grateful to have a cozy place to stay while my next direction in life and work became clear. I knew it wouldn't be long; it had never been.

Mom and I tolerated each other pretty well. I had come to accept that our relationship was the way that it was after years of work with forgiveness, compassion, and understanding. Sweet feelings of love never emerged. I hadn't thought about trying to feel love for Mom. I appreciated that she had done the best that she could and that her life had been challenging. We were seemingly worlds apart in politics and lifestyles; the exception was that we both loved needlework. I experienced her as always ready to fight and argue. That was her way of connecting, and it often wasn't subtle. At dinner, she would ask, "Don't you want to argue about this?" Even though I understood what was happening, there was tension and distance between us, not connection.

It was quite an adjustment for me to live with someone, since I'd been single and lived alone much of my life. It was for Mom as well. There was bickering and arguing and a mood of melancholy, which duplicated our home environment when growing up. All of my years of learning and coaching about how to be effective with other people helped with navigating our disagreements and my ability to coax feelings of compassion within myself. Yet, feelings of closeness or tenderness were lacking; tolerance was the operative state.

My daily activities included revitalizing my coaching practice and pursuing job opportunities. However, there wasn't traction advancing a clear direction. I wanted out but had no sense of where to go.

I surrendered to this new realm of not knowing what to do next, and the inability to force myself into action, and was thoroughly exasperated.

Without looking for it, months into this situation suddenly came clarity: Obviously, life, what I call the divine, had other plans for me than the ones I was trying to make. I was cemented in these circumstances to develop a loving relationship with Mom. I didn't know what that would feel like or how it would happen.

Opening to these feelings required me to listen for guidance. I traditionally engaged in practices to advance to some state, stage, or way of being. However, my true nature was inviting me to turn within, not try to change or develop myself, but to accept who I truly am—loving, peaceful, and happy. And to see and experience Mom in the same way—loving, peaceful, and happy.

To experience meaningful love for Mom meant *trying* was not an option. I was only going to experience this love by engaging as if my life depended on it.

First, I asked what I wanted to feel, and the answer was love. Then, no matter what Mom said or did that annoyed me, I told myself that that was merely a thunderstorm happening over there. It wasn't personal. I reminded myself that she is a loving, divine being in all circumstances.

"You know Obama wasn't born in the United States," the storm rumbled. The eruption occurred unexpectedly amid a dispassionate chat about the day's news. It took everything from me to stay where I was, perfectly still, fully feeling the emotions, and keep my mouth shut. I reminded myself she was being a thunderstorm and was divine. I shifted my focus to feeling the love-in-hiding, silently saying to myself, "love, love, love." It was similar to the experience I imagine Odysseus in Homer's *Odyssey* had as he was tied to the mast of his ship and passed the sirens trying to seduce him with their sweet voices to his death. My sirens were my thoughts, emotions, and instincts to get away or respond in kind. My mast was reminding myself to love. After a few minutes, I calmly changed the subject.

I had thousands of opportunities to remind myself to love! I would not let myself succumb to the sirens; giving in would be an invitation to them to continue singing and to bury love.

After many months of staying tied to my mast, there was a dramatic shift. Mom offered a topic to argue over, and my reaction was a spontaneous eruption of internal giggles! I had not been triggered in the old way. I knew immediately that my authentic love for her had emerged, the one that had always been present, yet hidden in the background, obscured by a lifetime of patterns of behavior, thoughts, and emotions between the two of us.

After that, the loving experience remained in the foreground more consistently; whatever she did or said fell to the background and didn't matter. I would see or think of her and feel love. She still acted in her usual ways, and sometimes habitual emotions arose, but over time, the intensity diminished. I had finally been able to be with the loving being that was ever-present.

A few months later, I received a job offer in Dallas, and I moved. I missed her terribly and returned to visit her as often as I could. I was hungry to share experiences and spend time with her. I had truly, madly, deeply fallen in love with my mom, and was experiencing love as I had never before.

She lived a little over a year after the move.

My love for her continues to grow more vibrant and precious. The divine's plan was much better than mine. I'm forever grateful.

The Vertical Life
By Ashe Owen

I had the right length, now I just had to find the right beam. Inside or outside? Under the upstairs deck, a joist beam. The tears come in fits, thinking about what I am about to do. This is the only way out of this pain. It consumes me and follows me through every waking moment. As I sit on the edge of the bed with the rope in my lap, I start to write my last letter. The tears come uncontrollably now. I only get through the first sentence before I pick up the phone and call my sister.

This was five years ago. I was going through the dark night of the soul, that was for sure. I couldn't think about anything else except my misery. It's funny how the darkness sucks you in when that is all you think about. Suicide appears to be the only way out and somehow better for everyone who loves me. I couldn't love myself, so how could anyone else?

Fifteen years before my dark night of the soul, I was working in a cubicle. I quit that job of 16 years to move to Atlanta to pursue a sales job. I had never worked in sales, and I didn't make any either, so I was let go. Luckily, I did not move my family to Atlanta. Instead, they stayed behind in Colorado, and I moved back to face an uncertain future.

I have been a musician most of my life, and my dream was to become a rock star. I decided when I got home that I would pursue music full-time. This is not an easy decision at the age of 40. Both moving to Atlanta and becoming a musician are risky life choices.

Now, becoming a musician at any age is difficult, but doing it at 40 with a family in tow is even more of a challenge. I was lucky—I ended up working at a dueling piano bar and playing in a band. Eventually, I was hired on full-time at the piano bar and was a full-time musician. In two years, I had reached my goal.

I was having the time of my life! I was out partying with the band and the patrons at the bar, and loving all the attention I was getting from the ladies. This was when I started to cheat on my wife. I was also drinking a lot, smoking pot, and doing other substances which will be left unnamed. Suffice it to say, I was in my 40s acting like I was in my 20s.

You would think that after achieving the goal of changing careers at 40 and doing something you love would be enough to satisfy someone, but deep down, I still wasn't happy. I was so self-focused that I was missing the little things with my family, while attempting to fill a void that could not be filled. I kept trying to fill that hole in an endless cycle of guilt and shame.

My physical health was now failing, my marriage was falling apart, and the girl I was having an affair with was finished with me. My career as a musician was at the lowest it had ever been, and I was in a deep depression. By the time I was holding that rope in my hands and writing out a suicide letter, I was getting divorced and feeling the pain of losing my family and home. I was feeling broken-hearted because the affair I had hoped would be more was ending, and I was facing kidney failure, starting dialysis, and the death of my stepfather. This was my darkest moment, and the only way out that I could see was suicide.

I wasn't aware of the toll it was having on those around me, in particular, my wife and children. I was unaware of anyone else's pain—completely unaware of anyone else's needs except mine—and this had been going on for years. No one could be feeling as bad as I did.

My mom took the brunt of my suicide rants, and I know that was especially hard for her. One day, when I was in a particularly low state, she had a friend of hers call me and talk me off the ledge, so to speak. He recommended I seek help from an old high school friend of mine who is a grief counselor. He has a retreat center where I spent five days, and that is when my life transformed. I was immersed in spiritual, emotional, and physical therapy. My life has never been the same since.

I would love to say that everything I was dealing with magically disappeared, but that was not what happened. I got divorced, continued dialysis, my girlfriend did not come back, and my stepfather did not come back to life. I will say that I sincerely love myself and that asshole that got me here. It is easy to love yourself in the moment, but sometimes harder to love the person from the past that made those mistakes you feel guilty or shameful about. It was hard for me, at first, to forgive myself for my past behavior, because it caused pain for others as well as myself.

However, it was those mistakes or lessons that put me on the road to find out who I truly am, and I would not change a thing.

It has been inspirational for me to look back at this journey and see how far I have come. I was living a horizontal life, only looking at what was on the surface not diving deeply into myself and taking a look around. I found that the deeper I went into myself, the more capable I was of going deeply into others. I now live a vertical life, diving below the surface—where all of the good stuff is.

Happy Practices For Hard Days
By Lisa Paquette Yee

Recently, all the balls I juggle on a typical day as a mom and entrepreneur hit the floor and bounced. For every ball I rescued, another two rolled out the door and into the weeds, until it started to feel like I wasn't being planted but buried in life's dirt.

I mean—seriously! Do you ever have days like this:

I stepped in cold cat puke getting out of bed. My son couldn't find the rubber boots he needed for the day's pond study field trip. The virus making its way through my house was leaving a trail of dirty dishes and germy discarded tissues—ugh. We spent hours in waiting rooms investigating my daughter's sore throat, which turned out to need immediate, costly surgery.

And that was only on the home front. In a single day. In a string of days like this.

At work, the team developing my upcoming Soul Prompts game was waiting and wondering what to do next. But I was feeling off-track. And I was pretty sure my creative muse had packed up and left town.

Of course, when things suck, I have besties to give hugs, and coaches to talk through solutions (and they did). But I also had to remind myself that happiness is an intentional decision. We can create our own grace. I created mine by returning to some of my favorite wisdom and practices that help me ground and remember who I am and what I value most:

#1 - What Sets Your Heart Free?

Years ago, I was on retreat with the deeply wise Barbara Sher (referred to by some as the "godmother" of life coaching). She reminded me that a good old-fashioned cry can be the first step to lightening up.

(I know! I know! I gave Barbara the same stinky side-eye you're giving me. But in a world that reveres stiff upper lips, this childhood practice is being forgotten.)

The technique is simple: find yourself a quiet, private spot (a washroom cubicle is dandy in a pinch). Settle yourself and fold your hands over your heart, inviting all the unhappy to come bubbling up. More often than not, the tears will follow.

If that feels too uncomfortable for you, I am also a fan of Julia Cameron's "Morning Pages" exercise. Anytime you need to, sit down and do three pages of longhand, stream-of-consciousness writing. Even if you have to start with, "I don't know what to write," don't lift your pen, don't pause. Write.

Morning Pages walked me through four years of my Dad's cancer journey. So I can say with authority that this practice can help you get out of your head and relieve the burden on your heart.

#2 - Be The Light You Need

When you're feeling cranky or heavy, it's tempting to want to flop down and wish for someone else to make you feel better. But what if you could learn to see unhappiness as an invitation to fill yourself up with magic?

Give some thought to what light you're craving. Then go out and create it for others (or yourself). It may be exactly what you need to flip the switch on a funk the way I did one bitterly cold winter morning.

I got the call that schools had closed for a rare third day in a row. My heart sank. The kids already had cabin fever, and I was in dismay at the thought of another day of refereeing and bickering. And I needed to work! But more than that, I needed a break and so did they.

So I woke them up as if it was a regular school day. Drove my usual route. And surprised them with a trip to our favorite quirky local coffee house. We sipped hot chocolates and played board games until we were ready to go home.

The joy of this unexpected excursion was so pure and deep that my son asked me to be sure to share this story with you. And I find myself again grateful that I listened to the crazy idea my heart whispered on that cold morning. Find a way to be the light you need.

#3 - Trust the Wisdom in Your Heart's Whispers

Sometimes easier said than done—I know. However, tuning in to your higher self's wisdom is a practice vital to daily happiness. Your higher self is your present, past, and future self. Her wisdom whispers through your heart. And she has all the knowledge and permission you need for daily happiness.

One quick way to tune in is to tweak the "Morning Pages" exercise by turning it into a higher conversation. Do this by writing down a question. Then, without pausing to think or let your brain kick in, start writing down whatever comes to you.

Not a writer? Grab your smartphone and hit the audio record button. Out loud, ask your higher self a question like: "Higher self, what is one thing I can do to feel happier today?" Then start talking. Flow and let go as you answer your question.

The environment for your conversation doesn't have to be precious or perfect. Amazing conversations with my higher self have come about while washing the dishes. I've talked to her in deep meditation. In noisy mastermind groups. Quiet moments of writing. And over coffee with friends through a deck of Soul Prompts cards pulled from my purse.

Go ahead! Try creating a conversation with your higher self in a way that feels fun to you.

#4 - One Thing I Know To Be Absolutely True

You already know the way to happiness, although you may not be aware of it. So it never hurts to tuck these practices in your back pocket for a rainy day. And when it comes? Reach out for support. Remember to hold yourself with kindness and a sense of humor while you fish those dang balls out of the weeds!

Valentine's Day A Gift And A
Lesson In Self Love
By Cheryl Peterson

The moment I saw him, I knew my vision was true. My excitement about seeing him after several months of health problems vanished in an instant. His body language told me everything. The lack of tenderness when he saw me dimmed my spirit. Instead, I intimately felt his strain and anxiety at being in my presence. I felt like he was hiding behind his arms full of pink roses, chocolates, and a Valentine card. He laid them on the table and motioned for me to come over and acknowledge the gifts like it was an obligation and not a gesture of love. I was stunned. I felt like a knife had pierced my heart. I could barely breathe. I felt like a stranger in his presence, even though we had been together for the past six years. Pink roses, and not my usual red? Did the other woman get my red roses? I carefully opened the card. After reading it, I fought back tears of overwhelming emotion and struggled to keep my composure. The card said nothing about love but wished me every happiness. It felt like an ending. I knew what I needed to do.

In that instant, I allowed myself a moment of reflection and asked spirit for guidance. "You can do this," spirit replied, "You are loved and guided." It was the same voice I'd heard in my dream. My mind flashed back to the dream I had a few days before when I was awakened in the middle of the night by a female voice. Was this my inner-self trying to get my attention? The voice insisted that I wake up, and then revealed to me that he was with another woman—much younger, married, and living some distance away. The voice even informed me that I knew her name. Stunned, I could not get back to sleep. I tucked the thoughts away, not wanting to believe them, but knowing deep in my soul, the words were true. I finally needed to trust my intuition.

We had planned a road trip for Valentine's Day and as we headed out to his car. I could feel his tension. After a long and uncomfortable silence while we drove, I said, "It's good to see you." He did not respond. At that moment, it occurred to me that I had been so wrapped up in my health issues over the past few months, I had not focused on us at all. Could this be why he was so cold at the moment? "What have you been up to?" I asked. Once again, I could barely breathe knowing what was coming and what I had to accept. He replied that he had been writing music with a friend. My inner voice was strong and insisted that I tell him now. With all the courage I could muster, I said confidently, "You're seeing someone else, right?" With a cold, harsh tone, he replied, "You don't know her." His words pierced my already wounded heart. I shared the dream I'd had from a few days ago and what was revealed to me. He was stunned. He kept driving without a glance towards me. I said, "You had so many opportunities to tell me. We could have ended this relationship with more respect than this." He remained silent, turned the car around, and took me home. His parting words to me were, "I did not mean to hurt you." And the relationship ended. Just like that.

This is my story. It is like millions of stories about love, loss, and betrayal. But we do not have to become our stories. Here's what I have learned and what inspired me to move forward.

Over the next month and many sleepless nights, I recalled all the times I let myself down in relationships and settled for less than I deserved. It was all of the little everyday "hurts" that I let erode my spirit and dim my light. Repeatedly reviewing every possible scenario, I examined every outcome and the emotions that paralyzed me. Betrayal—that word evoked such intense emotion. Betraying myself was one of the most painful experiences to work through. Then, there is forgiveness. How easy it is to forgive others, but trying to forgive myself felt like an insurmountable task. I stayed in the relationship when it no longer served either one of us. I truly believed this ending was a gift, a reprieve, so both of us could find the happiness we deserved.

I spent many hours meditating, writing, reading, and going over all of the whys. Knowing that I needed to take personal responsibility for the relationship's end, I had to own my role in it. I needed to forgive and uncover the shadows and darkness inside of me to move towards the light and heal. I allowed spirit to guide me in the direction for my highest good, and I deliberately replaced fear with love. I was no longer afraid to stand in my power. I felt a renewed sense of purpose, and my usual enthusiasm for life began to return. With the support of my "earth angel" friends and the power of spirit, I felt empowered to move forward fearlessly.

I learned again that self-love and self-acceptance are key to a conscious relationship with myself and others. I felt a renewed sense of spirit—a coming home to myself and my purpose. My renewed sense of self-love, trust in my intuition, and amazing courage inspired me to share this with others. I trust that all is for my highest good. When tears come, I breathe in love and light. I know I am swimming in hallowed waters where many have gone before, and I am not alone. We are not alone. Our souls are awake.

Love, joy, and happiness are waiting for us. Trust that they will come.

You Are More Than An Observer
By Nicole Piotrasche

The idea of writing for a book called *Inspirations* both scared and, well, inspired me. Writing this story has provided an opportunity to mine my life for the richness I thought was missing, and I hope that telling you what I've found will encourage you to become an archeologist of your personal story, to go on a journey of discovery that will surprise you.

How I Got Here

Later, I'll tell you where *here* is, though that might become clear as you read the *how*. I am a forty-one-year-old adult child of an active alcoholic. Long ago, in a lifetime I have yet to understand fully, my mother chose alcohol as a go-to coping skill, a way to numb whatever pain she had experienced. My experience in addiction is that it's a choice that becomes a chooser— eventually, the line between the decision made and the power the addiction holds blurs. She chose to drink to escape, and now alcohol wraps her up inside and out.

Around age 12 is when I remember feeling the impact that my mom's drinking had already had on our relationship. It had always been a factor. I hadn't had the capacity yet to process and articulate my feelings. This time was a hinge to a door of understanding and growth that was opening to me. I was blooming, and for reasons that I'm only now beginning to understand, she despised that. The next decade of my life was a constant battle.

I'd characterize myself as a pretty good kid. My grades were all right, and I never got into any trouble. I don't have any wild party stories or tales of ditching school to go get high. I stayed right in the middle of the road. On the surface, I'd say my world was boring. Beneath all of that was a bottomless powder keg of emotional and psychological abuse. I never knew where the fuse was, if it was lit, and how long I might have before the explosion would happen. As a teenager, a child, I tried everything I could—every combination, every formula—to get her to leave me alone. Every day was a game of "If I, then she…" I thought if I could find the right combination, she would stop drinking and be a mom.

Nothing ever worked. Somewhere between the words she hurled at me and the ineffectiveness of my efforts, I began believing I was nothing. I never wanted to die, I just wanted to stay out of the way of everyone. I decided that I didn't matter, that I'd sit in the shadows and watch, believing that was the only way I would ever be any good. It was how I thought I could love people best. Stay out of the way became my silent mantra.

I Am Here Now

Seven years ago, two things happened: I began the long process of what I now call soul recovery, and I met this kid. Through a variety of healing modalities, I began the journey of walking back toward myself, and I had a reason to get in the way. I was discovering beautiful pieces of who I am that had long since broken off, and I was learning what it means to show up in the world of a kid who suffers from deep depression and debilitating anxiety. I found empathy, humor, and wisdom. As I worked through the trauma of my childhood, I began feeling space inside me for compassion, forgiveness, and understanding. I engaged this relationship from a place of being fully present for the first time I can remember. To this day, this and all my relationships require that I am nothing more and nothing less than me. This means I participate, I enter in, I play, and I work, and I experience and allow others to experience me.

At first, this was scary. There was uncertainty, and I struggled with perfection and the fear that I wasn't good enough. I'd cave sometimes, crawl back into myself. Thankfully, I found myself surrounded by people who saw me, knew the me I was, and could see the beauty of the me I was becoming. When you experience life fully present, no cave can contain you any longer. I can't stay in the cave for long, it suffocates me. Now, when I feel the urge to crawl back in, I stop and breathe, get grounded, and remember who I am.

The Choice

I was struggling recently. I had allowed that old belief to rent space in exchange for my passivity. For a few weeks, I was stuck in it. I was working through it, reflecting on the circumstances that triggered this in me, when I had this realization: If you'll allow yourself to be a part of it, the universe masterfully weaves together threads—the lives of people it knows will bring life to a soul in desperate need. There's no time wasted in worrying about appearances or rules. Each strand is layered over the other just so, creating exactly the right tapestry, in the perfect design with precisely the right colors, that the one soul it seeks to wake up will see it and be overwhelmed by the love and care poured into the effort.

Each of us is a strand in this tapestry. We are all brilliant, vibrant pieces of a creation designed to wake each other up. We encourage each other most simply by allowing ourselves to be. When we allow that for ourselves, we see the world around us differently. We notice people, even when they are not able to see themselves. We hear and see and experience everything at deeper levels. Somehow this magically creates space and invites those around us to find themselves, to simply be. It is miraculous, and it is our greatest calling. I invite you to this journey, and I want to hear about it.

Inspired Synchronicities
By Anna Pitchouguina

Life brims with the profound, the mundane, and every frequency in between, spinning a delicate web of intricately connected synchronicities and contradictions. Inspiration, in Wayne Dyer's words, means to be "in spirit," surrendering to the driving force that navigates us away from the mundane and into the profound. Through my experiences, I have found this to ring true.

Operating in the logical head space and studying in the first year of my law degree, my 19-year-old self was confronted by an anomaly. My mum came home, produced a business card, and in a thick Russian accent informed me that I must get in contact with a woman called Marion. "She has a good energy and spirit," my mum said, "She will take you to Thailand for free, and you will translate from Russian to English at an international conference about spirituality and well-being."

I thought my mum had gone mad. I asked how she came across Marion in the first place. It turns out that the two of them frequent the same naturopath. Marion happened to be in the area and dropped into the naturopath's office. Mid-conversation, Marion asked the naturopath if he knew anyone who was fluent in Russian. "Coincidentally," the naturopath was finalizing my mum's appointment.

After one long month, when I could no longer bear my mother's persistent reminders to get in touch with Marion, I finally caved in—mostly to get my mum off my back. I ended up meeting Marion and her husband, Brian. They talked about energy, spirit, past-lives, and the Akashic plane. This was a few dimensions removed from contract law, which I was studying at university. Nevertheless, curiosity and a free holiday to Thailand won me over. It's worthwhile to mention, however, that I did read Eckhart Tolle's *The Power of Now*. I came across the book "coincidentally" when I was house-sitting for a friend of mine called Shanthi (keep this piece of information in mind, it will become relevant later).

I translated at three seminars in Thailand for Marion and Brian. I became deeply involved in my spiritual quest and even wrote an undergraduate thesis on Madame Blavatsky in the field of mysticism. I embarked upon the long journey from head to heart.

Marion and Brian became like family to me. Brian's daughter, Stacey, is now my best friend. At Stacey's 30th birthday party, I was confronted with a strange question from her grandfather, "If you were to borrow my car, would you return it to me in the same state you found it?" to which I said yes. "Good," he said. "So why aren't you doing that with our planet?" Another anomaly. I was lost for words, so he continued, "Talk to my son Brian, he's in renewable energy—ask him for a job."

I didn't like where I was working at the time. It was legal, it was mundane, and I felt uninspired. I also remembered from past experience that it's easier to deal with anomalies sooner rather than later, so I called Brian and asked him if he had a job for me. "Coincidentally," he was looking for an Executive Assistant.

I was interviewed by Brian and his business partner Noel, who took great interest in the high school I attended. I queried his curiosity and was informed that his daughter is studying at the same school. Brian also chimed in and said, "Yeah, and his ex-wife is the head of strings there." Cue anomaly here. "Shut the front door!" I exclaimed. "Your ex-wife is Shanthi? She was my music teacher! I have house-sat your former matrimonial home! I know your daughter!" It was also during that house-sitting that I came across *The Power of Now*—my prequalification training for translating for Marion and Brian.

The planets had all lined up in one straight line, and it truly did seem that everything came together and fell into place. I could see every single one of my decisions and experiences as single threads that wove into a complex tapestry. My 16-year-old self, playing the viola under Shanthi's instruction, could not have ever envisioned that ten years later, I would be working for Shanthi's ex-husband. Nor could I have possibly known that Shanthi's ex-husband could be the business partner of Brian, with Brian being the husband of Marion, whom my mum "coincidentally" met through a naturopath. An anomaly indeed.

The plot thickens. I receive a call from a recruiter called Nikki. I did a reference check for a colleague of mine with whom I had worked at the law firm, prior to my employment with Brian and Noel. After the reference check was complete, Nikki asked me if I needed help with securing legal employment. I did feel a yearning for a legal career, but I didn't want to leave the job I already had. I told Nikki that she wouldn't be able to cater to my two-day per week availability. She refuted my comment—her best friend (and director of a law firm) was looking for someone part-time. It was written in the stars, and it worked out as it had meant to.

Wide Awake: A Collection Of Songs And Poems From My Bedside By Colleen Porter

Cycle Through

From the upcoming "Sacred Songs for Sacred Circles" book, featuring original songs and music by Colleen Porter (share song with acknowledgment, but not for reprint or audio recording).

Let your bare feet sink
Let your roots run deep
Let your burdens pass through
Cycle through, cycle through.

Let your arms reach high
In connection with the sky
As you give your love away
Let them sway, let them sway.

Let the soft breeze blow
Away the pain you used to know
Let the old stories go
Let them go, let them go.

Feel the cool water run
A new journey has begun
Follow ease where it goes
Let it flow, let it flow.

Let your face greet the sun
And remind us we're all one
Collective beams so bright
Shine your light, shine your light.

Feel the wash of warmth above
It's your turn to live and love
All of earth's supporting you
Cycle through, cycle through.

Let your bare feet sink
Let your roots run deep
Feel the wash of warmth above
You are supported, you are loved.

Let life and love pass through you
Cycle through, cycle through.

Without a Cloud in our Sky

Imagine a world without clouds…
    No changing, no shifting
        No rising or lifting.
Each sunrise the same, no artwork at night…
    No colored explosions reflecting the light.
No reason to look up with wonder and awe…
    Or imagine new worlds in formations we saw.
No dragons or turtles that live in the sky…
    No watching them gather, let go, or glide by.
They invite us to think beyond static and still…
    And open our minds beyond earth, beyond real.
Each inspiring minute they shift, re-arrange…
    On their magical journey of courage and change,
As we see the same beauty, yet differently see…
    Their constant creations that play in the breeze.
How lucky are you, how lucky am I…
    That we don't know a world "without a cloud in our sky".

A thought for sprouts and buds…

Most people will applaud your blooms;

but few, if any, will see and appreciate the work that comes before.

The digging deep, the removal of obstacles,

the pulling out of invasive plants,

the building up of rich and fertile soil.

Yet the condition of the soil you surround yourself with is everything:

Affecting every seed, every root, and all beauty that will ever have the chance grow there.

Your quiet attention to the part that no one sees,

deserves great self-applause and admiration.

It's Easier

It's easier.
It's easier to be asleep.
It's easier to be asleep than awake.
It's easier to be complacent than aware.
It's easier to be quiet than risk conflict.
It's easier to blend in than to be different.
It's easier to justify than to be honest.
It's easier to reject differences than consider them.
It's easier to assume than to listen and understand.
It's easier to assign a label than value.
It's easier to dismiss than acknowledge.
It's easier to ignore your own needs than to take time to meet them.
It's easier to push down and forget than push forward and heal.
It's easier to stay with routine than make hard changes.
It's easier.
It's easier to be asleep.
It's easier to be asleep than awake.
But it's better to be awake.

Awakened Woman

The awakened woman opens her eyes and sees the world in vibrant colors, even when the darkness falls.

She has a fire in her soul that cannot be doused, a purpose in her step that cannot be stopped, and a truth in her tongue that cannot be stilled.

She can no longer piddle in the petty…for her eyes see, her heart leads, and her hands heal.

With power in her belly and creation in her womb, she is rewriting her story and the story of hushed women everywhere.

She has laid down to rest that woman that used to shrink and play small…standing in her place as the woman who rises to speak and be seen.

She stands firm upon the earth above judgment and division. She recognizes truth and good in the collective all, but is aware of pain and injustice…seeking to lift the forgotten and oppressed.

She is clothed in the present, wearing robes of love…knowing *love* is the only glory that ever mattered or ever will. Her eyes can never be closed again.

My Second Chance
By Elicia Raprager

I was finally maturing. I stopped running away from my problems and making excuses. I survived. My kind mother-in-law bought me a shirt with the phrase, "Remember where you came from" printed on it. She found it fitting, and I did too. My happiness and newfound strength stem from escaping the fog of depression, panic disorder, and more. I feel for others who are caught in its grasp. There is hope. I want you to get through this. I hope this small piece of my story inspires and uplifts you.

I wasn't true to my passions. I was an artist and a writer who seldom painted or wrote. I had several unfinished projects, and others I hadn't started. After my husband picked me up from work, I drew four loose, abstract pastel drawings. Those were solely for me. I hastily drew without thinking or sketching. The first couple were dark and concerned my husband. The last two were stronger. I wouldn't say I felt better, but I felt a sense of release and self-awareness. Afterward, I wrote thank you cards to everyone who helped me earlier.

Earlier that day, I was at work. My performance had been slipping for a while, but I didn't think much of it. I was getting through each day and week. The abnormal rhythm and heat in my chest warned me I was about to have a panic attack. I tried to hide it. I stifled my breathing, but it became louder. A few teammates who became my friends walked over to me. One held my hand and told me to breathe. Another placed her hand on my shoulder, and the last one wheeled me in my computer chair to an open conference room. Leadership followed.

It was a Friday. The friend who transported me asked what weekend activities I was looking forward to. Everyone took turns answering the question. Also, we discussed self-care routines. I decided to return to weekly therapy appointments temporarily. For a couple of months, I was going biweekly. When everyone cleared the room, it was just my leadership and me.

My manager suggested I do things over the weekend that were good for me. The first thing I did was peruse the cute little store downstairs. I wandered in a saddened, confused daze. The owner continually asked me questions. He probably thought I was going to shoplift. That wasn't my agenda. I was lost and trying to figure out what was good for me while wondering how to get back to my regular self.

I looked at every object in the store two or three times. There was a bright yellow scarf. My caring manager loves the color yellow. Classy, vintage purses caught my eye. Those reminded me of my good friend who models. I stopped at a small selection of blank cards. I bought one each for my leadership and the teammates who helped me.

It wasn't the first time my conditions rendered me helpless. When the cameras appeared at my brother's wedding reception, my pained face came out of hiding. Again, my inner demons told me it was a lie and that I wasn't meant to feel happy. I left the building and finished my cry. My mom and other close female relatives came to console me. I half cried, half hyperventilated, and guilt consumed my shortened breaths. My depression interrupted another joyous milestone, and the camera captured my shattered soul.

When I tried to isolate myself, so as not to bother anyone or embarrass myself, my support system came to me. I'm thankful they showed me they care, they're there for me, and I matter. Their message was well received and needed. I tried to only let in pleasant experiences. I limited time spent watching the news and stopped watching horror movies years ago. I sought out joyful videos, enlightening books, and meaningful conversations.

I shared what I learned about mental health. I started blogging about my struggles and accomplishments. No victory was too small. I remember posting a video of my clean dining room and kitchen. At the time, that was a huge win for me. I used to wait for the day to pass. That day I was determined to be productive. I put on music, lit a candle, and sang to rock songs while I washed the dishes and swept the floor. I even wiped the table and scrubbed the refrigerator. Close family and friends knew what a big deal that was. Soon after, my posts were shared and supporters told me I inspired them. In truth, they motivated me. The more they said I helped them or they were proud of me, the more I wanted to share with them.

My wise cousin once told me you see the good in others that you want to see in yourself. I find that fitting. I see kindness and determination in my friends. I see affection and protection in my parents and grandparents. I witness strength in my loved ones. I took on these traits.

I try to be kind to everyone. I smile, compliment, and check in on people. I'm determined to be the best version of myself, live a better quality of life, and give hope to others. I'm affectionate to my family and friends. Staying locked in a warm hug provides long-lasting comfort. I protect my wellness and happiness from intrusive thoughts and unpleasant sensory. I'm strong for seeking treatment and continuing my existence when my mind fed me numerous ways to end it.

Acknowledging a mental illness and learning to understand it is empowering. You're taking back the power that seemed to flow out of your body when that illness swallowed you. You gain a unique power and strength from your new coping skills. You get a second chance. That's how I think about my life in treatment. It's a second chance for joy, love, respect, peace, and a fulfilling life. You're worthy of that life.

Share a smile. Stay inspired.

Reminisce, Reflect, and Seek Serendipity
By Elicia Raprager

In ten minutes of reflection, I went back almost 20 years. It was special to look at my current surroundings and be grateful. When I lacked control of my emotions, being silent and still was harmful to me. The moment I wasn't working on something, I was crippled by depression and anxiety. I've learned to set aside time for myself. I've learned to use it to my advantage. Now, I can enjoy the quiet idle moments. I can savor the tranquility. Please take a moment to join me.

My husband and I recently moved into our first home, and I've been enjoying being outdoors and taking care of our yard. This has been my top priority. The fresh air and sunshine clear my mind, and a calm mind helps me appreciate the present moment. I found what I believed to be a bunny den while I was mowing. There was a hole at one end. The entire length of the divot was covered with brown feathered grass. I cautiously mowed the outskirts of it. The past week or two, there have been two rabbits coming and going, and I was delighted to know there could soon be baby bunnies. Our yard is fenced, small, and peaceful. The rabbit parents chose a safe place for their offspring.

Once I finished mowing, I sat down on the swing and looked ahead. I enjoyed the gentle breeze. At first, I visualized what flowers I wanted to plant. I saw friends gathering for future occasions. Then, I reminisced. Many of my childhood memories took place in the backyard. My dad would be lying in his hammock with a large glass of iced tea that my mom made fresh and brought to him. Today, the sound of ice clinking puts me in a serene state.

Often, my two best friends visited me. My backyard had the best attraction—a tire swing. We took turns pushing each other. One of us would sit on top, another would sit in the opening below, and the last would push. Eventually, we became too big for it, and the rope aged and became worn. I later put one foot on the bottom of the opening and watched it fall to the ground. Shortly after, my dad surprised me with a hammock chair. He hung it from the large tree, on the opposite side of his hammock. In that seat, I read books galore. I caught up on recent adventures of *Harry Potter, Goosebumps, Dr. Jekyll and Mr. Hyde,* and many more characters.

My mom and I would go to the end of the yard and swing on our swing set. Mom always wanted to stay on the swings longer, but my arms and legs became tired more quickly than hers, and now I regret that I always asked to go back inside. This was the time I would tell my mom what was bothering me, who my latest crush was, and what we discussed in my favorite classes. I learned it was a reprieve for my mom too. She and my dad had filed for divorce. When we were on our swing set, she was free from the turmoil.

I tried to bring these sentiments to our new home. I'm not sure if our current city allows bonfires, but I hope we can have a raised, covered fire pit. While growing up, we sat around a fire most summer nights. The neighborhood children would come over and play hide-and-seek in the dark. I learned my signature move from my big brother. I wore dark clothing and laid on the grass close to the area we determined "safe." I was afraid of the dark much longer than most kids, and was especially afraid when I was outside. When I was playing with them, I had no fears. I felt like a normal child. In school, I learned I was quite different. When I played that game, I fit in. I'd wait for my opportunity and run to "safe." My younger friend mirrored this technique, and she got pretty good at hide-and-seek.

My mind wandered further back to my most memorable birthday. I watched my great-grandma playing croquet with my friends and me at my tenth birthday party. Not only did she give us a challenge, but she also won! She was 99 years young and jubilant. She had an amazing spirit and filled everyone with hope. It seemed like she would be with us forever. That's why it was devastating when she passed four years later. I'm grateful for all these memories. I can see her any time if I take a moment to recall those days. Her memory is alive and spirited.

I love this time of year, and being a first-time homeowner has helped me appreciate it even more. I'm inspired by nature's beauty. The peace I feel allows me to gain clarity. Two weeks after I spotted what I believed to be a rabbit's den, I mowed again and checked the ground. The hole was filled. When I saw a baby bunny flee from a low bush, I knew it was a den! They were safe inside, and they're residing in the foliage against our house. Just as quickly as the bunny jumped away, ideas for a new garden formed the same night.

My excited mind took me to the future once more. I started visualizing replacing the grass with stones. I'd plant tiger lilies and hostas with a bird bath as the focal point. Here, birds would find relief from the humid heat. I'd bring in rustic white benches, stools, or wood crates for potted plants. My ceramic angel, given to me by my maternal grandma, would find a home in this garden. Inspiration is all around us. Keep your eyes and mind open. Your next great idea or masterpiece may come to you when you least expect it.

Share a smile. Stay inspired.

I Am A Superhero
By Samantha Renz

In October 1974, I was evicted from the only home I had ever known. It was a warm, cozy place where all I had to do was sleep, eat, and grow. What a lovely place. On that 21st day of October though, my world changed. I was pushed and pulled, practically yanked out of my home. It was cold. There were bright lights and a sudden stinging pain on my rear. That is when I found my voice. The landlord, I call her mom now, says I had the biggest feet she had ever seen in her life. Insult to injury— smack me around and make fun of my feet? What a way to enter this foreign place. Skeptical at first, but I soon realized that using my voice got me held, fed, and what is that warm feeling—is it love? I liked it.

Fast forward, it seemed that using my voice over time was less and less effective. These taller people started shushing me and telling me when I could and could not use my voice. I learned.

As time rolled by, there were a lot of confusing and hurtful events. I saw big boy body parts, felt pain, experienced so much discomfort. I was told not to talk about it. I was threatened. I was made fun of. I started hiding. My voice got smaller and smaller, and so did I. The incredible shrinking woman? Is that my superhero power?

I am bi-racial—my father is black and my mother white. Around 12 years old, I was told not to tell. I was told to lie. We had moved to a small town; my parents wanted to protect us from the racist comments. I am a lesbian, by the time I realized, I was used to lying. I stayed in the closet for years.

Somehow, I learned to be invisible. Perhaps I thought that was my superhero power. I learned not to speak, to hide, and to keep all my thoughts and feelings to myself. It was safe. Maybe if I was invisible, they would all stop hurting me.

I grew up and recently realized that I gave up my voice years ago. As an adult, I have taken a step back. I have let others lead. I have kept my opinions to myself and watched as others failed because I did not speak up. I have felt the shame and regret of not being able to use my words.

Eventually, I couldn't even find them. I even started believing I had no opinions, or anything that anyone would want to hear.

I started reading books about letting go of shame and guilt. I read books that talked about vulnerability. I tried it with some close friends and my partner. I was amazed at the experience. There was no judgment, there was acceptance. Vulnerability—was that my superhero power?

I went to therapy and talked about what happened to me as a kid. I experienced compassion. I was told it was not my fault. I was comforted. I was given tools to cope. Honesty—was that my superhero power?

My shame started falling off; my heart started opening. I started feeling that warmth again—I was able to experience love. Real love, not the kind that I thought I had to earn.

I enrolled in a program. It was called Pathways Core Training. It was intense, but took me through a process of looking at my life. Facing what was holding me back and keeping me from being everything I wanted to be. I looked at my life. I looked at all of them, everyone who had hurt me. I looked at my unforgiveness. I looked at my anger. I looked at my fear. I looked at my whole identity crisis. I looked at the walls I had built.

I realized I had built walls so thick and so tall that the love that was trying to break through couldn't penetrate it. I started removing those bricks one at a time, made a small doorway, and the love started pouring in. The acceptance was overwhelming. The compassion was abundant. So much so that I started accepting myself and having compassion for me, and for that little girl who was so hurt so long ago. I keep her close to me now, and encourage her every day—that little girl was a badass, and she still is to this day. I found a little superhero inside me.

Through it all, I found my voice. In a few short months, I have learned what it takes and what it looks like to lead. I am the CEO of my civil engineering firm. I am launching a mission-based franchise line. I am writing this story. I am living bigger than I ever imagined. I have accepted that there is no other being in this world like me, and that I was created this way and experienced all of it so my story can be told and so I can empower women across the world. Every single one of us has it inside of us to have an immeasurable impact. We need to find our superhero powers. What are yours?

My superhero power is vulnerability.

My superhero power is honesty.

My superhero power is authenticity.

My superhero power is love.

When we allow our voice to be taken or we give it away, we give away the power. I found my voice and claimed my power. I challenge you to claim your power too. I am a superhero, and so are you. It takes courage to look inside. It takes courage to face our fears. It takes courage to be truly honest with ourselves about who we are and what we want. It takes courage to see ourselves raw and love every bit of it. I am a courageous, peaceful, and valuable badass. I am a superhero.

Summer Sojourn – Sidelined
By Marci Rosenberg

My plan was to escape Phoenix during the heat of summer. I was experiencing fatigue of mind, body, and soul due to the unexpected death of my mother, navigating the settlement of her estate, and managing a demanding career in a zoning and land use law firm. I'd daydreamed about freedom and adventure and had begun piecing together an itinerary for my "Summer Sojourn."

The first part of my journey was to be spent in Anchorage, Alaska, where my daughter and her husband live. During prior visits, we'd enjoyed the beauty of the Alaskan landscape and summer weather hiking, kayaking, and salmon fishing. The next leg of my Summer Sojourn would be visiting my sister in Portland, Oregon, enjoying farmer's markets, museums, art shows, and concerts. After Portland, I planned to visit cousins in Los Angeles, with a bike trip to Venice Beach and stand-up paddle boarding in the bay. From Los Angeles, I would board Amtrak's passenger train to Chicago, see the country from the comfort of a private sleeping car, and meet fellow adventure-seekers. With family there, I would have places to stay and people to play with in the Windy City. Next, I'd visit my hometown of Peoria, where a few friends still live, and three generations of my family are in the cemetery. I would visit them all. Last stop? Austin, Texas to spend time with my son, whose house, on a half-acre with a creek and daily visits from deer, is only a 15-minute drive from the coolest downtown in Texas.

On the second-to-last day before I left my job—not to retire, but to take time for self-care—I got a telephone call that changed everything. I heard the sweet cadence of an East Indian female's voice: "Marci, this is Dr. K. We got the results of your colonoscopy, and Marci, you have colon cancer."

Just like that, the visions of my Summer Sojourn imploded. New images of chemotherapy, radiation, hair loss, and the real possibility of dying flooded my mind's eye. I finished the conversation and hosted a private pity party for one where I asked some higher power if this was my reward for carrying the weight of responsibilities for settling mom's estate while struggling to meet the demands of my professional job.

Angry with the reality of my condition and afraid of the unknown medical journey ahead, I soon met with an oncologist and with a colorectal surgeon for a crash course in the digestive system and details of colon resection surgery. To my relief, chemotherapy and radiation would not be needed if the cancer had not spread. The next step was a CT scan to detect evidence of cancer in any other part of my body.

A few days before the CT scan, I received great news: my daughter was pregnant! My joy for her and her husband, and thoughts of my new role as a grandmother, were rays of light in my foggy, dark world: my first grandchild and the beginning of a new generation on our family tree.

The position of my emotional teeter-totter tipped again. A week after learning the happy baby news, the surgeon called to report the results of my CT scan. It was a Friday. I was alone in the kitchen preparing Passover dinner for 12 guests due to arrive in four hours. The surgeon's voice was clinical: the scan showed several nodules in my lungs. If it was cancer, it was metastases from somewhere else in my body, and the diagnosis would be terminal; no point in doing the colon resection.

Numb and barely able to speak, I managed to ask, "So, what's next?" He said that a PET scan would be scheduled to see if the nodules lit up any cancer cells. I insisted the scan be scheduled for that Monday.

The call ended, and I looked around my kitchen, taking note of what still needed to be completed for Passover dinner, now perhaps the last one of my life. In a state of reverence, I chopped walnuts, apples, and dates, then mixed them with cinnamon, sugar and grape juice to make one of the traditional foods for the Passover Seder plate. This mixture represents the mortar used by the Jewish slaves to hold the stones together as they built the Egyptian pyramids. I wondered, "How am I going to hold myself together?" My answer came from a hopeful place within, "Just keep moving forward, and live as if there is a tomorrow and many tomorrows."

Rather than negotiating some deal with God to let me live if I promised to be a better person, I made a deal with my unborn grandchild. "You keep growing, and I'll do whatever is required to make sure I'm here to welcome you when you arrive, and to be around as you grow up."

It was a beautiful *al fresco* Passover Seder, celebrated with friends of all faiths—Christian, Catholic, Muslim, and Jew. We shared our personal perspectives on modern day freedom and summoning the courage to wade through life's challenges—our personal Red Seas. I spoke only of my upcoming surgery with no mention of the possibility it would be canceled if I had terminal lung cancer.

The next day, I shared the frightening CT results with two dear friends. They shepherded me through three long days of worry and waiting. Finally, the PET scan was negative for lung cancer—I felt reborn!

At this writing, I'm six weeks post-surgery. Phoenix daytime temperatures are over 100 degrees. And I'm simply grateful to be alive. My Summer Sojourn was not supposed to include visits to doctors' offices, a four-day stay at the hospital, much pain, and months of recovery at home. Yet, this humbling experience has enhanced my elation and appreciation for my ability to travel to Austin later this month, and to Anchorage in August for a baby shower and again in December for the birth of my grandson—the beginning of my Winter Sojourn.

In Good Company
By Laura Rudacille

Before the day greets the sun, he slides his feet into fleece-lined slippers, wraps his body in a cotton robe, and moves to the kitchen. With deliberate motions, the kettle is filled and positioned to boil. An embroidered cloth is laid across the enamel top table. A plate, bowl, and mug are selected, and a napkin is nestled beneath the fork. At the counter, he cuts a grapefruit, then pours cereal and milk before selecting a chair which offers a spectacular view of the woods surrounding his house. A routine of gratitude and purposeful beginning, as the rays of daybreak begin to kiss the trees.

He was my grandfather, my Big Gop—the result of the mispronunciation of Grand Pop. He was a pastor, father, husband, artist, writer, scrabble enthusiast, and so much more. He demonstrated deliberate care to the details. He paid attention to the tiny things within the things.

I remember how it felt to share the road of life with my Big Gop. I can still feel his secure and welcoming embrace. I can envision him, backlit by stained-glass, as he delivered a Sunday morning message. I can vividly hear the wisdom as it permeated the sanctuary, opening minds and changing hearts.

In preparation for retirement, Big Gop purchased wooded land on a Pennsylvania hilltop. He worked in deliberate stages to fulfill the dream of building a home. I watched the unfolding with a child's eyes as he cleared trees from a selected acre and harvested stones from a spring-fed stream. Big Gop mixed each batch of mortar, and slowly, a puzzle of rock took shape and stretched toward the sky.

I'm certain Big Gop's reflective moments of accomplishment far exceeded the tipped barrels of concrete, slips on the forest moss, and smashed fingertips. I imagine his blooming smile, amplified by an idyllic soundtrack of nature, forest, and stream, as he positioned the final stone and completed his house.

Countless strides on the road became the place where my family gathered. The Woods, as we'd come to call it, was far more than a residence among the trees. The Woods was a testimony to a legacy of persistence and purposeful invested time.

Big Gop built his workshop beside the house. A refuge where an artist, absorbed in his craft, paid little attention to tin hands circling a numbered face. Woodcarving showcased his gift for patient discovery. Through an intentional and meticulous series of chip-chip-chipping away, he'd remove fragments and reveal the beauty hidden in a hunk of lumber.

After his passing, I spent an afternoon in Big Gop's workshop. I boxed unfinished projects and scraps like fine china. As I caressed his tools, seeking any tangible connection, my grief-swollen eyes landed on the sawdust-covered clock hanging on the wall. Hands frozen for as long as I could remember, the device had simply failed to thrive in a haven where magic flourished at the hands of a man who truly valued his minutes.

I knew a fraction of the man Big Gop was throughout his eighty years. Youth had masked my awareness to dig greedily into the gift of his presence. I wish I had been curious enough to inquire and investigate before our moments were shifted to memory. I'm fortunate to have touchable treasures created by his clever hands. Each Christmas, as I remove my hand-carved nativity scene from a protective cocoon of tissue, I reverently trace the etched wood, and for a moment, Big Gop's fingers link with mine.

Big Gop was good company. He was simply present and grateful in every action, and the time we shared influenced me deeply.

We are joined on the road of life by countless influencers. They provide companionship for the steps we are taking. We're drawn toward their intangible traits like sunshine, and invite their rays to infuse the whole of who we're becoming. We stroll together for a moment or a distance. We rest and restore in each other's company, then separate to seek another adventure.

We have the opportunity to get to know the individuals whose strides match ours as we navigate life's incredibly diverse terrain. We have a chance to hold space for the children who scamper past us in energetic discovery, leaving a trail of giggles and cookie crumbs for us to follow.

We're given openings to show compassion to the men and women whose story stops us mid-step, and opens an avenue for us to cultivate deep and meaningful understanding. We're offered moments to embrace the victors, of all varieties, whose courage champions us to fight harder and develop strength beyond measure.

Our influencers continue to walk with us long after their physical feet fail to carry them. Embedded in our memory and imprinted on our heart, their wisdom flows from our lips and carries on our breath to delight fresh ears. Recollections lighten our burdens in a surge of boisterous laughter or torrent of cleansing tears.

Big Gop's workshop clock hangs in my salon. Every day I see it, and I think of him. The tin hands still fail to keep time and are a perfect reminder of the gift in being present.

I encourage you to set a table for your one miraculous life, and take care with the details. Treat yourself to the gift of inquiry, patient listening, and nourishing silence. Link hands with the company on your road, absorb goodness, and embrace the beauty in every awakening sunrise and inspiring sunset. Learn and grow through each experience as you chip away and expose the truest expression of who you are.

We're doing life together after all, and we are in good company.

Silence
By GG Rush

The Land Rover bounced as it plowed through the thick brush and thorn bushes making its way further off the dirt track. My guide, Shaun, sat to my right in the driver's seat, simultaneously shifting gears, quietly giving our position on the radio, and steering over small trees. He looked over at me and smiled and raised his arm to signal to those in the higher seats behind me to duck as a large thorn branch got in our way. We'd been at this for an hour. The only words we had heard were the hushed voices on the radio. All around us birds and impala let out distress calls. Our tracker, Jerry, had left his perch seat on the front of the Rover and joined the others in the back just before we left the dirt track. A much safer spot. We were in hot pursuit of our game. Armed with only cameras and hot water bottles under our blankets we drove on in the early morning hours.

We were on a silent game drive. Part of a group of brave souls who had traveled the long distance to South Africa to discover ourselves—to lay bare our weaknesses, fears, and doubts about ourselves. We spent our time at camp in group discussions with three famous life coaches. Learning and listening and challenging ourselves. Our twice-daily game drives took us deep into the bushveld to be one with nature and learn to understand what the "real world" is.

And here we were in the real world. Our goal reached. We all sat silently as we took in the scene before us. A pride of lions. Five gorgeous lionesses taking in the morning sun. Ten fuzzy cubs yawning and stretching after a breakfast of impala. One cub possessively holding onto a leg that his siblings were not going to take from him. None of them seemed to care that there were silent observers watching them from inside a big tin can. Our being silent and at peace put the pride at ease.

This is the thing about being silent and being still. All of your other senses come alive. You can actually hear. You hear the sounds of nature all around you. You can hear your breath and heartbeat. You can smell the fresh air and feel the sun on your skin. You can taste and savor the feeling of pure joy at seeing a pride of lions in the sun.

Animals, Drums and Nature
By Michelle Ryan

The grandchildren were visiting the farm following a death in the family that was causing a lot of pain, anger, and fear. I worked with my younger granddaughter using drawing to support her grief. Big Sissy needed another approach to help her acknowledge her grief. She was almost eight, and had an aliveness that asked questions about the natural world and how things worked. She was deeply connected to her Native American and Irish roots, without the direct teachings in our family.

The house was filled with little sis and Momma, so I said, "Addy, it's your turn. Let's go out to the chicken coop."

Five years ago, we'd moved to a farm because of following spirit and grace. I had no idea that my retirement would be on a farm. However, the power that guides said, "Look, grandchildren are being born. Your husband is an amazing beekeeper. The house on the hill sold at the same time the county approved your bid on five acres on the open space." Small farm, beekeeper's wife it is.

I started my farm soul investment with chickens. The baby chicks were fun in the grass with two-year-old Addy in the spring. Building a coop, learning the chickens' ways and needs and their social structures within the flock were entertainment for me. I would sit in the run and watch and enjoy the chickens' interactions. I was still teaching and would share with my students the chickens' escapades, using photos from the farm as writing prompts, sharing chicken metaphors in staff meetings, and examining chicken idioms with my students learning English. The farm was tapping into my soul, my childhood memories, and ancestors.

I incubated eggs the next spring, and through grace, the grandchildren were present when the chicks began to hatch. We squealed in delight and danced around the kitchen. Only one chick matured enough to survive, so we kept her in the house to keep a close eye on her and give her social interactions. She was our first Rosie. Addy loved the name, Rosie.

That summer, my father's and my long-time dream came true. Spotting a trip to Ireland that included a ten-day condo stay in the small town of Adare and was within our budget, off we went to see the land of our ancestors.

Our lodging was a short drive from the small town of Bird Hill, where my dad's grandfather was born. My great-grandfather was a Falconer* of the manor house. As we sat on the rock marking the village of Bird Hill, I felt with amazement the full circle that had landed my father and me here. I felt the power of ancestry, whether I consciously knew it or not. My chicken joy—my chicken care—was beginning to take on more meaning and understanding. It was in my blood to care for birds, and I was following a deep family lineage without even knowing it.

Then we went to a historical village with reconstructed homes of times past for the Irish. Standing in a peat miner's hut, my dad recalled his grandfather's night dreams of being called out by his father to go get the peat. Sacred memories surrounded us. We walked into a farmer's home, which held a chicken box in the kitchen.

I innocently said, "Oh curious, they kept their chickens in the kitchen."

My husband laughed and said," Like us."

I didn't even realize I was doing the same thing back home. Rosie was in our kitchen. The unconscious is a powerful guide.

Sometime later, I faced another powerful loss myself. My support network suggested I create a howling tent for myself outside, so I could honor my grief and stay present to my feelings. It was natural for me to turn to the chicken coop. There was an entry to the building that held my chickens. I hung a large scarf to separate some space. I brought things in that made me comfortable and supported my grief: my drum, sage, candles, tennis racket, pillows, blankets, a rocking chair, a journal, tissues, and water. To my therapist, I committed to daily time in my grieving space. I found with regular attention to my feelings that I experienced freedom through the other parts of my day. Where I had been experiencing my grief sneaking up on me and feeling overwhelmed, this changed as I attended to my feelings. When they arose, I felt some sense of manageability with my feelings and connectivity with my daily routines.

This was where I brought my granddaughter, who was experiencing her first big loss through death, to share with her the womanly art of tending to one's self and feelings. I shared why I placed these objects in the room; why I came to the chicken coop, and what I did in it. I had her light one of our beeswax candles we made together from the wax Poppa gathered. I showed her how to light the sage and spread it through the space. I began to drum and sing. I spoke my truth about my feelings of loss. She began to drop her shoulders, flush, and cast shy glances. We were together in this space, held and okay while being a little weird and new. Addy let me know she was ready to close her grief time. I saluted with the drum.

She said, "Mimi, let's go hold Rocky." Rocky was this season's teenage chicken. I smiled.

As she held Rocky, she said she wished she could hold her chicken every morning to start her day like mine. I said yes, that would be nice. "You have Rhett, the family dog. Could you pet and lay with Rhett each morning to remember?"

"Yes, Mimi, I could. I will try."

She was ready to meet this present moment, to be with Mommy and Sissy again.

*Falconer: a person who keeps, trains, or hunts with falcons, hawks, or other birds of prey.

Serendipity At Work
By Michelle Ryan

Have you ever had a feeling of attraction to an activity or a change, but then thoughts came in to talk you out of the inspiration? The longing doesn't make sense. It is a new attraction that you haven't had before or a spontaneous one and requires a leap of faith. If you are like me, sometimes you leap without question and other times you fight and argue with the feeling in an attempt to rationalize its meaning. This is a story of the lessons in following those attractions.

A posting came for the International Women's Summit that an acquaintance liked. I noticed that this friend was tapped into the global force of women. My bank account was empty, so I just watched the advertisement. I was attracted yet confused.

My family needed me at home, as several deaths and emergencies had occurred. I had begun serious tracking of my grief process. Grief was not new for me for I had lost my mother at a young age. Then, my grandchildren lost a family member to a tragic accident. I began guiding our five- and eight-year-old granddaughters in age-appropriate ways to validate their feelings. I had cultivated sacred actions to support grief and loss experiences through my own losses and in my work with children.

While doing so, a voice said, "You need to write a book. Parents and teachers need this information. This is the purpose to all the grief you have experienced."

I shared the secret whisper to a girlfriend to keep myself accountable and to put power and movement to the voice of deep knowing. This was not the first time this voice had spoken to me, and I did not want to lose the moment, which I have lost in the past. At a deep level, I was scared.

My friend and spirit that I was now connected with recommended I read Elizabeth Gilbert's book, *Big Magic*. Also, my friend shared a podcast that Liz Gilbert had spoken on and told me that hearing her in person was powerful. I quickly listened to the podcast. My mind was blown. I looked into speaking engagements and again the International Women's Summit (IWS) 2019 came to my attention. Okay, this was getting interesting. By now, I was writing regularly. I was supposed to be at this conference.

I kept watching the Facebook feed and writing while riding the chaos of my family's grief to the breaking point. There was not enough space for me. I was outgrowing myself to the point of a scream. My current context was too small for me. I needed a bigger container.

Then the spirit rose up to meet me further. A surprise check came in the mail. I had discretionary money for me to run with so permission was granted. Little did I know, this was just the beginning.

Now it was clear, I was to be at the conference for reasons I didn't totally understand, but I knew the process of a spiritual journey was afoot as I walked through the airport and checked into a new environment without checking my past as extra baggage, or carrying the roles of a homeowner. I felt delicious freedom and autonomy. The other women began to show up to the hotel and introduced themselves through random tidbits of conversation.

"Hello, may I sit next to you?"

"My name is...."

"I am from...."

Two more women joined us, and I recognized a pattern developing between strangers, bonding with one another and being fully present in the moment in each other's lives and developing a deep knowing of one another. I'd see this pattern repeated throughout the weekend. We stayed present because it was so delicious to do so. I noticed the few times when I brought my back-story, it felt unsatisfying. There were great lessons in being present.

During our first lunch together, I walked through the buffet line listening to the buzz of the enthusiasm the morning speakers had stirred. Once my plate was full, I realized that the seating was quite organic. Many of us came from our homes without our friends. I walked to the next table that was filling, and the routine began again.

"What is your name?"

"Where are you from?" This time I added I was originally from Illinois because the ladies were speaking about the Midwest.

The woman across the table spoke up. "What part of Illinois are you from?" she asked. "Springfield."

Her eyes widened. Her forehead wrinkled. "Me too!" she exclaimed.

She said, "Oh my God. I know you. We were friends when we were young children. You lived two doors down from my grandparents, and we would play when I visited them."

A memory immediately rose of a cookie—a vanilla wafer with homemade green frosting. More memories rose from her grandmother's kitchen and playing at the telephone table.

We sat staring in amazement, unable to take our eyes off each other. Our hearts were speaking. We had been childhood friends. It was like looking in a mirror. There was joy and love greater than great due to the serendipity—which was the morning speakers' theme.

Our five-year-old selves played the next few days as our adults caught up and realized we would choose to be friends today. We still had parallel lives and the same interests because we had shared the same table 50 years later. I came with unspoken loneliness, and then I was reunited with a deep friendship and a community of women for my next leap.

So back to my original question: have you ever had a feeling you could not explain, that you may fight with but follow and later receive gifts greater than you could imagine? This happened to me. I may not know why, but I know I must continue to listen even through doubt that there is a greater story than I know of just around the corner.

The Start Of Something
By Bruno Salvatico

April 12th, 2015, a Sunday like any other. I wake up in a haze and with a sense of misdirection, both literally and metaphorically. It has been a couple of months that I've been struggling to find my way. I have been searching for a compass to point me in the right direction, and unfortunately, not only do I feel lost inside my head, but I am also having a difficult time expressing my feelings verbally. This morning I woke up perhaps a little more confused than usual, due to the previous night's festivities with my friends, Chase and Pat.

I wake up to the sun in my eyes. This happens every morning, and I often struggle to fall back asleep, so I lay there for some time to let my eyes adjust to the sunlight, and try to get my dry contacts back into place. Once I finally get up and stumble through the living room to the kitchen for a glass of water, I see Chase—who is also fighting a futile battle against the light— on my couch.

Pat seems to have taken more of a beating than Chase and I, so we agree to let him sleep in and get our day going by what is now high noon. Although it is a late start to our day, we decide to go on an adventure and drive into the beautiful Rockies without destination. To this day, the mountains still stun me. After almost a year of being in Colorado, they continue to re-energize my soul and fill me with something more spiritual than anything I could ever imagine.

Chase and I don't say much to one another; we sit back and enjoy the beauty before us. The sunshine finds the perfect balance as we drive with a whirlwind inside my single cab, making the snow-covered summits all the more majestic. You can feel wanderlust fill the air. This has always been an unspoken chemistry that Chase and I share; we bring it out in each other. Still, there is not a word from either of us.

The serene drive is exactly what we needed—a chance to get some fresh air and heal some of the collateral damage from the previous night. After several miles, I start seeing signs that point me in the direction of Boulder County.

"Want to go to Utah?" I say, jokingly.

Chase chuckles and responds, "You know that I'd love to, but I have to go to work tomorrow. Let's grab a cup of coffee in Boulder and walk around. It's a beautiful day."

He knows me well enough to realize that although my tone is playful, all it would take is a simple "yes," and the east face of the Rockies would be behind us in a few hours. That's the way it has always been—the more spontaneous, the better.

As we drive down the Foothills, we can now see the Flatirons. The scenery opens up and we make our way into the city. The main streets are filled with locals and tourists trying to blend in. Tulips line Pearl Street, and crowds surround the street performers. You can see that spring has come.

We park on 9th Street and start making our way to our favorite coffee shop downtown. We get our coffee to-go, and decide to make our way down a couple of side streets to branch out and continue what has already been an adventurous day. A few sips of coffee and some fresh air finally gets some conversation going.

"I don't want to be smart, I want to be wise. I want to live my life the best way possible and see and experience as much as I can," Chase muses.

I had heard or read this somewhere before, but it struck a new chord with me this time. It was exactly what I needed to hear at that moment, so elegantly phrased and summed up in such few words.

You see, up until that point in my life, or maybe up until that exact moment, I had been searching for something to kickstart me, to get me motivated, or what I eventually came to know as *purpose*. The problem was that I had been searching in the wrong places. I became reliant on materialistic things that only brought me momentary joy. As soon as I was old enough to work, I started buying what my family could not afford to give me when I was young. This quickly manifested itself into what eventually became a serious drinking problem and an inconceivable amount of debt for someone in their early twenties who hadn't attended college.

By the time I was 24, I had taken a good, hard look at myself and decided to move away from the small town I grew up in and head for

Colorado to cleanse myself of the toxic environment I had created. I quickly learned that although a new environment does help, you can't truly change unless you are willing to change your habits and your mindset, which is what I had unknowingly been struggling with that spring day. Although that particular day was the start of something beautiful, I had been pretty miserable up until then.

Chase's words that day, simple as they were, changed me. They became the anthem for the spiritual and mental shift that demanded I live up to the expectations that I believe to be meaningful. Some people call these moments *turning points* or *spiritual awakenings*. We all have moments like these throughout our lives, big and small. Only if you are lucky enough to be present for one of them, you may think to yourself, "This is it, this is the moment I will look back on as the start of something."

Breaking Free
By Chelsea Sandoval

I used to live my life in a box. No, I don't mean I physically lived in a box when I was little, I mean that my life was caged. I didn't know what the world around me was like. I didn't know how mean people could be. If I'm being 100% honest, I didn't know how to do things or how to think for myself. You see, I was raised in the Catholic Church. I was an altar server, a Sunday school student, and a teacher. I spent most of my life at the school or church more than I did at home. Now I'm not bashing the way I grew up by any means, so please don't think that. I had my grandparents bending over backward to make sure I had a good education; I had my mother working long hours, sometimes two jobs at a time to make sure that I had clothes on my back and the school supplies that I needed. But when I started to get older, I realized that something was wrong. My family was amazing, but I began to change. I wasn't going to church because I wanted to, I was going because I had to—I was almost being forced to. I felt my heart being pulled in a different direction; I started to break free.

This is hard for me to write, I'm not going to lie. I know that people will read this and not understand why I did what I did. I know some people are going to be straight up mad at me because I "pulled away" from the church. I am sad to say that some of those people will be my family, but I learned that even though I want to do what I can to please them, I have to do what is right for me. I have to think of myself from time to time, and I have to think *for* myself, rather than listen to what everyone else wants me to be or act or say.

That's the hardest battle I have ever fought. I am constantly fighting an inner battle with myself, even to this day. One side is telling me to do what will make my family happy, and yet the other side is telling me to live my life and follow my heart. Maybe my story will inspire you to break free from whatever is holding you back, whether it is family or yourself. Maybe my story will inspire you to live your life the way you want to.

I'm going to share with you a few different things that helped me when I was breaking free. These are steps that you can take, and they aren't hard. In fact, you may think they are the most straightforward steps in the world. But maybe you need to hear them. Perhaps you need some inspiration, and that's why you are reading this book. These two steps are: listen to your inner voice and follow that voice—but don't feel guilty.

Listen to your inner voice. Now I know that sounds like a bunch of BS, but it's true. You have two different voices. The first one is the one that you only hear negative things from. This voice always told me that I wasn't a good granddaughter because I didn't want to go to church, because I wasn't thinking or acting in the way I was taught. For the longest time, I listened to this voice. But then something started to change. I began to hear a different voice, one that sounded like mine. It told me that I wasn't a horrible granddaughter because I wasn't doing these things, I was growing up. It told me that when you grow up, things about yourself change. Your eyes and your heart start to open because you learn more about the world. You begin to learn about what makes you, you. You start to learn all these things that you didn't know about yourself. It was beautiful.

Follow that voice, but don't feel guilty. I'm not going to lie to you, this is probably the hardest thing in the world, and I'm still struggling with it. As I said before, I have always done things to try and make my family proud of me. But sometimes the things that I have done, I didn't want to do. I would think that I was a horrible daughter/granddaughter because I didn't want to do the things they wanted me to do. Until one day, I had a conversation with that inner voice of mine. I know that sounds crazy, but in talking with her, I realized that the reason I wasn't doing certain things anymore was that my path was starting to change. At first, I felt scared because I didn't know how to deal with that change. I decided to stop listening to my guilt and start listening to myself. At times, I still hear the guilt in the back of my head telling me that I'm probably breaking hearts, but I just tell it that if my family genuinely loves me, they won't care, they'll only care that I'm happy and healthy.

I could go on and on about my transformation, it is something that has changed my life. I look back at the person that I was, and sometimes I don't even recognize her. I know these steps may seem like they are pretty simple things to follow, but as a 24-year-old woman, I wish someone would have told me these things sooner. But here I am, figuring everything out, one day at a time. I challenge you to do the same. Sit down and talk to your inner voice, maybe give her or him a name, follow your heart, your dreams and, more importantly, if not most importantly, never stop figuring out who you are. I broke free, so can you.

Working With Gratitude
By Felicia Shaviri

I have always thought outside the box when it comes to most things like people, situations, trying new foods, sports (if they weren't life-threatening), and well, life in general. Being number seven of nine children, I learned early on to work with what I had and to make the best of things. I didn't waste much time complaining, and quite frankly, it was rare for me to feel stuck, limited, or ever think I had no options.

Of course, there were times when I would yearn to go, do, or have something, only to have one or several obstacles appear to get in the way. It didn't take long for me to realize it wasn't the end of the world because I couldn't have something right away. It simply meant space had been created for me to look at the options. After all, just because we want something doesn't mean it's the best thing for us. Sometimes (often times, from my experience), taking the longer more scenic route of life offers priceless experiences that can be deposited and withdrawn at a later date for our future self. It wasn't until after I became a parent and began sharing some of my childhood stories with my children that I realized how grateful I was for learning to be humble and appreciative for whatever I had.

I can remember being hungry, one of many times growing up. The gas had been disconnected by the power company due to an unpaid bill, but the electricity was still on, so there was light. Our kitchen appeared to be bare, with little to no food for our family, but I knew I could find and create something, I just didn't know what at that moment.

As I searched the broken cupboards, I would find a bit of Crisco Oil, several slices of bread, a container of yellow mustard, and a half block of government cheese (umm, the best cheese ever!) that had not been gnawed on by the mysterious rodent, Bo-Bo the rat.

I began to think about all of the delicious dishes I could make. Would it be a double-decker mustard sandwich, cheese and mustard sandwich, or maybe even a grilled cheese sandwich? I decided to go with the grilled cheese sandwich, which was going to be a challenge. I found the electric hot plate, but unfortunately, it was not working due to a short circuit in the cord. So, as I stood in the middle of the room, looking at my three ingredients, bread, cheese, and Crisco oil, I began to pace. A melody of sorts began to play in my head, "Bread, cheese, Crisco oil…bread, cheese,

Crisco oil…bread, cheese, Crisco oil…" and I could feel my body moving to an imaginary beat of the music being created in my head. Then I remembered I was hungry, and thought to myself, "If I make a grilled cheese, how do I melt the cheese?" I kept thinking about that question, over and over again.

I imagined how the grilled cheese sandwich would look, smell, and taste. I was so into thinking about how good this sandwich was going to taste, that could hear myself saying "ouch" as the cheese burned my tongue from the first bite. I could smell the aroma of the grilled cheese sandwich as it began to fill the small kitchen in our home. My eyes began to scan my surroundings for something, anything that could help me make a grilled cheese sandwich.

I suddenly felt an incredible burst of joy that made my heart dance the moment I saw it! It was the clothing iron, which sat upright on top of the refrigerator. Oh boy, oh boy! I found myself dancing around the kitchen, full of sheer joy, and I began to sing "Oh Happy Day" by the Edwin Hawkins Singers, over and over again, as I began making my grilled cheese sandwich. Of course, my belly was full, and when I shared with my siblings what I'd discovered, they laughed and enjoyed an ironed grilled cheese as well.

Although times have changed, and I currently have the means to make as many grilled cheese sandwiches as my heart could desire, with my choice of bread and cheeses, I will always be grateful for my humble beginnings and, of course, my creative genius. You see, there was so much I discovered about myself through that experience. I was stronger than I allowed myself to see, packed with an incredible amount of self-discipline, determination, patience, awareness, and creativity, to name a handful.

I was hungry, yes. And yet, instead of going to my mother or one of my older siblings to complain or ask why, I did something about it. I made grilled cheese sandwiches for everyone. The point of this story is that, sometimes, we may not have what we might think we want right in front of us when we want it. This is to include all areas of our lives, relationships, careers, children, money, education, and so on. There will always be options available to each of us; we need only to be open and willing to see them.

A Heartbeat Away
By Jonathan Siegel

It's past midnight, and I can't sleep. I lie in bed, feeling my heart flopping against my ribs with tears flowing down my face. I think about my sisters and brother, my nieces and friends. I'll miss my niece Rebecca getting married, Lillian turning eighteen and going off to college. I won't be around to see what Robin, Miranda, Petra, and Rachel create for their lives. I want to see my brother retire and grow old. There is much in life I expected to witness and experience, and I see it drifting by like a leaf in a stream, forever out of reach.

In 2001, a random summer virus played havoc with parts of my heart's electrical system. On October 19th, I received the first of four pacemakers. The first allowed me to continue life as before. I returned to the field of play as a competitive road cyclist. I was also a swimmer, skier, and avid gardener. Six years later, I went into heart failure.

After three days of labored, shallow breathing, I called my cardiologist and told him how fatigued I was. The next morning I nearly crawled into his office. I envisioned vultures circling overhead, anticipating a sure feast. At the end of what had become frequent echograms of my heart, the look on the technician's face told me what I already knew: my heart was seriously sick. One measure of a heart's strength is the ejection fraction of the left ventricle (LVEF). Normal is 55 percent and higher. On that day, mine was 12 percent. A new pacemaker that controlled both ventricles of my heart was placed in my chest, and I began a routine of drugs to protect my heart. From 2007 to 2015, I soldiered on. My LVEF recovered to 35 percent, primarily due to the bi-ventricular pacemaker and two drugs that protected my heart. I was able to ride my bike gently around the park and swim laps. Because of my athletic background and overall healthy lifestyle, I felt better and did more activities than might have been expected. Then the roof fell in.

The last time I rode my bike around the park, I had to walk and push my bike home two miles as I didn't have the strength to pedal and stay upright. Three months later, I struggled to complete one lap of the pool. On the return length, I was fearful of making it across the deep end. In both instances, I recall thinking the same thing, "That is the end of that."

I was driving to a massage appointment in the Highlands area of Denver, and the phone rang. I was expecting the results of my last check-up, and despite my declining vigor, I looked forward to hearing an update. Dr. Altman delivered devastating news. The structure of my heart was weakening at an accelerated pace. My valves were leaking, and the septum (the central wall dividing the left and right ventricles) was extremely weak. The septum is akin to a backbone for the heart. It provides a structure around which the heart pumps and valves open and close. My heart couldn't pump efficiently enough to provide oxygen to my blood or circulation to my organs and extremities.

I needed a heart transplant.

In the winter of 2017, my health declined dramatically. My sole form of exercise was walking around a nearby park. In March, I couldn't make it to the end of my street. I could no longer sleep on my side, as I had difficulty breathing. I'd wake up gasping for air if I slept on my back. I gained two to three pounds a week from fluid collecting in my lungs, belly, and legs. I was put on an end-stage IV drug for my heart (Dobutamine), and wore an IV pump so that I could live at home.

On July 2, 2017, gravely ill, I was admitted to the hospital. I had MRSA (a drug-resistant infection) which caused me to be taken off of the transplant list. In itself, it was highly dangerous and a threat to my life. I had a blood clot in my arm from the IV. That was also a threat to my life. On what I expected to be my last birthday, July 19th, my family came into town. I knew they were there to say goodbye.

Through tears, I watched them eat a dinner of mediocre pizza and salad. As I tossed and turned and tried to sleep that night, I begged the universe to continue my life. As I watched the sunrise the next morning, I knew I would win this battle. At the end of July, I was stable enough for a heart transplant.

A donor heart became available on August 7th. That evening, I was prepped for surgery, as a gaggle of friends and family loitered in my room. Around 2:00 a.m., I was wheeled out of my room to pre-op, the nurses on the cardiac care unit lining up to give me a send-off. I smiled at them through tears of joy. After a long wait, at 6:30 a.m., the lead nurse told me that the donor heart wasn't viable, and I would be going back to my room.

I was wheeled back to my room, devastated and bereft of hope.

As the days went by I waited for a donor heart. I could feel my body weakening; there was only a small window where I was still strong enough for a heart transplant. On the morning of August 28th, my cardiologist came in and had good news. A donor heart was available. Around 2:00 p.m., he confirmed that I would be getting a heart transplant. I spread the news, and my family was there as I was wheeled in for surgery.

The morning of August 29th, 2017, in a surgery my surgeon described as "plug and play," I received the miracle of a donor heart.

Labyrinthine Inspirations
By Brooke Smith

In the fall of 2016, I sent my daughter away to college. Three weeks later, my mom passed away with little warning. Simultaneously, the two most important women in my life had transitioned in different ways. I found myself stuck inside of my grief. I was choosing bitterness, resentment, sadness, and anger for my chicken soup, my comfort. These feelings were familiar to me. I liked them! They served me.

In my search to find peace, I attended a retreat on Maui where I was introduced to The Labyrinth. I walked labyrinths before but had never been given an explanation until I met Eve. She shared the labyrinth's history and intent. She told of the magical self-observations that the labyrinth can reveal.

Eve explained how to walk the labyrinth. Step inside, set your intention; as you walk, take notice of what you notice. That's all.

Simple, right?

Six of us are guided to the labyrinth. It's my turn to step in. I set my intention: be open. I have no idea what to expect, but I need the truth revealed. I want the magic. Being open is what I muster.

My first steps wind around curves and expanses. I feel uneasy. I'm withholding my emotions. I don't want them exposed to those walking alongside me. I'm overwhelmed, hands fidgeting, shoulders hunched. I don't yet understand how to interpret the journey—how to "notice what I notice."

I notice subtleties: trees; slight, warm breeze; shadows cast; yellow leaves fallen on grey stones, held in place by deep, red bricks.

I notice an off-kilter brick. Its displacement creates a wobble in the labyrinth's parallel lines.

I notice a spillage of pebbles over the side of perfectly placed bricks.

As I walk around, up, down, along straight paths, around tight corners, flowing aisles, I notice correlations to my stories which I have attached to. Reaching inside, and finding that difficult, my hesitations return. The aisles mimic my self-limitations.

"Don't step over a line. You may return to the beginning and have to start over."

Oh, Universe, please don't make me start over. I've already come so far!

A friend pauses to feel, and we all pause. We experience personal emotions through her vulnerability. She resumes her walk, and we all continue. It becomes easier to focus on my internal experience after witnessing her emotions, easier to delve into the soul of the labyrinth. Our individual experience is interwoven alongside one another in this lifeline; this lifetime.

I'm opening.

Walking along the prescribed path, I find myself facing people, locking eyes, sometimes holding my arms tightly against my body. Sometimes reaching out to someone walking toward me. Sometimes I want to extend. Other times I need to withhold. I am witnessing my interpretations of the moment. Every turn exposes an emotion, an open "yes," a resistant "no."

Approaching that familiar spill of rocks, I notice my life. If the labyrinth were my timeline, this spill represents my "now." Life has spilled, and still I walk. The spill will always be there. I can get sucked in, stuck, dwell on it. Or I can step over the spill and move on. Wisely, I continue my journey.

Truths are being revealed.

The labyrinth mirrors my soul.

Reaching center, I sit. Witnessing the canopy of trees, inhaling forest scents, and watching the outlying circles, epiphanies begin to occur.

I'm open.

As I watch outliers continue their walk, I view myself through my perception of their journeys. I notice *how* I notice this place: these people, myself, and my soul.

I notice I'm bored. It's lonely in the center. I feel an urge to leave. My controlling mind wants to stay until the labyrinth clears. Revelations tell me *I'm holding myself in this place, this bitterness, anger, resentment, sadness.*

I notice.

Get up. Get out. Stop holding yourself here.

I stand and begin my journey out.

As I reach the first curve, the words *just grieve* hit me as I inhale. I feel elation.

I had been repeating a lie: *I don't know how to grieve anymore.*

Now, a great knowing comes. *Grief doesn't need to be sad. Grief simply needs to be noticed.*

As I continue walking through my timeline, I begin spelling the names for whom I grieve in congruence with my footsteps. T-I-E-R-Z-A-H; M-O-M-M-E-R. They walk alongside me with every step; they always have. This *is* my grief. The grief needs to be recognized, accepted and noticed. *But it isn't necessarily painful.*

The labyrinth clears. Only my bestie and I remain walking the pathways out. She turns a bend, and we are facing one another. I don't want to be contacted. Not yet. Not while I process this new grief. I pause so we won't meet so soon, again trying to control my space. As I slow my pace, she quickens hers.

Whatever happens is intentional. The happenings are here to reveal something that we need to notice.

I relinquish control, surrender to the process, and continue to walk toward her. As we near each other, her path turns as mine continues, guiding us in opposite directions and granting the space I had requested.

I feel enraptured!

She finds her way to the exit.

I'm alone, at last.

Everything is provided in due time.

Alone, continuing my walk, I find myself bored and lonely once more. I decide after this next turn I'll leave the labyrinth, simply step over the lines, walk out, go. I've been shown what I need. It's time to leave.

At that next bend, I find myself at the exit of the labyrinth.

Universal perfection.

The labyrinth revealed my blocks and my truths.

Since the retreat, I have been inspired to build my own labyrinth. Wherever I can assist in humanity's soul exposure, I'm all in! Both feet, walking.

Similar to the friend whose vulnerability assisted in my self-exposure, our individual participation assists in the growth of all humanity.

What inspires you?

Take action! We need you.

How I Learned The LGBTQ Community
Can Keep Its Spirituality
By Matthew Steadman

It was 4:30 AM on August 6th, 2016, and I was standing in front of the mirror in my bathroom. My wife and son were both asleep in the next rooms. I finally said the two words I had tried to ignore, suppress, pray away, and make "not me."

"I'm gay."

That night, I sat my wife down and read her a letter explaining everything. What I thought was going to me being thrown out ended in us hugging and her explaining she wanted me in our son's life, supported me and wanted the absolute best.

From mid-2011 to that early morning, I had been on a downward spiral into depression, anxiety, and self-hatred I wouldn't wish on anyone. Every day was grueling from the time I woke up until I went to bed. The peak, on September 6, 2013, was when I attempted suicide.

Through the worst of the times, I had always clung to my faith. Although I have a firm foundation in my beliefs and, being a pastor's son and grandson, I've always found other religions to be intriguing and inspiring. By studying all the world's main religions, it lets me see the beauty in people. In this same regard, I hadn't realized that coming out of the closet would change my faith and spirituality, too.

I am blessed enough to live in Dallas, Texas. Coincidentally, it is home to the largest LGBTQ-friendly Christian church in the world, The Cathedral of Hope. I had the opportunity to visit and hear the words of Reverend Dr. Neil G. Cazares-Thomas. His love, respect, and inclusion worked in symphony that Sunday morning, in conjunction with his biblical knowledge and passionate tone, and it sparked something in me.

As I looked around and saw same-sex couples at church, arms around one another or holding hands, I realized it was something I never knew existed. In this setting, it wasn't anything out of the ordinary. I looked up at the vaulted ceilings and a thought struck me, "*This* is how it's supposed to be." I realized that the exclusive tone Christian churches sometimes proclaim through sermons and conversations over so many years had driven away thousands of people.

A shift is taking place within the LGBTQ community, and people are reclaiming their faith. For years, there has been a frustration, irritation, negative, and pessimistic view of any religion. It stems from the feelings of being unwelcome and rejected. We are rejecting that exclusive tone.

Even for young LGBTQ individuals, it is a time of transition where having a solid foundation and ability to ground yourself is vital. However, whenever the time comes and someone re-finds their spirituality or faith, the effects are powerful.

On Valentine's Day 2018, I hit my rock bottom. I realized that I was miserable in every area of my life—from a physically and emotionally abusive relationship, to a job I had thrown my whole self into that ended up being a scam. However, as time went on, I've realized that every single instance in my life and others' truly do happen for a reason.

I knew that cloudy February 14th that something had to change, or I wouldn't make it to 2019. A mere six months later, I had saved up and hidden enough money to move. After another "episode" by my then-boyfriend, I let him know I was moving. In only six days I moved from the Dallas-Ft. Worth suburb of Lewisville to the middle of North Dallas. And in the next five months, I accomplished more things than I ever thought possible, met people I know were meant to be in my life, and was propelled into positions and opportunities I knew could happen over years, but not in mere months. I learned anything is possible!

One day, I felt things lift. My usual had become me worrying, obsessing on ruminating thoughts, and working myself into a panic attack at least once a day. Slowly, I noticed things were changing. Without the use of any medication, one day I realized I was finally in a place where I felt comfortable. The depression, the anxiety, the PTSD symptoms that had popped up, all of them were under control. I was starting to feel like myself for the first time.

I realized I had learned the most important aspect of the whole journey, and that was reclaiming the power of my mind. It wasn't until I had embraced my faith and spirituality that things truly began to change.

My practice included meditation, affirmations, gratitude journals, prayer, and church.

Once you accept yourself, who you love, and how you fill up your spiritual tank, it changes your perception. There's a peace in knowing that you are good with the one person who matters the most—yourself.

In the peace of accepting yourself, rejuvenation of reclaiming your spirituality, and finding solace in the moments of re-finding your spirit, there can be a shift. It's not about what people think. In fact, you'll suddenly realize they don't matter. You're at peace, and once you find that cornerstone, it allows healing to begin in all areas of your life. You can cope with situations, and even in the worst scenarios, you realize you can take a step back and look at the situation objectively and find a solution with a clear head and no panic.

Don't be timid or feel you need to continue hiding. There is a sense of change in the air, and things are changing for the better, rapidly. Although, for decades we've been pushed aside and told that side of us was "off limits," or that we were "distorting" and "twisting" things. On the contrary, I know that every person needs that aspect in their life in some shape or form, whether that be God or the vast wonderful power of the universe that helps guide you. In the end, it's the knowledge that the grace that comes from a healthy spiritual life is just as important to LGBTQ individuals as anyone else.

I learned in reclaiming my faith and spirituality it's one of the most beautiful moments to happen in your life, and it spurs on deep healing of the mind, body, spirit, and soul. For any LBGTQ individual who thinks they have to give this aspect of themselves up when they step out of the closet, let me be the first to tell you—you don't!

Now, it's your turn. Reclaim you. Reclaim your spirituality. Reclaim your faith. It's the most powerful thing you can do for yourself and others in the LGBTQ community.

Sitting Tall in the Saddle
By Janice Story

"Look into the eyes of a horse and let it awaken your heart"
~ Janice Story

About six years ago, I was introduced to a young army veteran, Adam Rowland, by my good friend Brandi Lyons. Rowland, as he preferred to be called, had been working with Brandi at The Horse Rhythm Foundation, an amazing organization founded by veterans, which employs horses in their therapy program. By the time I met him, Rowland had become a proficient rider and was seeking to take his horsemanship to the next level. My husband Kent and I invited him to try his hand at sorting.

Ranch sorting is a competitive sport in which two riders on horseback work together to move ten numbered cattle from one round pen into another in less than sixty seconds and in numerical order. If a cow gets through the gate out of order, you are disqualified. To excel at sorting, you must not only be a skilled rider—you must have a great horse as well! It is incredibly tough, and we keep a herd of cattle at our ranch all winter to practice and perfect our skills.

Rowland took to sorting from the first time Brandi brought him out to the ranch, and he soon started coming for lessons with Kent a few times a week. Over time, his understanding and skill continued to grow, and in February of 2014, we took him to his first competition.

Now, you may be wondering where this story is going and what's so inspiring about it, so let me fill in a few details that I left out. Rowland was on his second deployment in Iraq, stationed about thirty-five miles northeast of Baghdad, when he suffered a blunt force trauma to his head that resulted in a brain injury and loss of vision in his right eye. He was transported to a military hospital in Iraq, where he would spend about thirty days before being sent home. It appeared his recovery was going quite well, so the army placed him back on light duty. Rowland worked extremely hard to learn how to function with the use of only one eye; however, shortly after returning to full duty, he started experiencing severe stabbing pains in his head. When he returned to the doctor, he was given ibuprofen and sent home, but his condition continued to worsen and eventually took the sight from his left eye as well, leaving Adam Rowland completely blind.

The first time he rode at our ranch, Brandi and Kent put a bell on one of the cows so Rowland could hear where it was, but that didn't work as well as they had hoped. They had to figure out a different way. Rowland started riding Shooter, my old Palomino gelding, and Kent learned how to communicate to him where the cows were. For example, if two cows were close together, Kent would call out, "Inside cow!" or "Outside cow!" Rowland learned to tell from the sound of their hooves which one he needed to sort out; he would then give Shooter the cue and push that cow out of the herd.

I will never forget that first competition Rowland and Shooter took part in. There were a lot of riders warming up in the arena, and horses were everywhere. Rowland wanted to gallop some, and Shooter always took such incredible care of him. I swear that horse knew Rowland was blind! This not the case with many of the people there—aside from me and Kent, few knew Rowland's story or who he was. When it was their turn to enter the pen for that first run, the announcer asked everyone to please be quiet so that Rowland could hear Kent's voice spotting for him. The crowd watched, awestruck by his riding and the incredible teamwork of these two men and their horses. I don't believe there was a dry eye in the arena that day!

Rowland and Shooter continued their sorting partnership, and the following year Rowland earned a well-deserved belt buckle from AZ Sorting Productions for champion beginner sorter. What an accomplishment! Ranch sorting is a tough sport when you can see what you're doing, let alone when you're riding blind and chasing cows you cannot see. One day Brandi and I decided to try sorting with our eyes closed. Brandi ended up in the back of the pen, and I got so dizzy I thought I was going to pass out. Neither one of us was able to get those cows where we wanted them to go.

Kent and I have taken Rowland on many trail rides, and we have felt so honored to witness his strength, courage, and willingness to trust. He will ride out into a field and ask the horse to run at full gallop, trusting both us and the horse to stop him before he comes to a row of trees. Here is a man that has simply refused to let his trauma stop him from living a full life. It has not been an easy ride, and there have been struggles, but Rowland continues to rise and inspire others, and overcome all obstacles that have been placed in front of him. It is no doubt the same fearlessness he displayed while serving our country, so that the rest of us can continue to live in freedom.

Rowland's dream is to own a ranch someday where he can train horses and help other veterans learn to enjoy and heal their lives. I have no doubts that he will indeed be successful in fulfilling his purpose and mission. Thank you, Rowland, for being such an inspiration to us all. And thank you for confirming to me, yet again, that the work these majestic animals and I do together is healing hearts and lives, one person at a time.

Silence Is Golden
By Cathy Stuart

In 1992, I was living in Michigan, working as the executive for a Realtor® association, and had just completed a Total Quality Management class at the community college. The last class assignment was to write a personal/business marketing statement, outlining where you wanted to be in three years. My marketing statement had the following criteria: a membership-based association, a warmer state, more money than my current salary, and time for family. I also added quiet bubble baths for me.

In less than two months, I was offered an opportunity in Arizona to interview for the executive director position with a Realtor® association. The current executive director was leaving to pursue her dreams and thought of me for her position. I was offered and accepted the position. I then remembered the marketing statement and realized my request had been granted.

I had been communicating with angels since the age of seven, so it was no surprise to me that they would give me a message about my new position. Messages from my angels would come in the way of a gut feeling or a knowing. I was getting ready to move when my angels told me that this position would be for only 18 months. I, of course, inquired, "What happens after that?" The response was, "It will be okay. We will guide you on your path." I shared this message with my husband. He said that he trusted my intuition and he supported my taking the job.

We moved to Arizona and—almost 18 months to the day—the association and I agreed to part ways. It had been a cloudy day. As I got closer to home, the sun came out, and a song came on the radio: I Can See Clearly Now, by Johnny Nash. I knew everything would be just fine.

After I left the association, I had two offers to interview at similar jobs. My intuition told me to decline. I remember being told, "We will guide you on your path." I did not know or understand what this new path would look like, but I knew that it would be revealed to me in a short timeframe. I just needed to trust. The following week, I received two angel books: one from my mother, *The Angels Within Us* by John Randolph

Price, and one from my friend Michelle, *Ask Your Angels* by Alma Daniels. My sister sent me a newspaper article about an angel store in Detroit. Last, I saw a PBS show with Patty Duke about Tara's Angel Store in San Luis Obispo, California. Just like trusting that I was to move to Arizona, I trusted that I was to open an angel store. My friend Michelle, my family and my angels were all in agreement.

My next request for guidance was, "Where do I put this angel store?" While on 5th Avenue in Scottsdale, I happened across Kiva Courtyard. I recognized this courtyard. Eighteen months prior, on the morning of my interview with the realtor association, I stopped in Kiva Courtyard to sit by the fountains to calm myself before my interview. It was such a peaceful setting, so it was no surprise at all that I had been led back to this courtyard. I made an appointment with the landlord. He had one space available. I looked at the space and said yes. The day I was to sign a two-year lease, I sat across the table from him and said I could not sign it, as my intuition told me that there was a better space available. The landlord told me that the night before a tenant had given notice, but that space was larger and pricier. I looked at the space and that was where, on October 1, 1994, Angel Wings opened its doors.

In 1998, the owners of Mishka Productions, a company that hosted conferences representing some of the biggest names in the spiritual community, came into Angel Wings. They were interested in putting flyers in the window regarding a class that Doreen Virtue, a revered Angel Intuitive, was offering. They wanted to know if I would be interested in bringing Angel Wings items to the class via a booth in the back of the room. I jumped at the chance. Thereafter, whenever Doreen was in town, Angel Wings was present. One day, Doreen needed an extra person to help out in the class. She asked if I would come and sit with a person in the audience and share a reading. I never intended to become a part of her class as I was quiet about my ability to communicate with the angelic realm. My initial answer was no, but Doreen was persistent.

Later, at one of Doreen's events, I was approached by Elsa Ramon of Channel 10 who was doing a story about Doreen. Elsa wanted to include in this story one of Doreen's students doing a reading on her. Elsa shared with me that she had been told she needed to see me for this reading. I recorded my reading with Elsa for her story, and it aired on Super Bowl

Sunday in 1999 for 4 minutes 44 seconds. In the angel world, 444 represents "angels present." This story launched my Angel Reading and Mediumship career.

They say that silence is golden. My message to you is to stay present to your dreams. Create a vision board or road map similar to what I did in my marketing statement. It would have changed the entire direction of my path had I told my husband I could not take the risk of losing a job after only 18 months. In choosing to follow my intuitive gut instinct, by becoming still and asking for the guidance of my angels, more wonderful opportunities presented themselves than I ever could have imagined. My angels responded with a booming voice—all I had to do was listen. Silence is, indeed, golden.

Rising Phoenix: From Toxic Relationships to Manifesting True Love and Happiness
By Lisa Thompson, PhD

To say our relationship was complicated is an understatement. I was thirty years old when it happened. In the pit of my stomach, I knew I was in over my head and near the bottom of the barrel. The man, who would in a couple of years become my husband and the father of my first-born child, had pinned me to the floor and threatened to break my arm as he held it behind my back, twisting it to the point before the break. His anger was intense. Fear paralyzed me.

The thought running through my mind was, "How could I be here? Why is this happening to me?" The relationship had worn me down. I didn't know how to respond to being pinned on the ground except to try to get out of it. Fortunately, he let me go before my arm broke. I don't even remember what caused the argument. What I remember is his face changing in front of me. It turned bright red and he looked demonic, possessed. You would think it would have been my wake-up call to end the relationship. It wasn't. This was the beginning of my nightmare.

I woke up the next morning after the "incident" with my mind racing. This was my first relationship where my partner had been physically abusive with me. I was used to other types of abuse in my relationships, mostly emotional, which I wasn't aware of at the time I was in them. Here I was, an intelligent woman with a PhD, in a relationship with someone that clearly had anger issues. I thought about how I had gotten there. Why did I deserve this kind of treatment? I thought I was above this type of behavior. It happened to other women, not me. I even secretly judged those abused women. How could they not leave their partners who were so cruel to them?

Over the next few years, the abuse continued with cycles of him asking for forgiveness and trying to redeem himself. There were times I thought I had caused his anger and deserved the abuse. Mostly, I was in a state of shock. I didn't know what to do or how to get out of it. After nearly five years in this relationship, I had given him an ultimatum about how he was treating me. Only a few months later, he crossed the line again. Now was my moment to fight for my seven-month-old baby girl and me. I had to leave him for her sake. I didn't want her growing up thinking this is how a man treats a woman. If I couldn't do it for myself, then I had to do it for her.

With the help of friends and family, I finally left the abusive relationship. It would be another eight years with my second ex-husband before I was able to turn myself around. We met before I had even begun to heal from the first marriage, and we found out I was pregnant only five months into our relationship.

The relationship with my second husband was rocky. He wasn't abusive like my first ex, but I felt controlled, and I was not allowed to be authentic. When I decided to leave my second marriage, I knew I needed to change what I was doing. I was forty-two years old with two ex-husbands and a single mom of two children with two different dads. I had to heal myself if I was going to be able to have a healthy love relationship. I wanted to be able to share my life with a partner who would reciprocate my love, and experience the joys of life to the maximum. It was time to be happy and fulfilled. It was time to be the role model of love and healthy relationships for my children.

Learning to Love Myself

To be able to attract and marry the love of my life, I had to fall in love with myself. I had to acknowledge I didn't have self-love in the first place. I had to come to terms with my familial relationships and the stories that went along with them. I had to come to terms with three decades of unhealthy relationships with boyfriends and 12 years of toxic marriages. I had to stop making all of those relationships wrong. I was in them to learn valuable lessons in love and self-worth.

My focus turned to healing myself. I got back in touch with my spiritual side, using tools and skills I had learned over the years from my spiritual teachings to dig deep to find the wounds that were keeping me from attracting true love. I had to rediscover who I was. I had to become whole and healthy. It took almost a year for me to get to a place where I could say that I loved myself. My life improved. I was having fun with friends, traveling again, making money, and calling my own shots. I was rising like the Phoenix from the ashes, owning my power. I was free. Once I embraced my self-love and worthiness, I met the love of my life.

Four years later, I am still doing the work to go even deeper, but now it is from a place of wholeness and observation, rather than judgment and victimhood. My love relationship is like none other than I have ever experienced. It's filled with friendship, respect, trust, compassion, and love. We resonate together on the highest frequency. We are an inspiration to our friends and family members. We continue to cultivate the soul love and happiness we share daily. Last year, we committed our lives to each other in a wedding ceremony in Thailand—a dream come true.

My Healing Journey
By Chantalle Ullett

It all started subconsciously at my birth. One has to go through a period of tragedies, trauma, and dysfunctional events before understanding that not everyone goes through it. At times, growing up wasn't easy or pleasant. I was physically, mentally, and sexually abused by a variety of people who were part of my life in my youth. It took many years to understand the different layers of guilt, shame, hatred, and rage it created, including the negativity, as well as many years of therapy, forgiveness and inner growth to realize it was part of my path to becoming the person I am today.

Part of my healing journey included going back to school to become a Licensed Massage Therapist. Talk about challenges. I was 37 years old, and married to a wonderful husband with two beautiful young girls. In that decision alone, I became consciously aware of my healing journey.

As a Licensed Massage Therapist, I was required to take continuing education classes. I've taken many different classes over the years. However, the most impactful ones that have helped transform me on this journey were *The Bodytalk System*, which seeks to address the "whole person," be it emotional, physical or an environmental body-mind-spirit connection, and a *Linking Awareness* course. *Linking Awareness* is done through the heart connection of one sentient being to another where you experience deep communication and healing. Working with *Linking Awareness* and the people who come to participate in the different journeys, have proven to be where most of my transformational healings have happened. I have had the opportunity to travel to different parts of the world making connections with various sentient beings.

In South Africa, it was with elephants, white lions, horses, and Adam's Calendar, a series of circular monolithic stones resembling Stonehenge located near the town of Kaapsche Hoop. In British Columbia, it was with horses, cats, and dogs. In Hawaii—horses, birds, and the land. The most significant healing shift for me happened when I traveled to Indonesia in 2017.

Loesje, the Linking Awareness founder, invited me to participate in this particular journey where we would be in Indonesia for a month. I humbly accepted. We traveled to Bogor, Sumatra, and Borneo. While in Bogor, we connected with various people and amazing animals from around the world. My favorite was an otter. Then, it was off to Sumatra, where we had deep, meaningful encounters with the Sumatran elephants at Way Kambas National Park. Finally, we spent six days on a Klotok boat in the South Kalimantan waters in Borneo and connected with the orangutans at Camp Leaky.

While we were in Sumatra on our second to last day, sitting in presence with the Sumatran elephants, Desty, a seven-month-old male elephant approached me at the end of the day. Everyone was enjoying free time walking around and interacting with the young elephant. As I walked up with some fellow participants, Desty ran up to us and bumped into me. At first, I didn't think much of it. The second time he did, my inner voice spoke up and told me Desty wanted me to massage him. I thought that this was physically impossible. How was I supposed to massage a seven-month-old elephant?

It took a few moments to quiet and center myself to make it possible to work holographically with the animals. Desty approached bumping me a third time. Loesje, the organization's founder, spoke up confirming my realization. With some guidance from Loesje, Desty, myself and a surrogate for Desty energetically worked together releasing the discomfort, pain, and trauma Desty had sustained to his right hip during his birth. As we worked, releasing his pain, time became nonexistent. We became one. What I felt was astounding.

Not only could I feel the restriction in his hip, but I could also feel the entrapment, bondage, pain, and restraint the herd and I shared. Suddenly, a sense of calm washed over us, followed by a gut-wrenching scream coming out of me, freeing us both to find our inner voices. After the session was over, both Desty and his sister, April, thanked the surrogate and me. April swirled her trunk toward my throat and Desty wrapped his trunk around my hand. What I hadn't realized until discussing the event later that evening with Loesje was, as April swirled her trunk towards my neck, she removed the energetic remnants of the umbilical cord which was wrapped around my neck at birth. It wasn't until this specific moment occurred that I truly understood that I wasn't speaking my truth or being true to myself. Having had this particular encounter with these majestic mammals, removing the invisible cord enabled me to grow bolder, stronger, more courageous, and even more tenacious than ever before, allowing me to let go and shed many fears—fears of standing tall, and being heard and seen for the person I am.

We all have choices to make in life. Having chosen this singular moment, a metamorphic healing transpired. I am forever humbly grateful for everyone involved during this specific time.

Sixty Dollars In Change
By Monet Vincent

One of the most selfish decisions of my life turned out to be my greatest journey. I was twenty-three and addicted. I had been using drugs since age twelve. One night, I ran into an old friend, and we began spending a lot of time together. Soon I was falling in love with him. As our relationship grew, we decided we wanted to be together. He had one condition: "If you want to be with me, you can't be using drugs anymore."

We decided to leave everyone and everything behind. Gathering up all the money we could find, we bought two Greyhound tickets to Texas. With two bus tickets, the clothes on our backs and sixty dollars in change, we began our journey to a new life. We said to each other, "If we can do this, nothing can stop us."

Within moments of arriving in Fort Worth, it started to sink in. We had nothing and nowhere to go. What were we going to do? Where could we go? It was cold. Why didn't we bring coats? Finding our way to a local bar, we ordered a pitcher of beer and tried to figure things out.

Having grown up in a Christian family, I knew we needed to find a church. We found an address and started the long walk across town. We walked for miles. When we reached our destination, there was no church, no people and no help. Our feet and legs were burning, and it was getting dark. We had to move on. We headed back to the bus station where we began. Pretending to wait for a bus, we grabbed a couple cups of chicken broth from the vending machine and waited until morning.

The next day, we walked around the city looking for shelter. We came across a historic church. We knocked on every door; not one was open. No one came. Frustrated, we found a corner in the courtyard. It was a perfect hiding spot to spend the night.

Cuddling up, we attempted to get some sleep. Shivering, my partner covered me with his flannel. By morning, a wedding ceremony had begun. We planned our escape. Waiting for the right moment, we quickly strolled out without being noticed.

We couldn't do this anymore. We needed to find a real shelter.

We discovered one not far from us. Excited and hopeful, we lined up and waited for check-in time. Checking in, they told us we would be in separate quarters but could meet up for breakfast at 7 a.m. We would be allowed to stay three days, but on the fourth day, there would be a six dollar charge.

The sleeping area was vulnerable, cold, with concrete floors and shared bathrooms. The iron bunk beds were uncomfortable. I felt like I was in jail.

The next morning, we met in line for breakfast. We had only three days, and we needed to find jobs. We had nothing but pocket change, and it was dwindling down. We set out on our search.

A homeless man approached us, asking for change. We told him, "Sorry man, we're in the same boat as you."

"Well ya'll don't look like it," looking at us up and down.

"Don't judge a book by its cover," we responded. We turned and walked away.

The homeless man stopped in the middle of the street and hollered back at us. "If that's the case, there is a place you can go."

We turned, staring and asked, "Where?"

"There is a place in Arlington," he continued. They'll put you up, feed you, and help you get jobs. It's only an eight dollar bus ticket west of here."

"Why aren't you there?" we asked.

"I blew it. Three strikes and you're out. You have to follow their rules; no drinking or drugs allowed," he said.

We thanked him and then headed to the bus station. We had exactly sixteen dollars in change left, just enough for two bus tickets.

When we arrived in Arlington, there was a yellow cab outside of the station. We described the place we were looking for, but the driver had no idea where it was. We walked about a half mile when a red Ford truck pulled over.

"Need a ride?"

"Yes, we are looking for this place that will help us." We repeated what the homeless man told us.

"I know exactly where you're talking about. I will take you there. My name is Wilford."

With excitement, we hopped in. "Oh thank you!"

For the first time, I felt we were going to make it. Wilford took us to the Arlington Life Shelter. When we got there, a notice was on the door: *Not taking new residents until Monday after 3:00 pm.* No problem, one more day outside won't hurt. We will wait here on the porch until morning. After a short time, Wilford showed back up to check on us.

"Couldn't you get in?"

"Tomorrow we can. We will sleep here on the porch."

"You can come with me for the night, get some rest and have some dinner. I will bring you back in time for check-in." What a blessing he was.

We checked-in the next afternoon. The shelter was a good place. We were there for about two months. We received counseling on a personal and professional level. We were able to find jobs and saved up enough money to move into a weekly hotel. Eventually, we were able to get an apartment, a home and much more.

That was eighteen years ago. We have built a wonderful life, we have a beautiful daughter, and I have found my purpose in life. Despite the heartache and struggle, the life lessons and strength gained still drives me today.

Today, I teach others how to achieve their greatest potential and renew their strengths. I connect with people in their darkest times and help them see that there is hope and they are worthy. From the depths of despair, we persevered. Today we get to give back as we were given.

A Lesson Or A Test?
By Allison Voth

No one can predict what shall come,
the start, beginning, or end.

Is it a lesson or a test?
Difficult times & health paused in a breath.

It hurts in my chest,
A deep breath is a test,
Are they going to starve me to death?
No food, no water, just rest.

I learn to hold in my mind's eye,
my goals & positive thoughts.
Did I learn it or choose it?
*It **is** a choice to think this or that.*

Doing the best I can,
life doesn't always go to plan
The Universe provides what is
meant for my highest good.

This is meant to be,
So I can be a better version of me
I'm saving my strength for recovery.
I see myself doing the things that I love after this,
with the people I love.

I learned to let go of the little things.
Learned to be okay with the present moment,
no matter how hard it is or may seem.

Shift perspective & I see a rainbow
Shift perspective & I see black
Shift perspective & I feel good
Shift perspective & I feel low

Shift to a higher place & stay in the sunshine,
It's warmer there.

Sitting alone in my office, wondering how I would get through the day, I could feel the stress building in my body with its dense vibration, stealing my attention. My thoughts were telling me this is a bad day. I was managing the heavy workload of two positions single-handedly as a civilian with the Royal Canadian Mounted Police. During a challenging phone call with an external client, I could feel pain growing in my left shoulder blade. It felt like a muscle cramp, so I stood up to stretch it out. Within minutes the pain increased sharply with every breath. My intuition signaled something isn't right, indeed.

Fortunately, the hospital was across the street, so I walked over there doubled over in pain and truly wondered if I would even make it to the doors. My old friend returned to make a most unwelcome visit with me—anxiety. After a variety of tests, the nurse advised I am experiencing a "spontaneous pneumothorax" in the left lung. "A what?" I replied, stunned and somewhat curious. The nurse seemed pleased with the news, like any investigator when they realize they've cracked the case. The conundrum was that I presented no risk factors. Little blisters on the lung lining popped, causing it to rupture. Every inhale fills up the chest cavity, deflating your lung like a saggy old party balloon. Rest was the Rx. Now that the suspect was identified, the case was closed, and I could go home and restore my equilibrium.

Like a thief in the night, there was no warning until it was upon me strangling every breath with the hands of pain, verily, robbing me of my life-force energy. Every breath was a test. The emergency doctor advised, "It's worse than the last one, we must insert a Heimlich valve to drain the air building in your chest cavity." Frozen in my body, yet aware, I went into a trance-like state from the anesthetic ketamine. The days blended with heaviness from the pain-killing substances' deep slumber. After five days, it was removed, and I felt overjoyed to simply take a bubble bath without the accessory. The offender was on my watch list, and I was keeping notes.

If the third time is the charm, it certainly disarmed me. Like a prolific offender, it came back with its signature move—the knock-out punch just when you're getting up from the last attack. "We need to perform emergency surgery to stop the threat!" the doctor advised. At a different hospital, the thoracic surgeon specialist was to perform the reconnaissance mission with scope technology. Two days later, a bed opened up for my transfer during a rare snowstorm in Vancouver, Canada. The ambulance struggled on the roads, and my beloved father and my best friend rushed to blanket me with their comfort.

The surgeon walked in an introduced himself, "Hi, I'm Dr. Bond, Dr. James Bond," and offered a handshake, sans dry martini. I laughed and was pleased to meet the agent, finally! I was bumped three days in a row, starving each day for potential surgery, unable to shower due to the quarantine from the hospital transfer and barely able to walk more than a few meters without being dizzy from the plethora of drugs coursing through my body. So, I picked up a pen and paper and started journaling my experience. I wrote the poem noted above. I made a list of the things I wanted to do when I was out of the hospital, and took pleasure in my imagination, reliving them with fervor. Mundane moments were transformed into rare precious pearls through my new lens of gratitude, and I clutched them to my chest like priceless treasure.

After surgery, I would mentally assess every physical sensation in my body and analyze it in an attempt to predict its return. You see, the alias of disease is fear. Fear is the creeper in the shadows, lurking, threatening to suffocate you with its cloak and silence your heart. I transmuted the fear into a positive challenge activity with the British Columbia Lung Association's stair climb event, climbing 48 flights of stairs. Nine years later, I have raised thousands for research programs and conquered that fear.

Looking down the dark alley of that winter, I see the anxiety, fear, and grief shadowed by the light from my spirit. The blackness was my greatest teacher. It was a lesson, and I passed the test. Step by step, I moved into my future, colored with a fresh perspective and filled with the scent of inspiration, like an exquisite rose. Inspiration and expiration, that's what breath is. *Is it a lesson or a test?* It's both. Be *inspired* or expire. It's that simple.

Water Is In The DNA
By Nanette Waller-Stafford

Have you ever closed your eyes, took a deep breath, and plunged into the cold deep waters of the unknown? Just swallowed your fear and jumped? We are all told to follow our gut instincts to our goals. Is it truly that easy? Yes!

I was living in Pawhuska, Oklahoma, working for the Osage Nation as Director of Social Service on an interagency position between my federal employer and the tribe. My two-year interagency term was coming to a close, and I was searching for a new position. As luck would have it, a friend called and asked if I would be interested in moving to South Dakota. It was the position she currently held that would be open, as she had been selected to be the Supervisor of Mental Health at the Rosebud Sioux Indian Health Service Clinic. She recruited me to apply to be her replacement. Getting to work on filling out the numerous pages of a government application and submitting it by the deadline was not difficult. But waiting to hear if I made the certification list for an interview caused some anxiety. Once interviewed, the wait to hear if I was selected was extremely nerve-racking. And that was the easy part! Now, all I had to do was pack up my belongings, rearrange my life, and moved to a state I'd never visited and work in a job I'd never done. I did it all without any hesitation. I seized that opportunity to start a new career as a therapist at the Indian Health Service Clinic in Fort Thompson, South Dakota on the reservation serving the Crow Creek Sioux tribal members with enthusiasm and excitement.

It was early in January of 2000 when I made my journey to South Dakota. On the day I was driving to my new life in Fort Thompson, it was a below zero cold day and had recently snowed a foot. Looking back, I suppose it would be unusual if there weren't any snow on the ground or if the temperature had been above freezing in January; May perhaps, but not January. The start of the day was breathtaking as the sunlight was dancing on the freshly fallen snow, making it look as if silver sparkle had been sprinkled all along the landscape. My anticipation of the day was as shiny as the sprinkles of sparkle.

I turned off the interstate into Chamberlain, the closest town to where I would be living. As I drove through town, I was pleasantly surprised to find it was larger than I thought it would be, and had all the amenities I would need: food, gas, and entertainment. So far, so good!

As I drove on, I located the state road that would take me to Fort Thompson by way of the long hill out of town. The long hill would take me to my new place of employment and new adventures. Like the beginning of a rollercoaster ride, you go up and up, and the flutter of anxiety creeps in and then hangs on for dear life. The further up the hill I went, and the further the outskirts of town became, the tighter the anxiety clung to me. Slowly, the town totally faded behind me, and I was left in the silence of the road, as I continued to travel upward. Silence, until the loud voice of fear broke into my thoughts and amped up my anxiety to levels that had my heart racing and my head throbbing, reminding me the rollercoaster ride had not yet ended. The words of fear heightened the knowledge that I didn't know anyone in the town I had just left, and I certainly didn't know anyone on the reservation where I would live. Now the voice became louder, insistent and questioning: "What possessed you to pack up and move hundreds of miles away from family and friends? Why work in an area where the only person you know in the entire state is a three-hour drive away? What makes you think you will be a good therapist? What were you thinking?" Still driving onward, the voice of doubt was now shouting; the anxiety became more intense. The doubt and the intense, anxiety-driven rollercoaster continued chugging up that long hill.

Then, I topped the hill.

The Missouri River winded along its banks with the sun glistening off its water. I pulled over to the shoulder of the road. I watched the water moving onward, quietly and calmly to new destinations. I breathed. On my right was a turkey, strutting to meet up with the rest of the flock. On the left was a pair of mule deer, stopping long enough to ensure I wasn't a threat before continuing slowly on their way. I relaxed as I watched them disappear into the trees. An eagle flew overhead. He slowly circled over the Missouri River: a majestic bird in flight, easing my anxiety. I marveled at the sight as the eagle rose far above me, disappearing into the sky. I gave thanks for the eagle, delivering my prayer of gratitude to the heavens.

Peace overcame me, and the voice of doubt was quieted. I was reminded of the family stories of my ancestor's travels. I realized this journey into new territory along the Missouri River was my fate. The path had been laid generations ago by my great-great-great-grandfather, John Colter, who had traveled on this river while a member of the Lewis and Clark expedition. How fitting that the plunge I made into the cold deep waters of the unknown brought me back to my roots that are tied to the Missouri River and the ancestor I feel the closest to whenever I am near the Missouri.

Rollercoaster ride done. The voice of doubt: quiet. Anxiety: gone. I sighed, relieved.

In this place and in this time, I *am* where I am supposed to be.

The Earth Pot
By Patricia Walls

Many years ago, the spirit that talks to me told me that they wanted me to gather pieces of the earth and put them into one pot and focus prayers of healing on it.

It seemed like an immense undertaking. How in the world was I going to gather pieces of the earth from my little spot in Texas? This was long before Facebook, but luckily it was during the time of the Internet. At the time, I was immersed in the world of Reiki and, as luck would have it, or as spirit would direct, I had contacts all over the world. So, I sent out a request for those contacts to send me a bit of earth from their place in the world. I was amazed at the number of people who responded. As the earth came in, I put a teaspoon of it in the pot and put the rest in a basket. Each article was labeled as to where it came from.

When Facebook became popular, I made even more contacts and gathered even more earth. It was amazing and humbling how many people participated in this gift to the earth.

One day, I received a call from a woman who wanted help for anxiety attacks. In conversation, I learned that she made pottery from scratch, even collecting the clay from local riverbeds. Her pottery was beautiful and filled with love and healing. When I told her of my task, she gifted me a pot that she said she was directed to make many years ago and didn't know why. Her vision in making the pot was a bird shaman holding a bolt of lightning. When we started to work together, she understood. I have always worked with shamanic teachings as well as lightning energy. I was so grateful that the earth would reside in such a love-filled home.

At the time, I worked at a college, and the professors would bring earth from their travels. One beautiful professor thought of me on her journey to Italy. She brought this envelope to me and said, "Baby, there I was on my hands and knees in the Colosseum in Rome trying to scoop some earth from the cracks in the cement. My husband asked if I had gone crazy! There wasn't much dirt there." I could envision this 70-year-old grandma in her high-dollar suit on her hands and knees gathering earth for the pot with diamond-encrusted fingers. I was in love with her for that act of kindness and compassion.

As clients would come for sessions, I found that some of them were following their intuition and heart and coming for the connection that the earth afforded them. One young woman told me that she was East Indian by blood but born and raised in Australia. Her parents moved her to Texas in her teens, and she had never gone back to Australia or to the land of her DNA. I was blessed to have earth from both places and offered to give her some. As I opened the packages for her, she smelled each one, and the look on her face was priceless. We spent hours on the floor opening each package to experience the essence of the earth.

Since that time, I have had the pleasure of gifting earth to many people. I receive such joy from reconnecting them to their place of birth of the place they consider home.

Sometimes "home" is a place that we have never set our feet on in this lifetime but have a strong tie to it from other lifetimes or from DNA. Sometimes, "home" is a place where one of our other selves lives and we need that connection to them through the earth.

For a time now, I have been feeling that the pot and the earth inside her were suffering. I wasn't sure what she wanted me to do other than pray for her.

Here it has been raining for four days. My yard is practically a lake. Today, as I came to my room to sit, pray and contemplate what the day has for me, I looked up at the pot and felt a need to sit with her for a while. I clearly heard that it is time to release the earth back. She wanted me to release all the earth through the water. How perfect could it be? I sat and went through the pot, silently giving thanks for the years of love, patience, connection, and prayers. I held the earth in my hand for a long time, including each rock and piece of bark that found their way inside. I thought of setting aside those stones and bark and releasing the loose earth into the water. The Mother had other instructions. She told me that everything needed to be released, cleansed.

I lovingly cradled the pot as I walked barefoot outside to the back of the property. The rain was still falling, and the water was cold on my feet.

The Mother reminded me that it's the cold that wakes you up and makes you pay attention. I emptied all the contents of the pot into the water and watched as it sank. I even opened an envelope that was sent that contained the seeds of desert willow someone had sent for the pot and released them to the water. I wonder if they will take seed somewhere along the earth or if they were too dry.

Now, the pot sits on the shelf empty waiting for new instructions. I still have the baskets with packages of earth waiting for new instructions. Shall I keep them for those who come to make the connection? Shall I put new pieces in the pot? I will wait for new instructions.

I Hear Voices
By Jamalyn Warriner

W hen I was a child, I had two imaginary friends: Bambi and DoDeDom. I have no idea where I came up with these names, but they were my constant buddies. As I got older, the voices faded away and were replaced by real friends. It wasn't until I was in my mid-thirties that I realized there was a place for both real people and the voices that so lovingly guided me through the hard times.

I don't know if this voice is God, my parents, relatives that have passed, or angels but they have always been with me. I have a non-stop, running dialogue in my head from the second I wake up until the second I go to bed. These voices have guided me through work, raising children, deaths, buying a house, dating, and even clothing choices.

My mom told me that the voices were from the devil. I told her the devil wasn't that nice. She said he was tricky and could fool me. I know right from wrong, so if I heard I should kill people, I wouldn't do that. She asked how I knew it wasn't my voice. My reply was, "I am not that nice." If I make a mistake or a bad decision, I would say to myself sarcastically, "Boy, that was a good one," or "Really? I can't believe you did that!" The voices are always encouraging and comforting. When I told my dad about the voices, he said, "That is your gut talking; listen and pay attention, your gut doesn't lie."

A thousand times, I have not listened when I should have. A thousand times more, I have listened and was so glad I did. These voices are so much a part of me that I barely recognize they are there. I have written notes to people and read it afterward and thought, "I didn't write that. I've never even had that thought." When the person receives the note, they tell me, "Your note was exactly what I needed to hear," or "After reading your note I don't feel so alone; I know you understand." On occasion, I felt like a fraud because I knew they were not my words, yet I was receiving the credit.

I am convinced the voices have saved me multiple times. I was driving home from work one afternoon, and I heard, "Change lanes." I wasn't paying attention, but I moved over a lane anyway. A few seconds later, a truck pulling a trailer of golf carts hit a bump, and one of the windshields flew off and shattered on the highway. It would've shattered on me if I had not listened. On multiple other occasions, before I left my house, I heard, "No," or "Not yet." Even if I were late, I wouldn't leave until I heard that it was okay to go. Once there was a two-seater plane that missed the runway and crashed into the highway right where I would have been if I had left earlier.

When I hear messages for others, sometimes I am hesitant to tell them, but I know I wouldn't hear a message for them if I was not supposed to let them know. Although sometimes for strangers, usually the messages I receive are for the people closest to me. I received a message at work for one of my best friends. I told the voices, "I'm not telling her that. She'll think I am crazy." "Tell her." "No." "Tell her, now." I gave in and gave her the message. She read it, burst into tears, and ran off. I was thinking, "See? I should have kept my mouth shut instead of saying something."

The message stated that when she was in high school and broke her foot, her dad knew how it happened. Her boyfriend (who her dad and brothers didn't like) dropped her off a few houses down the street. While pulling away, he accidentally ran over her foot and broke it. She told her dad she broke it coming down the stairs. Her mother passed when she was 13, and her father raised her along with help from her aunt. There was more to the message, but she read it all and came to me later that day. She said that there was no way I could have known about that because she had forgotten all about the incident. Her dad had since passed, so she called her aunt and read her the message. Her aunt said, "Yes, the Taylors told your dad. It happened in front of their house. I told him not to say anything so you wouldn't continue to date your boyfriend out of spite."

My daughter's friend lost her boyfriend to an overdose. His parents needed to know the passcode to his phone, and my daughter asked if I could help. Later that day, the number "1461" popped into my head repeatedly, almost like a mantra. Incidentally, that was the correct passcode. I'm always shocked when things like that happen. Another time, I told a co-worker, "Congratulations, that's great you haven't smoked for three weeks." You could hear the proverbial crickets. "No one—and I mean no one—knew that I smoked so I *know* I didn't tell you. How did you know?" Stammering, I said, "You must've told me. How else would

I have known?" I am still learning when to say something and when to keep things to myself.

I have no idea why I have been entrusted with this gift, but I feel blessed. As a child, I thought everyone had voices that talked to them. I am encouraged every day, and am never alone. I pray that I use this gift to the best of my ability and that I hear and interpret the messages I receive clearly in hopes that I can inspire others in the way the voices inspire me.

Shadows
By Leanne Weasner

As time goes by, the journey within is unfolding. With the mind still in silence and the present upon me, I see things in a different light. I used to think being alone was lonely, but I have discovered something extremely valuable along the way—me.

"The key to your destiny lies within; the lock is in the mind.

Courage is the gift that will unlock your greatest treasure, you."

Who are you? A simple yet complex question to answer. As we journey through this winding road called life, we are given two choices—victim or survivor. Covered in armor, a façade is created when we apply the mask. When days are dark and nights turn black, it is frightening to see the light of day when the pain within has buried your soul. Have you ever felt so broken inside that your thoughts became reality, and in return, you don't know what reality is? Have you ever danced with the demons in your head, replaying traumatic events turning into depression and anxiety? Victims of abuse—sexual, emotional, verbal, and physical. Victims of trauma—illness, loss of a loved one, tragedy, grief, infidelity, and abandonment haunt the mind when the shadows of sadness never go away.

Standing in front of a mirror, with nothing but your naked soul staring back at you, stripped of all labels, possessions, and everything you have criticized yourself for believing you are—tell me, who are you?

"The mirror tells a story, one in which the mind creates."

Standing in front of a mirror, sadness consumed my soul as I looked at the only person who had the power to change my story. Scars others had left in my soul stared back at me. When words cut deep into a soul, they have a mysterious way of being branded in the mind. When emotion is attached to the mind, scars bleed. We are more alike than different. Some hide pain, others self-inflict. Childhood traumas create the illusion and mold the setting of our environment. For me, this is where it all started—a little girl and a dream. I grew up in a small, disarranged home. My bedroom consisted of a twin bed in a corner of my parents' bedroom. Living out of a clothes basket, I can still smell the scent of my clothes, a combination of cigarette smoke and our neighbors' wood stove. As I lay my head on my pillow, I can still hear the pain of Mother's tears. As I would watch at a young age, the one thing she avoided was the mirror. She had little self-worth and no confidence. A golden heart placed in darkness; she never gave herself credit or value for the beauty she possessed. I will always remember her beauty for the love she held for my father. She always saw the best in him. Touched by an angel in the physical, my father lost his wings the day she passed.

As the pain from my childhood grew with me, and the void of being loved and cherished as every little girl dreamt of, I set out at a young age. Falling in love with a dark soul with a drug addiction would soon become a valuable lesson. His darkness consumed my soul, left completely broken and scarred, compassion for him had filled my soul.

As I ventured into my next relationship, the sadness within blossomed into a beautiful bouquet of brokenness. Blessed with a beautiful daughter, married in 2007, my dream had finally become a reality. Everything I had ever wished for, but the love I had yearned for inside was hard to attain. Standing in the shadows, I knew in my heart what I had to face.

Alone for the last five years, I hit a wall of breakdown. I was consumed with the pain others had instilled in my soul. The soul is like a puzzle. Every soul that crosses our path leaves a puzzle piece behind. It is our journey, how we fit these puzzle pieces together, that transform us into who we are as human beings. Always believe that if a puzzle piece has left sadness in your heart and scars in your soul, they have also been scarred by many damaged pieces. Kindness is the *key to strength*, for we never know what one may be facing alone. Forgiveness in your heart is the *key to light*, to all who may have hurt you. Your light shines brighter when forgiveness is given. In the end, your light is your guide to love, loving you.

doubt to *faith*

weakness to *strength*

anger to *forgiveness*

depression to *breakthrough*

broken to *beautiful*

Powerful words that changed my life. Words are only words until we love ourselves enough to implement them into power. Darkness will always shade the light of the beautiful soul you are until you have the courage to go deep within. Living through the pain and struggles I have endured in my lifetime has made me who I am today. A heart full of gratitude to the darkness I faced and to those who left scars in my soul. I am blessed to see the world in a different light. A heart full of compassion, empathy, and unconditional love for all who cross my path in need. I am blessed to be able to help change lives for those who cross my path, working with them to go deep within their soul, finding their way back to self-love and healing. There is always purpose in pain, and we all have a story. Finding the courage to heal is a gift that will enable you to help change another's story.

"To rise in glory and be victorious in survival, you must feel it, own it, overcome it. Conquer."

Instilled with great strength to change my story; the mirror never looked so beautiful, for I cast my *shadows* into light.

"Be you, be brave, be bold, be beautiful, be magical, be unstoppable, but most of all, be unforgettable."

When We Say Yes, But We
Want To Say No
By Jondi Whitis

One day, I began to notice how people would share that they'd gone ahead and done something or said yes to something they didn't want to do. It made them angry, doubt themselves, and frustrated, asking, *"Why do I do that? What's wrong with me?"*

Why, indeed? Why *do* we do or say yes to things we don't want to do?

Discovery 1:

After years of pondering, here's what I came up with:

"There's always a good reason for that—I just don't know what it is, yet."

That's right. Apparently, people *always* do things for good reasons, although it's usually not obvious to them what those reasons might be. And they tend to repeat what they think is working (which might be another word for *feels comfortable* or something so-called *normal*).

I needed a better life experience than that. What's exciting about a life of repetition, doing things we don't want to do?

I started putting what I noticed to work, both for myself and the people who keep asking me why they kept saying yes or doing things they didn't want to do. I simply turned my 'discovery' into a question:

"If there were a good reason for this (behavior/action/choice/habit)—and I bet there is—what might it be? Could I take a guess?"

People liked that, but were often hesitant to come up with more than one or two *extremely* predictable answers. So I went back to the drawing board and came up with a way to deal with that, too:

Because we're creatures of habit and all tend to think inside the box, our brains are comfortable offering either the first answer that comes to mind or the same answer it's given you every time you've asked in the past, for example:

Q: Aargh! Why did I do that?

A: Because I'm too tired to fight about it.

In other words, patterns, habitual responses—whatever is on the tip of our tongue. We tend to think in comfortable patterns—*inside the box*!

Discovery 2:

So, I discovered an easy way to get *out* of the box by playing a game. Simply take something that feels bad and make it a game, and it's guaranteed to feel better. (Mary Poppins told us this.)

Here's how it works: As soon as I ask the question, "Why did I do that?" I begin immediately blurting out answers, and sure enough, after four or five answers have gone by, I start getting the good stuff—the truth!

Truthful, useful, and relevant answers start tumbling out when we're actually thinking, instead of going through the motions and old assumptions. This is what we call *thinking outside the box*, and it's surprisingly easy to do. (Did I mention it also feels great to know the truth?)

Try it with me. It's efficient, sometimes shocking, and can even be astonishingly fun.

The Blurt Game

1. Choose/Focus upon a specific event where you said or did something you didn't want to, and have no idea why you agreed to it. (*Ex: I said, 'Yes, I'd love to' when I actually wanted to say 'You must be joking.'*)
2. Repeat your question, quickly, out loud.
3. Now ask: If there was a good reason for this (decision/choice/answer you gave), what might it be?
4. Snap your fingers! Literally, snap them, then say "Blurt!"
5. Jot down each answer quickly.
6. As soon as you've written down the answer that came to you, repeat the process, asking the question out loud, snapping your fingers, and saying "Blurt!" then answering and writing down whatever came to mind. Do this at least five or six times.

7. Now take a look at your answers, especially focusing on the last few more insightful ones:

Example:

Q: Why did I say yes to her?

Blurt Answer 1: It's easier to just do it.

Blurt Answer 2: I'd rather do it than explain myself to her.

Blurt Answer 3: I don't want her to think I am selfish.

Blurt Answer 4: I felt ambushed and couldn't think straight.

Blurt Answer 5: I hate confrontation.

Blurt Answer 6: I am afraid to say no.

Presto! Additional information about why we do the things we do, and with it, compassion for ourselves and a clue about how to correct our path, either now or in the future.

For those of you who know how to tap, this is the perfect time to take the compassionate truth from your list and tap with it. For those who don't yet, that's easy to fix, and I will happily show you how.

In the meantime, *everybody* can feel better fast by using this little game to find your truth.

See how your perspective on this frustrating pattern changes, and how swiftly your pattern of doing or saying what you don't want to do, morphs into something more comfortable, pleasing, and truthful. Remember, there is always a good reason for everything we do, it's just hiding under all of our auto-pilot thinking and patterned responses. Playing The Blurt Game can be transformative! I'd love to know how this works for you, so please let me know.

To new adventures in being yourself!

Mount Everest Is Just Around The Corner
By Jan Wilson

Living your life your way takes understanding, patience, and planning. There will be times, more often than we would like, where movement forward comes to a standstill. Not allowing these times to stop us can be a challenge, yet we can get through them. The key is to take the necessary time to adjust and replan when needed.

Like many others, I have a bucket list. However, unlike others, I only had (yes, had—we'll get to that later) one item on my bucket list—climbing Mount Everest. I shared this with my daughter one day, and she told me she was okay with me following this desire, but she had one condition. I couldn't take on the adventure until I was ready for this life to be over. After all, climbing Mount Everest is not easy and can be full of potential injury or even loss of life.

You need the right mindset to begin planning for this. Thinking about the adventurers that have gone before me—those that have succeeded, those that have not, and some never to be found—does not sway me away from this goal. So, my daughter is willing to allow me to make this trip of a lifetime when the time is right, and I'm truly ready. And yes, I will know when I am ready, just like I know there will be many years before that time comes.

As I reflected on this future adventure, thoughts began to swirl, and I realized I didn't truly know what a bucket list was or what it was for. Many of us will create a list of things we want to try or learn or places to visit. In fact, a bucket list can be a list of anything we want to accomplish, including being our true selves or working through what we need to work through—the challenges, risks, and triumphs we face. With this came the realization that I have had a bucket list my entire life. I've been fortunate in that, when there was something I wanted to do, a place to travel to, or something to learn, I did it. No, it didn't always happen the moment I thought of it, but I did eventually do it, with Mount Everest remaining, so far, the one item on my bucket list, though I no longer consider it a bucket list item. It is a goal, a dream, a desire that I intend to fulfill when it is time. This was a decision I made for myself—recognizing I didn't need to create and maintain a bucket list.

There are a variety of ways to create your bucket list. By following my example, you can identify something and do it immediately, or take the time to set a goal, research, and plan. Or, you can create a written bucket list, create a vision board, put reminders on your calendar, or go so far as to create a formal project plan.

Remember, whatever method we choose to keep track of the things we want to do, we are not climbing Mount Everest alone. We have a support team—our "sherpas" who are there to offer a hand or advice when it is needed and when we remember to ask. In our hearts, we know we can rely on our sherpas who may or may not have made many climbs of their own. Regardless, to each of them, we will be forever grateful. While we are appreciative to our sherpas for their experience and support, we must also remember that the biggest support has and will come from within.

As we've all been climbing one version or another of Mount Everest, we must also acknowledge that each struggle, each opportunity, each lesson has led us to where we are today. While the view from the top may not be what we expected, in moving forward, we can take the time to plan our next climb. Being aware that there are summits and places to rest, not merely taking the time to rest, but to understand the lessons learned and to make any needed adjustment to our plan.

Climbing Mount Everest remains something I will do someday, but I no longer refer to it as a bucket list item. That is a decision I've made for myself. I expect to continue to identify things to do that I haven't done before or even to re-experience a previous adventure, making adjustments based on what I learned and, perhaps, setting different expectations. But, with each, I know that whatever it is will inevitably include the growth of mind, body, and spirit.

Whatever method you've chosen to create your bucket list, take time to check and add what's missing or what needs continued support in living your true self. Keep in mind, living your life your way is dependent on you, yet you don't have to do it alone. Allow yourself to lean on others— family members, friends, and the higher power that you believe in. Knowing that every plan may give you pause and make you feel like you have to put on the brakes and remain in the known, take heart and push into the unknown. While uncomfortable, it leads to moments of success and times for celebration, and yes, can also lead to disappointment and sometimes heartbreak. Give yourself time to adjust and replan when necessary, and rely on your support team, whomever or whatever it may be.

Remember, be patient, be willing to change, breathe, and open your heart to all the possibilities.

Author Information

Rollie Allaire: is an experienced holistic life and wellness coach and soul healer. She has worked with women who have experienced childhood trauma, sexual trauma, domestic violence, critical incidents, compassion fatigue, and grief by supporting and guiding them as they retrieve the lost parts of their souls and achieve wellness, joy, and success. Since 2001, she has drawn on her extensive career background of clinical psychotherapy skills, in combination with chakra work, Crystal Reiki, Akashic Records reading, and Moon Medicine teachings to facilitate her clients' journey to wellness. You can find Rollie at her website www.rollieallaire.ca

Kim Andrews: is a Spiritual Leader, story shepherd, and peacemaker. She guides seekers into a deeper experience of themselves so they can lead a life overflowing with peace and joy. She is passionate about storytelling and its ability to help us heal and transcend our wounds, whether we boldly and bravely embrace the stories of our lives with and by ourselves or in a public forum. She is the Spiritual Leader of Unity Spiritual Center in Sachse, Texas. Her website is www.kimfortheworld.com. You can reach her at kandrews@unitysachse.org.

Linda Ballesteros: As a Certified Franchise Broker, Linda Ballesteros taps into her 30-plus years in the banking industry, as well as her coaching background, to support and guide her clients. Her unique approach to match clients is achieved by finding the up-and-coming franchise that is best suited for each client's individual passion and skills. This allows her to empower those seeking to build a solid financial future and leave a legacy through business ownership. You can also hear Linda's interview skills on one of the many radio shows she has hosted over the years. Contact Info: Mpowerfranchiseconsulting.com
Linda@mpowerfranchiseconsulting.com
facebook.com/MpowerFranchiseConsulting/
facebook.com/AllThingsFranchising/ linkedin.com/in/lindaballesteros/

Pam Baren Kaplan: Certified Professional Coach, specializes in pet loss grief recovery. As founder and facilitator of *Paws to Celebrate*, she has helped heal the broken hearts of thousands of people. Pam is affectionately known as, "Leader of the Pack." She has developed a highly interactive, supportive, and healing global community for grieving pet parents to work through their grief and tell their unconditional love story. Pam works with clients worldwide. In her upcoming book, *Tails of Unconditional Love*, Pam guides you on your journey through to the other side of grief recovery. You can reach her at pam@pawstocelebrate.life

Brooke Bensinger: is a school counselor and owner of B-Squared Tie-Dye. In both roles, she assists individuals of all ages to gain self-confidence and feel empowered as they transition through life's milestones. Her passion is using creative arts as a catalyst for personal insight and transformation. You can reach Brooke at bsquaredtiedye@gmail.com. www.facebook.com/bsquaredtiedye/

Kristi Blakeway: is a school principal in Maple Ridge, BC where she lives with her husband Shawn, and sons, Jaden and Cole. She is the Founder of Beyond HELLO, a student run initiative that helps Vancouver's homeless reconnect with friends and family. TEDx Speaker and winner of the YWCA Women of Distinction Award for Connecting Community, Kristi encourages everyone to step outside their comfort zone, engage in soulful conversation and connect with compassion. A storyteller at heart, she welcomes the opportunity to speak and inspire. She blogs regularly at www.hopefullearning.com and www.beyondhello.org. She can be reached at kblakeway@beyondhello.org.

Meredith Brookes: The author wishes to remain anonymous. For more information, please reach out to the publisher.

Jenny Cabaniss: is a software engineer in the telecommunications industry, with a master's degree from the University of California, San Diego. She is also an equestrian, an ordained minister, a Reiki Master, and a professional card reader. She enjoys finding new ways to tap into her intuition for the benefit of others. You can reach Jenny at jennycabaniss2016@gmail.com.

Jeannie Church: is a divorce mediator, coach, and healer. She has successfully helped hundreds of couples achieve a mutual understanding about how to separate their marriages. Jeannie is passionate about inspiring people to radically heal themselves as they go through a divorce. With a Master's in Somatic Psychology, she brings a holistic approach to compassionately working with the stress and trauma of any major transition. When she's not mediating, you can find her communing with nature and her gong or on a shamanic journey somewhere. truedirectiondivorce.com/ truedirectiondivorce@gmail.com birdbrown.com/ 720.722.4159

Tami Close: is a 45-year-old mother of three. Her sobriety date is June 17, 2011, and she has eight years sober. Tami is passionate about recovery, and believes there is much healing that happens when we connect to each other through our stories. It is our darkest moments that shine the light on who we really are if we are willing to look within. Tamiclosetolman@gmail.com.

Gilda Jill Cook: is a Holistic RN who devotes her time to working with those recovering from emotional and physical traumas. She is a wife, mother, grandmother, pet-sitter, gardener, and joyful pet mom to Audrey the cat, and retrievers Maggie and Daisy. She now makes her home in the desert southwest with hopes to one day have a small cabin with land for more animals, flowers, and a mulberry tree. You can learn more about her work at www.ClarityHolisticHealth.com.

Joann Cooper is Transformation Coach of RenuU Your Ideal Wellness. Having 11+ years' experience in the wellness industry, Joann knows how to transform others back to the person they want to be. Joann has been a true entrepreneur for over twenty six years. Eleven years ago, she found herself overweight and started her journey through weight loss, losing 37 pounds in four months. That's when RenuU was born. She now enjoys coaching and helping others to success. She is married to Tony and recently celebrated 21 years of marriage. Fur babies Phoebe and Lola absolutely run the house. www.RenuU.us

Liz Dawn: is the CEO and co-founder of Mishka Productions/Celebrate Your Life events. Liz works with the top spiritual and personal development teachers of our time including Deepak Chopra, Dr. Wayne Dyer, Caroline Myss, Byron Katie, Gregg Braden, Neale Donald Walsch, Dr. Joe Dispenza and the list goes on. Liz is deeply committed to uplifting the consciousness of the planet one amazing event at a time. To learn more about Celebrate Your Life events, visit: www.CelebrateYourLife.com

Cecilia Deal: Cecilia Deal is a best-selling author, speaker, and Certified Professional Coach. She has helped organizations and individuals get focused on purpose-driven business and navigate successful transitions. She helps them clarify their message so they can communicate effectively and make more aligned decisions. This allows her clients to create a path for growth, and have work and business be the vehicle in which they fulfill their purpose. When she's not working with clients, she's hiking with her dogs and embarking on new adventures. You can reach her by visiting her website at www.findingwanna.com.

Kandice Den: is a Transformational Coach. For over 25 years, she has helped thousands of clients develop better, fuller lives. She now works exclusively with women who are ready to reconnect with their heart's calling. By uncovering limiting beliefs and structuring a plan to reach their goals, she helps them use their talents and gifts to lead them straight to their lifelong dreams. She passionately believes that when women shine, the whole world benefits. Whether a woman's goals are personal, business related or global, success is possible. You can reach Kandice at www.bethelightcoaching.com, or by email at kandice@bethelightcoaching.com.

Katie Elliott: was an educator for over 30 years prior to becoming a free-lance writer. Her passion is to encourage others to find happiness and serenity, no matter the challenge. You can reach Katie at: katie.elliott.100@gmail.com.

Juhl B. Estar: is a Relationship and Life Empowerment Coach. She assists individuals, groups, and businesses with aligning to who they authentically are through expanded awareness and consciousness. Her passion is to create the opportunity for illumination and insight by allowing life experiences to become the connection to the Creator within. You can reach Juhl at www.JuhlBEstar.com, juhl@juhlbestar.com, or 503-798-8077.

Ana Evans: is a speaker/author/energy healer. She practices Reiki and various indigenous practices to help people find health and wellness in the wake of trauma. She is passionate about story-telling as a primary modality for healing, believing that within each of our stories are the keys to our own wellness and is working to develop workshops designed to assist others in telling their own story. Ana can be reached at www.givegreatness.com.

Benjamin Evans: is currently spending his days as CDL driver, developing his skills as a natural empath while traversing the beautiful landscape of the US. He is walking the recovery road within loving community and learning from his experience with addiction and mental health struggles. He is deeply passionate about telling his story of healing to a world in need of hope and light.

Kathryn Ferguson: is a high school teacher and MS advocate from North Vancouver, British Columbia. She is a self-described "Kindness Ambassador" who hopes to spread a little more positivity into this wild world. Kathryn can be reached at: kathrynn@telus.net.

Lori Verbin Flaum: is a first time author with a lifelong passion to live a creative life. She is an avid crafter/sewist and sells her wares through Etsy and local boutique shows. You can reach Lori through her Etsy shop www.RyeGoods.Etsy.com

Karen Gabler: is an attorney, intuitive coach and psychic medium. She is also an author and inspirational speaker. Karen is passionate about encouraging others to live their best lives. She provides clients with intuitive guidance regarding their personal and business questions, facilitates connections with their loved ones in spirit, and conducts workshops on a variety of spiritual and personal development topics. Karen earned her Bachelor of Science in psychology and her Juris Doctorate from the University of Hawaii. She enjoys reading, horseback riding, and spending time with her husband and two children. You can find Karen at www.karengabler.com.

Sarah Gabler: is 12 years old and will be in eighth grade. She loves playing with her family and traveling to new places. She enjoys acting, singing, dancing, and horseback riding. When she grows up, she intends to be a motivational speaker or work in fashion design. She loves em-powerring people, even if they don't reciprocate! She began exploring spiritual teachings and soul empowerment concepts when she was ten years old, and believes it has made her a better person today. It also has motivated her to find ways to help others on their journey to live their best lives.

JG Delos Reyes Garcia: is a Philippine-born, former Washingtonian (DC) living in Hawaii. She's a healthcare professional and the "fur mum" to James Dean, her mischievous Bichon. When she's not binge-watching *Law & Order: SVU* and *TED* Talks, she's reading Gibran and Rumi, baking cupcakes, practicing yoga, or thinking about the meaning of life. Bali is her happy place where she lets her hair down. Her blog is her creative corner written with newfound self-awareness and evidence-based data. Connect with JG and share her latest bucket list journey – to visit the Seven Wonders of the World @ https://jggarcia.com and @missjg_garcia

Kim Giles: is an outstanding entrepreneur specializing in helping young and old learn to use the many choices in communication and problem solving applications. She writes colorful and straightforward novels, short stories and blogs to achieve her goal of helping others help themselves. She is brilliant in her field and hopes to motivate others to find the confidence and to use the tools they have right in their own realm of understanding. You can reach Kim at Kimgiles76@hotmail.com or on Instagram @Phxwriter5

Rach Gill: an inspiring writer and lover of poetry, photography, and dancing. She helps support others by inspiring them to find their passions in life by her writing. You can reach her at Rachel_gill@email.com

Dina F Gilmore: (aka Ashwani) is a certified Shamanic Practitioner, Licensed Massage Therapist, Reiki Master Teacher, Photographer, Filmmaker, Scriptwriter, and multiple bestselling author of "When I Rise, I Thrive, Healer and Life Coach." Gilmore thrives to inspire and empower others through multimedia resources utilizing her creative gifts as a visual healer. She created Mobile Shaman to share the healing art of Shamanism across the country in our modern-day society. Gilmore leads Shamanic Journey Circles, teaches various healing classes, is currently pursuing her degree in Digital Media Journalism and created Empowerment Productions for the visual art of storytelling.
www.empowerment.productions
empowermentproductions33@gmail.com
shewhohealsplenty@gmail.com

Michelyn Gjurasic: is a coach, an artist, and a healer. She is a certified Emotional Freedom Techniques Practitioner and Master Hand Analyst, and she exhibits her original pastel landscapes and portraits. Michelyn helps individuals and groups to recognize their gifts. Her passion is alchemy: inviting together seemingly contradictory opposites into a new awareness of self and purpose. You can connect with Michelyn at www.Michelyn.com.

Scott Goodell: is a health and fitness advisor. He helps individuals of all ages embrace the challenges of being bullied. His passion is to raise awareness and spread hope for originally unique people who face harsh criticism for sharing their God-given talents. He understands there are challenges facing the world, and would love to help others feel comfortable in their skin. He speaks to groups of all ages. You can reach Scott Goodell by cell: 832-773-7981 or by email: scottieg713@yahoo.com.

Nikki Griffin: is a certified Autism Travel Professional, who owns a travel agency in Calgary, Canada. Since embarking on her happiness journey, Nikki has found and married the love of her life and finds joy every day with her hilarious daughter and witty son. Nikki is a best-selling author and enjoys writing blog posts, newsletters, and social media content for other small business owners. Her passion is helping others succeed! Boost your brilliant self, engage your sense of adventure, and enjoy a more fulfilled life! Connect with Nikki at nikki3griffin@gmail.com or follow her on Facebook @divinewanderlusttpi.

Elizabeth Harbin is a psychic medium, Reiki Master, certified hypnosis practitioner, professional card reader, an ordained minister, and author. In 2016, she became a radio talk show co-host where she uses her psychic medium skills to provide insight to questions from call-in listeners. Her humor and quick wit have made her a sought-after guest speaker and panelist. Text her at 214-545-0072.
Facebook.com/ElizabethHarbinpsychic
Facebook.com/ElizabethHarbinEventPage

Suzanne Harmony: is an author, teacher, psychic, and medium. An epiphany led Harmony to publish, *Leap of Faith...From Fear to Fulfillment*. Experiential guidance to create positive life changes is

accentuated with others' personal accounts of their leaps of faith. Her self-help memoir, *Because I Didn't Tell*, published with pen-name, I. Katchastarr, details the horrific events of her young adult life. Gems of self-forgiveness and pearls of wisdom serve to soothe, help, and heal readers. Her desire to be of service is fulfilled through writing, public-speaking, her Reiki Practice, and shared adventures.
ReikiAndHarmony@gmail.com www.HarmonyHelps.ca 1-705-494-0001

Julia Hawkins: is a full-time college student pursing her degree in Education. She hopes to mirror the skills she learned from her favorite teachers to make a difference in the lives of her students. You can reach Julia at: julia3hawkins@gmail.com

Patricia Haynes: is a writer, speaker, tarot reader, spiritual counselor, world traveler, photographer, and unabashed Egyptomaniac. She's also a genealogist, paralegal, and investigative researcher. Some of her photographs have been displayed in several newspapers, books on Egypt, and in the Petrie Museum of Egyptian Archaeology in London. She has written many articles for legal publications, and in books on Egypt. She finds travel and researching ancient sites and people to be the most inspirational and healing phenomena anyone can experience. The more you learn about the world, the more you learn about yourself! You can reach Patricia at phaynes@eyeofhorus.net.

Dr. Debbie Helsel: is a Heart 2 Heart Healing and Heart 2 Heart Connections Practitioner, additionally trained in Reconnective Healing and Reiki and working with crystals. She has a Doctorate of Metaphysical studies through the Alliance of Divine Love Ministry. Debbie serves as Executive Director at Back to Nature Wildlife Refuge in Orlando, Florida. Since 1990, Debbie has dedicated her life as a federal and state licensed wildlife rehabilitator and public educator. www.BTNwildlife.org

Dr. Vicki L. High: is a best-selling author, life coach, counselor, speaker, founder of Heart 2 Heart Healing, Reiki Master Teacher, and former mayor. Her books include *Heart 2 Heart Connections: Miracles All Around Us,* and as a contributing author in *When I Rise, I Thrive* and *Healer.* Dr. High boldly journeys into healing, counseling, empowerment and spiritual insights. She shares wisdom and helps people architect the lives they've dreamed of. Her gifts connect ideas and concepts, creating patterns. She lives through her heart, inspiring each person to live their purpose courageously. Vhigh4444@aol.com www.heart2heartconnections.us www.empowereddreams.com FB: @heart2heartprograms @ce2oinc @stoptraumadrama, @kalmingkids, @empowereddreams

Lisa Holm: is a Psychic Medium, Animal Communicator and Spiritual Healing Practitioner. Her passion is to facilitate clarity and alignment with life purpose, enabling people to creatively and joyfully live in harmony with Source. She loves empowering clients across the U.S. and internationally through classes, clairvoyant counseling, intuitive readings, mediumship, animal communication and spiritual healing. Lisa has studied with medical intuitive Tina Zion, Hay House author and psychic medium John Holland and the Church of Religious Science. Lisa also teaches Intuitive Development, Animal Communication, and Mediumship Mentoring. You can reach Lisa at 360-786-8617. Website: www.lisaholm-psychic.com

Jillian Holper, CCHt, LC: is a mother of two, wife, Clinical Hypno-therapist, Empowerment Life Coach, and published author. After pursuing her first degree in Psychology, she decided to return for a second degree in Occupational Studies in Holistic Health Care with a concentration in Mind-Body Transformational Psychology. Today, and for the last several years, Jillian is doing what her soul had always longed for. She feels honored to have a trauma-informed practice where she assists and empowers clients to overcome subconscious blocks and actualize their goals for mental, emotional, spiritual, professional, and physical well-being. You can reach Jillian at www.EleMentalHealingCoaching.com, (928) 793-3990, or Jillian@EleMentalHealingCoaching.com.

Rosemary Hurwitz: is a married mom of four young adults, and she is passionate about an inner-directed life. She is a best-selling author of *Who You Are Meant to Be: The Enneagram Effect* and is co-author of several other best-selling inspirational books. She has a Masters in Pastoral Studies, and is an accredited Enneagram professional, who gives private life-coaching sessions and workshops. She assists individuals with emotional wellness and purpose through deepening awareness of their unique personality to essence. You can reach Rosemary at www.spiritdrivenliving.com or rosepetalmusic@gmail.com

Foxye Jackson, RN, CA-SANE, CRM: is a forensic nurse, Reiki Master, transitions coach, intuitive reader, ordained minister, and author. Using metaphysical knowledge, the power of Reiki, and psychic intuition, she helps individuals navigate life's transitions and heal from various traumas. Her primary experience is with the traumas of sexual assault, domestic violence, and mental abuse. Foxye's purpose is to assist individuals with understanding and healing the soul. Her classes and intuitive readings are excellent for those beginning their journey of enlightenment and aware-ness. To reach Foxye:Please text 469-333-1728 or email peacewithfoxye@gmail.com. Facebook: Facebook.com/FoxyeJackson or Facebook.com/groups/ispeakfoxye. Instagram: @ISpeakFoxye and @PeaceWithMarcusandFoxye

JamieLynn: is an empowerment coach, founder, and host of the Breakthrough & Summit, founder of Arise Empowered LLC. Empowering lives one voice at a time, and host of Awareness Talks—bringing insight and action to your life. JamieLynn is also a best-selling author, energy healer, and thriver of sexual and emotional abuse. JamieLynn empowers those around her by holding them accountable to who they say they areand who they have the possibility of being. To connect with JamieLynn: jamielynn.ariseempowered@gmail.com

Vanessa Johnston: is an End of Life Doula, trained, and pursuing certification through the International End of Life Doula Association. She offers individualized and intersectional emotional and spiritual support for people and their loved ones experiencing palliative and/or hospice care. Her passion is to help those who are dying approach their final milestone with love and meaning instead of fear and anxiety. She seeks to be a compassionate companion and serve as a witness in sacred service to honor the final chapter in other's stories. You can reach Vanessa on Facebook @DenverEOLDoulaLLC or by email at

EOLDoulaDenver@gmail.com.

Cindy J. Kaufman, MEd, EdS:, brings her background in counselor education and more than 20 years of hospice volunteer experience to her work as a Certified End of Life Doula. She serves as a compassionate companion for life's final journey, honoring her clients' choices about end of life care and assists them with vigil planning. Cindy is also an ordained interfaith minister, officiating ceremonies, funerals, memorials and life celebrations. She is trained in home funerals and green burials and can assist clients with these options. Cindy is based in Denver, Colorado. Contact her at (720) 989-1929, cindy@heartspeak2u.com, or www.heartspeak2u.com

Susan Marie Kelley: a freelance writer, began a spiritual journey twenty years ago when her spirit guides began speaking audibly to her through her husband, Dave. Her first book, *Spirits in the Living Room,* is a humorous and heartfelt memoir that chronicles Susan's life from her painful early years to a life filled with joy. Her second book, *Ravens in the Back Yard,* is based on the ancient teachings of the Creator Gods, and explains how Susan learned to use the magnificent universal laws to create and manifest her heart's desire. Susan also holds metaphysical workshops and blogs regularly to help others on their journey. You can reach Susan at https://susanmariekelley.com.

Amy King: is a certified Life Coach and owner of Your Phenomenal Life LLC. Her 12-month coaching program can help you transform your life. Whether starting over after illness, divorce, death of spouse, job loss, or are simply desiring a healthier way of life, she can help. Amy's greatest joy is using her experiences and the personal challenges that she has overcome to help women move past their personal blocks to becoming empowered to live the Phenomenal Life of their dreams. You can reach Amy King by text or phone at (916) 975-3017.

Julie Lalande: is a Canadian freelance writer working to inspire others towards self-discovery. Her work explores life circumstances where people have had to learn to cope, heal or surrender. Keen interest in storytelling has led Julie to a path to find untold stories and to move them into written form. The journey to healing requires self-acknowledgment, and realities kept buried only sicken the soul. Julie can be contacted at juliemlalande@gmail.com.

Barbara Larrabee: has had success in the equine industry and founded a multi-million-dollar direct sales company. She has a diploma in Personal

Nutrition from Shaw Academy and is an Ambassador for the Dallas Holistic Chamber of Commerce. Always wanting to uplift others, Barbara is a global sales leader in the network marketing profession. As a Longevity Coach for over seven years, she is passionate about educating people on wellness solutions—including weight management options and ways to influence genes and DNA—that may be outside the box of traditional western medicine thought. You can reach Barbara at Your-Longevity-Coach.com, barbara@your-longevity-coach.com, Facebook.com/barbaralarrabee.5.

Michelle LaRue: helps people promote their businesses through social media marketing. She is a reformed engineer with a passion for wine and words. She lives with her daughter, the namesake of her business, and their little cat, the supreme ruler of the household. You can reach Michelle at www.sonjablueproductions.com, 703.651.2953, or michelle@sonjablueproductions.com.

E. Chloé Lauer: is a travel coach, speaker, and author. She helps people get off their couches and into the world, finally experiencing the adventures they have dreamed of for years. Her passion is to debunk the myth that travel is expensive, scary, and overwhelming to plan. You can reach Chloé at https://www.chloelauer.com.

Kenneth Laws II: has been on a spiritual path to understand the unexplainable, his awakening, after a series of life-altering events that occurred in his life in 2013. It was not until then that he started to understand the meaning of oneness with all and accepting all with no judgment, as well as his humanness. He has been inspired to help others by way of sharing personal experiences of pain and joy. He has a blog at www.simplyindescribable.com and can be reached at ken@simplyindescribable.com.

Anne Mackie Morelli: is a former Canadian National track and field champion and Olympian, who now is a writer, educator, public speaker and registered clinical counselor. She is passionate about inspiring and instigating others to maximize their talents, strengths, and leadership abilities for the greater good. As a Christian, Anne strives to practice generous kindness, inclusivity and justice. You can reach Anne at her website, The Stones Call, www.thestonescall.com, by email at eanne.morelli@gmail.com, on Twitter at @EAnneMorelli, or on Facebook at www.facebook.com/asacredexchange/

Sarah McArthur: is an Intuitive Life Coach and Certified Aroma Freedom Practitioner. Her passion to empower others to live their most authentic and free lives was birthed out of the wisdom she learned on her own healing journey. As an Intuitive Life Coach, Sarah focuses on helping others identify core beliefs and negative belief patterns that are no longer serving them, and she uses Aroma Freedom to transform negative thoughts and feelings into growth and expansion using essential oils. Sarah's Facebook page is Restoring Hope Forward, and she can be contacted at restoringhopeforward@gmail.com

Ghene't Lee-Yong McCormick: is a Nature Immersion Guide, Life Coach, and Educator. She assists people in reconnecting with nature and thereby reconnecting with themselves and each other. Her passion is bringing people to the outdoors and rekindling their love of nature and self. You can reach Ghene't at info@ghenetmccormick.com and www.adventnature.com. By phone (texting is preferable) 7862038600.

Stacey Moore McGown: As an educator and entrepreneur, Stacey McGown is empowered by making a difference in the world. She explores all avenues to find solutions in leadership, education, and living a quality life. Her commitment to the reporting principles of truth and leadership was influenced early in education when she was a reporter for the Cat's Tale. She attended Baylor University. Stacey's goal is to make the world a better place, one relationship at a time.

Paula Meyer: recently retired from a position as events director for a *New York Times* bestselling author. She has more than 30 years of experience as an event/workshop/meeting planner and as a procurement/contracting specialist, and 12 years in author/speaker management. After recently becoming a widow at 54, Paula's goal is to help other widows get back in the game of life and realize there is still so much to learn and love with the time we have left. Paula travels internationally and lives in Washington, Colorado, and Florida. For information on her travels and grief workshops for widows, go to www.gpeventworx.com.

Tina Miller: is an energy practitioner who practices Frog Medicine, using various energy modalities to help her clients release what does not serve them and to expand their self-awareness. She lives in Phoenix, Arizona with her husband, two dogs, and five fish. Together they have seven children and ten grandchildren. She loves to hang out with family and friends, hike, read, and do crafty things. This will be her first published work.

Meaghan Miller Lopez: is an Artist and Creative Advisor specializing in self-discovery and intuitive ways of knowing. Informed by neuroscience, psychology, quantum and metaphysics, Meaghan offers original art, personal guidance and intuitive art-making experiences that encourage the embodiment of inner wisdom. Her work helps people make space in their daily life to bring personal creative projects into existence. Meaghan's purpose is to activate and inspire all people to experience their life as a work of art. Find out more online at www.touchstonestudioart.com or search @meaghan.miller.lopez

Roseann Minafo: is an up and coming author inspired by her life as a single mom, now married to the love of her life in her 50's. She shares her home in Oakland, California with her husband, two fluffy mutts and a cranky old cat. Her new position as an empty nester has given her time to write, quilt and contribute to her husband's acting career in community theater. She prefers to be off stage working with the actors on their costumes and quirky creative hats. Roseann loves traveling and recreating dishes at home. Non-fiction is her favorite genre, in both life and reading! roseannminafo@ymail.com

Aerin Morgan: is an artist, designer, avid world traveler, and animal lover. When she's not working as a freelance art director and product stylist, she can be found climbing Mt. Kilimanjaro, strolling through the markets of Bangkok, or photographing the streets dogs of Istanbul. She is passionate about protecting the natural environment, as well as improving the lives of animals. She is a staunch supporter of animal rescue and works with local organizations in their education and adoption efforts. Aerin is currently writing her first book, and mapping out her next great adventure. You can join her at: www.aerinmorgan.com.

Luann Morris Morton: is an herbalist, LVN, CST, ordained minister, author, and professional card reader. She is passionate about teaching the health uses of herbs and essential oils. You can reach her at: https://herbal-lu1105.vistaprintdigital.com. A special thanks to: Bill Morton, Gussie Allmer, Elizabeth Harbin, Jenny Cabaniss, Linda Jeffcoat-Ballesteros, The Tribe, and Kyra Schaefer at As You Wish Publishing.

Kiauna Skye Murphy-Ballard: born in 2007, is about to enter sixth grade in Denver, Colorado. She is an artist, athlete, amazing friend, and daughter. She loves being creative, imaginative, listening to and creating music, swimming, basketball, volleyball, circus, theater, plays the cello and trumpet. Her home is full of wonderful pets, and she is an animal lover. Kiauna is a "Reiki baby," and was attuned to Reiki 1-Master in the womb—her touch, humor, and perspective are truly magical. Kiauna is a master of creating a vision and manifesting it into reality.

Kira Murphy: is an Acupuncturist, with a Masters of Science in Oriental Medicine. She owns a storefront named Ki Healing Center, in Denver Colorado, (Ki-Denver.com) offering various types of healing treatments, on-site and distance. Ki healing center was named after Kira's beautiful daughter Kiauna, whose nickname is Ki. Kiauna has been the inspiration to her life. Kira practices gentle acupuncture and esoteric healing. Kira loves to channel and draw a person's unique, one of a kind, sacred soul symbol through meditation. Kira Murphy L.Ac, MSOM 303.947.4563 / TrueHealthAcu@gmail.com / http://www.TrueHealthAcupuncture.com.

Georgia Nagel: is an animal communicator and sacred activist. She lives, breathes, and shares the sacred connection between our spirit and the earth. Her personal journey has been intertwined with animals, nature, and earth wisdom. She believes that if we share the unconditional love from animals and nature, and apply it to those we encounter, we will together shine a brighter light upon this world. Georgia has authored two books: *Pet Talker, Listening to Those Who Speak Silently* and *Maurice the Goat Finds His Real Family*. Georgia can be reached at www.georgianagel.com or gnagel@arvig.net, 218-841-6730

Barbara Nersesian: is a high school teacher working with autistic teens. She is also a Certified, Professional Life Coach who works with professionals who have been struggling to reach their goals. As a teacher, she strives to improve the life skills of her students. As a coach, Barbara is a catalyst who inspires, motivates, and draws out the passion in people wanting to make a change in their lives, whether in the workforce or in their private lives. You can reach Barbara at: 520-235-4128, Email: nersesianassociates@gmail.com, or www.nersesianassociates.com

Nicole Newsom-James: is a teacher, designer, and heart-centered realtor. Her studies include healing the body through studying the spirit. She combines both eastern and western philosophies and techniques which remove energetic blocks from her client's lives and environments. Nicole also works with real estate companies to shift the energies of the properties they want to sell. Her passion is to guide her clients through the storms of life via education, designing a supportive environment, and locating their dream home. You may reach Nicole at 918-443-0592 or via email: nicolenewsomjames@gmail.com.

Peggy O'Neal: guides and coaches others to discover who they are and to live their lives in alignment with their true nature. She has had a life-long sense that we could all live together peacefully, and once she became aware of wisdom teachings that supported her knowing, she integrated those teachings into her work. Peggy is a Certified Integral Master Coach™ and brings over 30 years of experience working with complex management, leadership, organizational culture, financial, and business development issues. You can reach her at peggy@peggyonealglobal.com.

Ashe Owen: is a professional musician and a soul session leader. He helps married men facing challenging life experiences love who they are and the asshole that got them there. His passion is seeing others light up. Ashe can be reached at Ashe@asheowen.com.

Lisa Paquette Yee: supports women creating happy lives and businesses which, considering where you're reading this, makes perfect sense. She's best known for Soul Prompts, the cozy self-coaching card deck with a knack for delivering wisdom so "weirdly appropriate" that it's become a favorite tool of clients and inspired her upcoming game. You are warmly invited to email hello@experienceyourextraordinary.com to connect with Lisa in Alberta, Canada, where she lives with two geriatric cats, three smarty-pants kids, and her creative husband, or visit her website, SoulPrompts.ca, where curious clickers may find Easter eggs of hidden treasure.

Cheryl Peterson: has worked for a non-profit organization and has defended women's rights for the past 36 years. She enjoys her work as a fiber artist and creates wearable art for sale at art shows. Cheryl is a Reiki practitioner, and practices guided meditations with individuals and groups. She was able to officiate her first wedding this year and is looking forward to expanding this practice. Powered by spirit, and inspired by *A Course in Miracles*. Cheryl enjoys sharing her love and light with the world. Cheryl Peterson, Morning Dove Designs—cherylswearableart.com or cherylmdd@gmail.com

Nicole Piotrasche: a rideshare driver and peddler of hope and whole-heartedness in Denver. Her passion is to facilitate others in reclaiming their own being through whimsy, wonder, and all forms of creative story-telling. Nicole can be reached at nicole.piotrasche@givegreatness.com.

Anna Pitchouguina: is driven by a passion for justice and creative expression. She graduated from Monash University with a Bachelor of Law and Bachelor of Arts (honors) and is also fluent in Russian. A dancer since the age of nine who became an instructor at age eighteen, Anna won the world championship in B-grade women's Latin same-sex Dancesport in 2018. Using the same skills she employs to make complicated dance moves seem effortless, Anna transforms even complex legal matters into concepts that are easy for people to understand. Anna has written an Undergraduate thesis on Madame Blavatsky and blogs at www.crossingfaith.wordpress.com.

Colleen Porter: is a music creator, lyricist, and playwright in Gilbert, Arizona, who is gifted with stories and songs that encourage empathy, love, and empowerment. This year, she is releasing some powerful songs, as well as a couple new musicals performed locally. In Gilbert, she holds Radiant Warrior events for women and looks forward to publishing story books and sacred songbooks. Follow her journey at colleenportermusic.com, or her artist page where you can subscribe/hear her music at www.patreon.com/ColleenPorter. Feel further inspired to facilitate, support, or be involved her creations? Contact: colleenportermusicals@gmail.com.

Elicia Raprager: is an artist and blogger. When her mental health declined, she returned to these passions. Although Elicia struggled, she challenged herself to remain positive. The best compliment Elicia can hear is, "you inspired me." She opened up about her mental health on social media and was overwhelmed by encouragement and gratitude. She prioritizes self-care for mental and physical health. Elicia will share her story in her future book, Share a Smile: Thriving in Life and Treatment. Elicia is published in the July issue of RAC Magazine. Stay updated by following Elicia Raprager at www.shareasmilewithelicia.wordpress.com

Samantha Renz: is a Civil Engineer and CEO of a civil engineering firm in Fort Worth, Texas. She is an entrepreneur, and pursues ways to help those desiring a second chance at life. She is passionate about developing and leading strategic growth, creating opportunities, and transforming lives. You can reach Samantha at Samantha@evolvingtexas.com.

Marci Zeisel Rosenberg: is an urban planning consultant. She helps property owners and their design consultants prepare plans, resolve potential issues with local neighborhoods and navigate the land development approval process. Her mission is to facilitate the creation of affordable housing and healthy communities. You can reach Marci at MarciZRosenberg@gmail.com.

Laura Rudacille: is an author, enrichment speaker, and certified restorative and chair yoga practitioner. She encourages growth-through-sharing, and champions women through every season of life. Thirty years in the salon industry taught Laura the value of good listening and human connection. Through writing, enrichment events, and live videos, Laura offers thought-partnering insight and candid humor shedding light on our similarities, and infuses positivity and possibility into every moment. Join her live 7:45 p.m. EST Sunday evenings in her private group for women's enrichment on Facebook, the AGR Hen House. www.LauraRudacille.com

GG Rush: Life Coach In Training, ggrush1@gmail.com

Michelle Ryan: is a mother, grandmother, retired school teacher with her masters of arts degree from CU Boulder in Multi-Cultural and Social Diversity Education specializing in Special Education and English as a Second Language. She has traveled with several nonprofits to Central Asia supporting people to people connections and self-esteem work. Michelle has thirty years of experience volunteering on the boards of three human-itarian organizations. She has facilitated women's retreats and loves being with women. She currently lives with her husband, a beekeeper, on a farm in Boulder County and spends her time listening to the Universe and creating.

Bruno Salvatico: is a community college Innovation Manager and an entrepreneur. He helps students and small business owners bring their projects and ideas to life. He has a passion for technology that will help make the world a better place, and loves to help those who want to be helped. You can reach Bruno at bmsalva90@gmail.com.

Chelsea Sandoval: is a college student studying the field of Psychology, and working towards her Wellness Coaching Certificate. She has a dream of helping those who suffer with mental illness as she does, and she hopes to change lives through her writing. Her passions include being a caring individual to all, writing and helping around her college as much as she can by being a part of multiple organizations around campus. She enjoys making a difference for her fellow classmates. You can reach Chelsea and read more of her work, both fantasy and growth pieces at ventureinwriting.com.

Felicia Shaviri: is on a mission to tell everyone within earshot or afar the importance of the role they play in the world. A former corrections deputy turned best-selling author and wellness coach, Felicia believes every person can turn their life around regardless of the circumstances. A native of Chicago's Englewood District, Felicia lives between Milton, Washington, and Henderson, Nevada. A professional fitness/wellness coach, Certified Life Coach, voice-over talent, and the founder of SheRox Fitness and Wellness, based out of Henderson, Nevada, Felicia has an incredible ability to connect with troubled teens and women. She has helped countless clients through her one on one, group coaching, and wellness retreats. www.sheroxfitness.com

Jonathan Siegel: From the brink of death, Jonathan Siegel is now an inspirational speaker and writer. He shares his story to inspire others never to quit and to create miracles. He lives in Denver, Colorado, where he has created a new life that includes cycling, skiing, and gardening. Visit his blog: jonathansiegel.blogspot.com or contact him at:

jonathan63siegel1@gmail.com.

Brooke Smith: authors books written for all ages including, Brinley Discovers Santa, The Mango Tree, The Tortoise and the Flair, and BUCKET (to be released Summer, 2019). She was born in Santa Cruz, spent years on Kaua'i, and finally settled in the mountains of Colorado where she lives with her husband and participates in the growth of her curious children. She is pursuing a career in life-coaching and currently hosts labyrinth retreats. Brooke is also a self-publishing consultant and works at the local library. You can connect with Brooke through her website: BucketOfWonders.com

Matthew Steadman: is an author, public speaker, and Accountability Life Coach who lives in the Dallas, Texas, area. His passion is helping readers and clients grow through accountability, self-love, and learning the power of their mind to transform their lives! www.MatthewSteadman.com MatthewJSteadman@gmail.com 972-269-3578

Janice Story: is a certified Reiki master/teacher; mind, body, and spirit practitioner; author and speaker; and Equine Coach who brings over thirty years of expert horsemanship into her work. Janice's compassionate and gentle spirit provides a safe space for others struggling with physical, emotional, and spiritual trauma. She works with a team of seven horses with whom she shares a strong connection and who were instrumental in her healing. Together, Janice and her equine team create an opening for healing and transformation that far exceeds that of human contact alone. Connect with Janice: janicestory.com and janice.story@me.com

Cathy Stuart: is a Certified Spiritual Counselor and Coach who offers angel readings, personal coaching, spiritual mediumship, chakra balancing, and Reiki. Cathy is ordained through the Madonna Ministry. By following her intuition and her vast knowledge of what most would call "life experience," Cathy has been assisting her clients for over 20 years in releasing emotions and patterns that have prevented them, in this lifetime, from moving forward to a life of peace, love, and harmony. www.universalwisdom.com. 623-363-2746

Dr. Lisa Thompson: is a scientist, award-winning interior designer, and life/love/soul coach specializing in Past Life Regression therapy and

Human Design. She works with clients to create environments that support them physically, emotionally and spiritually to release limitations and to access self-love, worthiness and inner wisdom. She owns two companies: Mystic Manta Coaching and Design Smart. She is the author of *Sacred Soul Spaces: Designing Your Personal Oasis* and the upcoming *Sacred Soul Love: Manifesting True Love and Happiness by Revealing and Healing blockages and Limitations*, available Fall of 2019. Lisa can be reached at www.MysticManta.com and Lisa@MysticManta.com.

Chantalle Ullett: is a Licensed Massage Therapist who specializes in treating the body, mind, and spirit with a variety of modalities including *Linking Awareness*, which creates heart-to-heart connections with other sentient beings, and, *The Bodytalk System*, which addresses the whole person. She has traveled the world working with sentient beings of all kinds, and has experienced deep, transformational healings with animals such as horses, cats, dogs, orangutans, and elephants, to name a few. Chantalle is a French Canadian residing in McHenry, Illinois with her husband and two daughters, where she practices her therapy and continues her lifelong healing journey. (815) 403-9106 chantalleullett@gmail.com chantalleu.massagetherapy.com

Monet Vincent: From a young age, Monet fell into a dark place leading from one bad decision to the next with no desire to change. She met someone she loved and admired who told her she could be more than the life she had chosen for herself. In time, she began to love and believe in herself. In healing and growth, a desire ignited to help those who felt there was nothing more for themselves than their current situation. To this day, she continues to find success and encourages others to love themselves and find their true purpose in life.Mvincent@ashleydfw.com 817-718-3046

Allison Voth: is an independent writer, poet, and intuitive entrepreneur. She has over 20 years' work experience in the federal government, including serving as a Border Services Officer, and five years volunteering as a Royal Canadian Mounted Police Auxiliary Constable. Her passion is serving the global community within the common unity that bonds us in the expression of unconditional love. She can be reached at honeyheartalli@gmail.com

Nanette Waller-Stafford: is a Licensed Clinical Social Worker. Her therapist career spanned from reservation areas in South Dakota to retirement in Muskogee, Oklahoma from the Veterans Administration Medical Center. She continues providing supervision for graduate-level social workers seeking their clinical license. She is married to a multiple-tour Vietnam Veteran, and supports his activities with the Creek Nation Honor Guard. When not participating in these activities, she and her husband are busy with their business of making boxes out of Eastern Red Cedar for Native American tribal members to protect dance regalia or NAC items. Contact information: nlwaller22@sbcglobal.net or 918-360-9275.

Patricia Walls: is a natural intuitive living in Texas with her husband and fur babies. Through her natural gift of communication, she works with all life to assist in healing, balance, and expansion. Her training began some 40 years ago in shamanism and evolved through learning and practicing many healing modalities. She has served as an international speaker, teacher, women's retreat leader, healing facilitator, and mentor. Currently, she continues her earth traditions by working with the elemental and animal world in making ceremonial drums and art. Her websites include PatriciaWalls.net, GalacticFrequenciesofLight.com, and WiseWombyn.com

Jamalyn "Jamie" Warriner: has spent her life trying to bridge science, spirituality, and the real world. She has studied Massage Therapy, Reflexology, Reiki, is a Certified Christian Counselor, a Reverend and a Heart to Heart Practitioner. She inspires people through her words and actions by sharing her insights. She has had a successful career in finance for a major defense systems company for 35 years and counting. She volunteered there for 20 years as the Community Charities Manager along with her finance job. Contact Info: JamilynWarriner@yahoo.com

Leanne Weasner: is based in the Niagara Region, Canada and spends her days as a Renal Aide in the kidney Care Program at the SCS Hospital. She is passionate about making a difference in other people's lives and believes her most precious gifts are her empathy and compassion towards others. Inspiring those on a journey to self-love and healing, Leanne draws from emotional intelligence, positive psychology and incredible confidence.

Leanne may be reached at lasinspirationalquotes@outlook.com. Visit her Facebook page L.A.'s Inspirational Quotes and healing.

Jondi Whitis: is a Master Trainer of Trainers in NYC and is passionate about helping people feel better fast. You can reach her at: www.JondiWhitis.com or Jondi@eft4Results.com.

Jan Wilson: takes her inaugural stroll into the world of writing with her contribution to this book. Jan uses her life experiences and desires to inspire, with the hope that they help others to understand that it is easier to overcome adversity when we embrace our strengths and abilities. She embraces a life of natural health and has received training in yoga, acupressure, Reiki & birthing services. She empowers others to create a safe and comfortable space in which to receive healing and support. 1stmetowe@gmail.com

Final Thoughts From The Publisher

It has been a true honor to work with the authors in this and all our other incredible books. At As You Wish we help authors avoid recjection, your words are our passion.

Visit us at

www.asyouwishpublishing.com

We are always looking for new and seasoned authors to be part of our collaborative books as well as solo books.

If you would like to write your own book please reach out to Kyra Schaefer at kyra@asyouwishpublishing.

Recently Released

Happy Thoughts Playbook

When I Rise, I Thrive

Healer: 22 Expert Healers Share Their Wisdom To Help You Transform

Life Coach: 22 Expert Coaches Help You Navigate Life Challenges To Achieve Your Goals

Selling Emotionally Transformative Services By Todd Schaefer

The Nudge: Life Is Calling, Wake Up by Felicia Shaviri

Upcoming Projects

Holistic: 22 Expert Holistic Pracitioners Help You Heal In A New Way

When Angels Speak: 22 Angel Practitioners Help Connect You To The Wisdom Of The Angels

45546260R00186

Made in the USA
Lexington, KY
17 July 2019